Talents and Geniuses

ALSO BY GILBERT HIGHET:

The Classical Tradition: Greek and Roman Influences on Western Literature
(Oxford University Press, 1949)

The Art of Teaching (Knopf, 1950)

People, Places, and Books (Oxford University Press, 1953)

Man's Unconquerable Mind (Columbia University Press, 1954)

The Migration of Ideas (Oxford University Press, 1954)

Juvenal the Satirist (Oxford University Press, 1954)

A Clerk of Oxenford (Oxford University Press, 1954)

Poets in a Landscape (Knopf, 1957)

Talents
and
Geniuses

THE PLEASURES OF APPRECIATION

Gilbert Highet

New York / OXFORD UNIVERSITY PRESS / 1957

© 1957 by Gilbert Highet
Library of Congress Catalogue Card Number: 57-11635

SECOND PRINTING

© 1954 by Oxford University Press:
Death of a Poet; The Decadent; The House High on the Hill; History on
the Silver Screen; I'm Going To Write a Book; The First Few Words;
The Look-it-up Shelf.

© 1955 by Oxford University Press:
The Unconscious Artists; People of the Caves; Bach; The Fascination of
What's Difficult; Pictures of War; The Trial of Socrates; The Animal
Kingdom; Ruler of the World; What's in a Name?; The Face in the
Mirror; Compulsory Reading; Summer Reading.

© 1956 by Oxford University Press:
Jolly Old Graves; The Bird on the Gibbet; Inside Aubrey; The Vergil of
the Insects; The Letters of Jefferson; The Magician; An Unknown World;
Scottish Words; English Shibboleths; The Birth of a Book; I Married an
Author; Permanent Books; The Mystery of Zen; Immigrants.

© 1957 by Oxford University Press:
The Indescribable City; Criticoses; The First Deadly Sin.

PRINTED IN THE UNITED STATES OF AMERICA

Lui qui nourrit ma plume
De mots et de chansons,
Lui qui vit retiré
A l'abri des salons,
N'a pas comme le coeur
Ce grand besoin de battre
Ni de se mettre en quatre
Pour montrer sa douleur.
On ne voit que le front,
Le front et les cheveux
Et les yeux sourcilleux.

—Jules Supervielle, 'Le Cerveau'
(*1939–1945*, p. 147)

Preface

―――――――――

THIS is a new selection from the discussions of literature
and the other arts which I have been broadcasting during
the past five years or so. (Every Tuesday evening at 9:05
from Station WQXR in New York City: other places, other
times, "from coast to coast.") These essays are not merely
transcriptions, but have been revised and partly rewritten
for this book. Two earlier volumes have appeared: *People,
Places, and Books* in 1953, and *A Clerk of Oxenford* in
1954, both published by the Oxford University Press in
New York. These books and the weekly broadcasts have
brought me a huge mass of correspondence from friendly
readers and listeners. I hope that this fresh collection will
not disappoint them.

As before, my thanks go to all those who have been kind

enough to listen to my talks and to express their interest; to the publishers and others who have permitted me to quote from works in which they hold the copyright; to the three experts and encouragers, Mr. Fon Boardman (representing the Oxford University Press), Mr. Andrew Stewart (of Denhard & Stewart and Harold Andrews Productions), and Mr. Stanley Bumbly (formerly Chief Warrant Officer, U.S. Navy, now senior technician, Nola Studios, Steinway Hall); and to the only listener who never misses a joke or a syllable, my wife, Helen MacInnes.

New York City   G.H.
June 1957

Contents

MUSIC AND ART

CHARACTERS

WRITING AND READING

Music and Art

The unconscious artists

IF you cultivate the sense of wonder, you can find beauty
in every living thing — not only in the obviously handsome animals like tigers and their domestic cousins, not
only in the most admired fish like salmon and in the most
elegant insects like butterflies, but even in the grotesques
of nature: the intricate lobster, the weirdly angular mantis, the humble but valuable protozoan, and that sinisterly
smiling survival, the crocodile. Yet, of all living things, of
all our companions on this planet, the most diversely beautiful are certainly the birds. Not only that. Although they
are so remote from us in ancestry and so unlike us in many
of their habits, in some ways they are, of all the animal
kingdom, the closest to men.

Of course, the true naturalist would deny this. Every

scientist is always wary of anthropomorphism — the mistake of judging that because an animal behaves like a human being, it thinks and feels like a human being. That is a valuable caution to bear in mind. Still, the remarkable thing about the birds is not that they sometimes behave like human beings, but rather that human beings often behave like birds. One of the fundamental activities of the human race is art: decoration, ceremonial, stylized play, call it what you will, it is art. The cave men painted splendid pictures in their caves; even the most primitive tribes love singing and dancing. All men and women on earth take trouble to decorate their homes and their bodies and their equipment, whether such decoration consists of a few brass bowls or of a glittering Cadillac. These activities are artistic. The only other living beings on the planet which consistently engage in the same kind of activity are the birds.

When we speak of the birds as artists, the first thing we think of is their singing. The scientists tell us that when a bird sings, he has one chief aim in view: to establish a home. He is warning other male intruders out of his territory; often he is signaling to a possible mate, whom he has not yet encountered; and then, after he has found her and been mated, he is expressing himself to her, and charming her, just as he does by displaying his plumage and by stunt flying. So far, no doubt, the song is purely functional, and scarcely artistic. But scientific observers are often forced to admit that it goes beyond that, into regions where it begins to look like music, like art. One of them, the French naturalist Paul Barruel, concedes that 'the song sometimes seems to be uttered purely for pleasure,' and he calls it 'the externalization of a certain state of well-being.' He adds that although most females are mute, some birds, after getting married, sing duets: the Guianan partridges harmonize so delicately that their utterance seems 'like a single song.' However, not all birds sing love songs—some birds sing comic songs. A male bird does not have to be Count Almaviva; he can also be the Barber of Seville, and let go with the 'Largo al factotum.' The olive-sided flycatcher's song consists of a very loud whistle, which can be transcribed as HIC THREE BEERS . . . HIC THREE BEERS. For sustained amusement, give me half an hour listening to a mockingbird. And how many composers have been charmed by the song of birds! One of the simplest bird songs of all makes the climax of Delius' *On Hearing the First Cuckoo in Spring;* it appears, together with other songs, in the slow movement of Beethoven's *Pastoral Symphony*. Vaughan Williams has a fine piece for violin and orchestra called *The Lark Ascending*. Respighi has arranged a whole suite called *The Birds,* and he has most beautifully introduced the song of the nightingale into one movement of his *The Pines of Rome.*

Next, think of the costume of birds: it covers every possible variation of elegance, from the plain but correct evening dress of the penguins to the dazzling elaboration of the birds of paradise. In tropical Asia there is a little creature called 'Mrs. Gould's Sunbird' (lucky Mrs. Gould!). It lives only on the nectar of flowers. It looks about the size of a goldfinch: its chest is rosy red, shading into golden yellow and then into pale green; its neck is dark crimson; its wings are dark green; its head is crimson, with three beautiful rich blue patches, and it has a long double tail of blue and black feathers. And, mark you, this is a bird in its ordinary working clothes. When the birds really dress up in order to get married, the result is nothing but astounding. One of the grouse — the sage cock — in amorous display looks like a nobleman of the Italian Renaissance painted by Bronzino. He has a white doublet, with two enormous yellow medals in the center of his chest; black breeches; white socks; and variegated brown and green wing- and tail-feathers. To show off, he droops the wings with nonchalant grandeur and unfurls the tail in a sunburst and produces something like a ruff of brown feathers behind his shoulders. His eyebrows are bright red. Some of the birds of paradise are more intricate and fantastic in their beauty than anything the most skilful artist could invent. And don't think the birds are not aware of their own beauty. They take care of it. When preening, they spread the secretion of a special oil gland over their feathers, and clean not only each individual feather but usually each individual barb and thread. Herons manufacture talcum powder to put on after leaving the water.

Everyone knows that most birds build houses, and very efficiently, too. Although not usually artistic, their nests are careful and often ingenious. The tailorbird puts nesting material inside a large leaf, then sews up the edges in a curve so that the leaf cannot unroll. The South American ovenbird, which weighs less than three ounces, makes a nest weighing between seven and nine *pounds,* out of a hollow ball of earth fixed to a branch. In Australia the rock warbler makes a long hanging nest and attaches it to the roof of a cave by spiders' webs; the reaction of the spiders is not described. On the Malay Peninsula the megapodes build artificial incubators: piles of vegetation mixed with sand which gradually decay and keep the eggs warm. The birds themselves are not as big as an ordinary fowl, but the nests can be eight feet high and twenty-four feet across, composed of five tons of material scratched together from a radius of several hundred yards. The house martin builds a neat little house of clay with a front door. A simple nest like that of the redstart means six hundred separate flights for material.

Some birds, however, go further, and build simply for aesthetic effect. These are the bowerbirds of Australia and New Guinea. They are perching birds, between eight and fifteen inches long, which look rather like our own woodpeckers, but are more handsomely costumed. Their specialty is unique. The males make clearings in the forest, and at their edges build elaborate arbors of grass and leaves. On the clearings and in the arbors they set out decorations, carefully chosen and grouped: the heads of blue flowers, shells or brilliant objects such as pieces of glass, cartridge cases, and even glass eyes (though these are harder to come by). The scientist who has studied them most closely, A. J. Marshall, shows pretty clearly that this is simply a variation of sexual display intended to attract the little female, to mark off each particular male's own territory, and to allow him a proper stage on which to display his plumage and his masterful poses. And yet Marshall is bound to admit that the birds seem to enjoy their arbors; that their building goes beyond mere functionalism; and that they display very marked discrimination, which can only be called aesthetic taste, in decorating their bowers. An American collector in New Guinea was making his way through the jungle without thinking of bowerbirds or ever having seen one of their structures, when he suddenly came on a place where the undergrowth had been neatly cleared away from an area four feet square, and a hut-shaped bower had been built beside it, about three feet tall and five feet broad, with an opening a foot high. 'This curious structure fronted on the cleared area. The impression of a front lawn was heightened by several . . . beds of flowers or fruit. Just under the door there was a neat bed of yellow fruit. Further out on the . . . lawn there was a bed of blue fruit. Off to one side there were . . . ten freshly picked flowers.' Later this explorer saw the architect returning to its bower. The first thing it did was to notice a match that had been carelessly thrown into the middle of its clearing. It hopped over, picked up the match and with a toss of its head threw it out of the clearing. So the explorer collected some pink and yellow flowers and one red orchid, and put these in the clearing. Soon the bird came back and flew straight to the new flowers. It took all the yellow ones and threw them away. Then, after some hesitation, it removed the pink ones. Finally it picked up the orchid, decided not to throw it away with the rest, and spent some time carrying it from one pile to another of its own decorations, until it found one where it would fit in with advantage.

Does that sound incredible? There are other facts about the bowerbirds which far surpass it. After one male has completed his arbor he must guard it, for if he flies off in search of food a rival male will wreck his bower and steal his decorations. Some species not only decorate their bowers but paint them, with colored fruit pulp, charcoal powder from burnt logs, and (near homes in Australia) stolen bluing. If a flower in the display fades, it is removed at once; and if a human being interferes, the result of his interference is rectified. One observer took some moss out of a bower and hung it some distance away in the forest. Time and again a radiantly colored male bird angrily put the moss back. And then the same observer conducted an experiment which I can only call brutal. He set fire to three of the bowers. In each case, a male bird flew out of the trees and perched close by the burning arbor, 'his beautiful head bowed and wings dropped, as though sorrowing over a funeral pyre.' O Science, what crimes are committed in thy name!

The bowerbirds are not specially intelligent; their artistic displays are no doubt connected with the activity of their hormones. At least that is the scientific, or mechanistic, attitude. But there have been many human artists who were not noted for their intelligence, and who worked best when their hormones were activated.

Much more could be said about the artistic ability of the birds. Their dancing is sometimes grotesque, often elegant. You recall the extraordinary scenes in Walt Disney's bird pictures in which happy couples, or even happy groups of birds, dance together in weirdly charming ballets. And certainly the most fundamentally beautiful thing about birds is their flight. The ugliest of them all, the vulture, looks fine in the air. Some of the crudest and meanest, such as the gulls, are sensitive artists when they fly. Even the fat, greedy, commonplace pigeon, so like vermin as it waddles along the ground, becomes, when it takes to the air, something like an angel. Birds of prey often court each other by flying a sort of dance-flight. Ravens will fly side by side, almost touching, as if yoked together, not altering their distance from one another during lengthy evolutions. Buzzards when courting pretend to be the predator and the victim. They fly in huge circles higher and higher; suddenly the upper bird closes its wings and plunges down toward the other, which turns on its back; the wings open to brake the fall, the claws lock in ecstasy, and then the two birds separate to resume their ballet. In such ecstasies, in such dangerous and delightful and unnecessary nonfunctional activities, we shall find the true origins of art, both in the birds and in ourselves. Much of the best art is produced by forces of which we ourselves must forever remain unaware, because they belong to a realm beyond reason.

People of the caves

IF we were asked to name the most primitive of all human beings, the people who were least like civilized men and most like animals, we should automatically say 'the cave men.' The cave men: they are a popular subject for cartoonists — low-browed and brutish, roughly bearded, barefooted and bareheaded, wearing only the skin of an animal, carrying an almost shapeless club, and usually dragging a skin-clad woman by the hair, they have become part of our popular mythology. Most of us know very little more about those remote ancestors, and care less. Just now and then, looking timorously into the future, we have a horrible vision of the remains of humanity reduced once more to living in small primitive groups and sheltering in caves. The dream passes before our eyes for an instant, and we shudder, and banish it with a prayer. Or, in a good museum like the Smithsonian in Washington or the Field in Chicago, we may come across a room full of the tools and weapons the cave men used. Then we gaze with astonishment at those long rows of stone axeheads, stone arrowheads, stone knives and hide-scrapers and engravers and harpoons, all chipped out of hard stone with infinite patience and amazing ingenuity; and it comes across our minds that these men were not really primitive at all. And as we look back over the history of our race, it seems to stretch further and further away into the past — never, at any period which we can recognize, buried in absolute darkness or total, animal savagery. No doubt there was some such era, but it was unimaginably long ago; and when we look at the relics of the cave men, we see that they must have been made by people who had minds, and memories, and a sense of organization and — most surprising of all — a taste for beauty.

We know far more about the cave men than the average person nowadays realizes. I used to think we had only a few remains of their work, from a few scattered places. In fact, we have thousands and thousands of remains; they come from many different parts of the world, as far separated as Norway and Kenya. More are being discovered every year, and the discoveries cover many different fields of life, most of which can be correlated to form large patterns of recognizable human activity. Of course there are still many, many questions to clear up; but many of the essential problems have been solved, so that we have some picture of much of the life of those remote predecessors.

Properly speaking, the cave men were the human beings who lived before the most important of the early inventions on which a stable civilization can be based: farming, or the regular cultivation of edible plants; the domestication of hoofed animals; pottery — and perhaps with it the invention of wheeled transport; and the revolutionary technique of grinding, polishing, and boring stone tools so as to make them almost as efficient as the later tools of metal. The cave men did not farm; they were hunters and fishermen, and their women collected wild fruit, vegetables, and grain. They lived lives rather like those of the American Plains Indians before the introduction of the horse. They did not domesticate animals — or at best only one animal, our oldest friend, the dog. They lived largely on animals; they thought about animals constantly; but they were hunters, so they treated even the horse as something to be stampeded over a cliff and then eaten. They knew something about clay and how it hardens in the fire; but so far we have found no real clay dishes or containers among their remains. We find it difficult to imagine life without the peaceful cornfields, the quiet cattle, and the dishes from which we eat and drink; yet for most of man's existence on the earth these things were unknown and undreamed of. Settled farming began somewhere about 7000 years ago, in the New Stone Age: that seems like a long time ago, but it is only about 200 generations from our own time. Our two-hundredth grandfather was one of the first farmers. But before that there was a long, long period — not ten times as great but something like a hundred times as great — during which our forefathers lived in caves and hunted the wild animals and made tools and molded the human mind into something recognizably like its present effectiveness. That was what geologists call the Pleistocene period, and historians the Old Stone and Middle Stone ages. Some of it was unbelievably hard and terrible, with much of what is now the habitable world covered with grinding ice and thundering glaciers — the sky no doubt gray and filled with whistling winds and the repeated drift of snowflakes and sheets of chill rain. At other times, the world we know was comparatively genial, with subtropical vegetation and animals, and with many of the waste places habitable and huntable. The North Sea was dry land where our ancestors shot long-vanished animals, the Sahara Desert was a vast parkland with water and grass and trees like the big-game-hunting sections of Africa today, and the now barren canyons and sagebrush plains of the American Southwest were wooded and well watered: not our world, but a hunter's paradise. The experts believe that recognizable men have existed on this earth for half a million years; and from 500,000 B.C. (give or take a few thousand) to the comparatively recent date of 5000 B.C., they were what we know as cave men.

Yet their life was more intelligent and complicated, we might almost say comfortable, than one would expect.

The cave men had lots of tools, and spent much time, many generations, in elaborating them. Their typical tool was the handaxe, about eight inches long, with two cutting edges and a blunt point. It was shaped not to be attached to a wooden haft but to be held in the hand and used for many different purposes. Thousands and thousands of these tools have been found scattered over half the world from India to Oxfordshire, often mixed up with the bones of the animals on which their users lived. It is not possible to hold one in the hand and to examine the many skilful little fractures and chips which go to form its shape and its edges, without feeling some sympathy for the careful ancestor who made it and passed his skill on to his sons. The handaxe was only one of a wide variety of tools. By the way, something of the continuity of our life is shown by the fact that customs of the Stone Age survived to well within recorded history. Only the other day I was reading a Latin play in which a wicked servant got into a terrible jam: he was caught, as we should say, 'between the devil and the deep sea,' but what he said was 'I am caught between the altar and the stone' — a proverb which must go back to the days when the priests used stone knives in sacrificing, like the Mexican priests with their obsidian knives in the days of Cortez. And of course there are still primitive tribes in remote parts of the world who use stone and wood and bone, but have never learned how to work metal.

The cave men may have gone naked in summer; sometimes they may have worn only a single skin garment, as in the cartoons; but a long, long time ago they developed something more like clothes. They made needles, with eyes, out of bone; and bodkins, doubtless to bore holes in skins, out of bone and ivory; even buttons have been found in the caves; and there is one statuette of a Siberian cave girl wearing a skin suit, with trousers and a hood.

And did they live in caves? Yes, but not only in caves. The men were hunters, so they followed the game. Sometimes the game moved into areas where there were no caves. Then the hunters did what our own sodbusters did during the first hard winters, and what the Russian settlers in Siberia sometimes still do: they lived in holes in the ground, roofed over with anything to keep out the rain. More and more subterranean homes of Stone Age men, dug out of the earth, have been found recently — many of them with the bones and the tusks of the finest of all big game lying in them, the mammoth elephant. In southern England explorers have discovered one pit-dwelling which contains 15,000 flint tools: a very old hunters' clubhouse.

In their little houses and in their caves, was all darkness? No, there was the fire, there were lights. In the Chinese caves we have found remains of beings who are closer to apes than to men, but there are traces of fire there and many primitive stone tools. From a later period there are many caves with burned clay, charred wood, and carbonized bones. In the dim recesses of caves which were then, and are now, completely dark, we have discovered beautifully drawn and colored pictures, for which the artists must have needed artificial light. The lamps themselves have turned up: little stone saucers with a lip, which would hold burning oil or fat.

The artists . . . surely they are most wonderful of all. It is understandable that our remote ancestors should have been brave hunters and ingenious craftsmen who worked hard at practical things to make themselves efficient. But it is much stranger that they should have become such admirable artists that their work is still hard to equal. They drew, they painted, and they produced exquisite sculpture. One of their small masterpieces is a horse's head carved in ivory, with ears laid back, nostrils flaring, and mouth wide open; the differences between the hair on its muzzle, the hair on its cheek, the hair on its neck, and the hair on its mane are indicated by different angles of engraving, with a subtlety which would be astonishing nowadays. Probably there was a long tradition of sculpture in wood and stone which went before and prepared for it. In a cave in the Pyrenees there are relief sculptures of bisons, modeled in clay which has been plastered onto the walls and carefully shaped. Elsewhere there are many engravings in stone and ivory, some of them with the flint gravers still left lying beside them: galloping reindeer and browsing elks and many other beautifully observed and recorded subjects. Above all, there are the paintings, found in caves like the famous one in Lascaux: paintings of bison, hairy mammoth, rhinoceros, and lion. In color, outline, pose, and action, in almost everything except possibly perspective and grouping, they are better than any animal painting which is being produced nowadays.

There are not many pictures or sculptures of human beings. This art comes from a world in which animals outnumbered, and almost dominated, men. The animals are drawn with care and love, while the men are usually mere outlines, thin, athletic, two-dimensional figures shooting or running. But there are two exceptions to this. There are several carvings of women from the world of the cave people, and one famous painting of a wizard. The women are almost the extreme reverse of our own pin-ups. They are enormously fat, nearly faceless, and yet they give a peculiar impression of vast power: they represent woman as the ideal of fertility and long life and repose, the power which preserves and restores and replaces and reproduces. The wizard is partly human and partly animal. Quite clearly he is a man engaged in a ritual dance, and painted as the Indian dancers paint themselves; but he wears the semblance of several different animals — a stag's horns, a horse's tail, the front paws of a bear, and a weird multiple animal mask. No doubt he was trying to give his fellow tribesmen all the power of all the animals which they wished to outrun and to capture.

Tools change and develop. Invention proceeds, sometimes almost too fast for us to cope with the new world it thrusts upon us. But the foundations of human life remain almost the same: will power, and intelligence, and the taste for decoration, observation of the external world of nature, the love of men and women for each other and for their family, and the mysterious subconscious source from which spring myths, and magic, and much of religion, and the arts — the power which created dancing and music and acting, the beginnings of epic and lyric poetry, and doubtless oratory and tale-telling also. This language that we speak is no older than six hundred years or so — perhaps twenty generations. The inventions by which we record and transmit it are about two generations old. Writing may be nearly two hundred generations old. But language itself, that ancient and marvelous invention, goes back far further. Although the caves are silent now, yet as we gaze at the paintings done by the men who lived in them, or handle their ingenious careful tools, we sometimes seem to hear the distant echoes of that wonderful thing which is both an instrument and an art: intelligible speech.

Jolly old graves

SEVERAL of the most delightful afternoons I have ever spent were passed in visiting a large number of buried tombs. I am not a ghoul: most cemeteries leave me cold and depressed. But these particular tombs were far closer to entertainment than to depression; to gaiety than to mourning; to love and feasting than to loneliness and emptiness; to sport and dancing than to the motionlessness of the inanimate; to life than to death.

The people who made the graves and the people who were put to rest in the graves have all been dead for 2000 years; their language is forgotten; their national origin is a mystery; many of their finest achievements have been obliterated. But one thing we do know about them, one thing is made brilliantly clear whenever we see their graves, and that is that they enjoyed life intensely and had very little fear of death.

These people are the Etruscans (or Etrurians). They lived in central and northern Italy during the centuries before the Christian era. Where they came from, no one surely knows — although many believe that they were immigrant conquerors from the Middle East. No one understands their language — although we can read the various letters in which it was written and recognize some of the names and words. We do know that they began to dominate north-central Italy about 800 B.C., and spread over the west-central regions nearly as far northward as the Alps, building fine fortified towns and castles, until they were almost the masters of the peninsula and ruled the sea west of Italy; then they were conquered by a number of enemies, the most dogged being their former subjects, the Romans; they were absorbed into Roman Italy, and they disappeared from history about the first century after Christ. (It is always a sobering thought to see a chair where a friend used to sit, or a house where he lived for some years, and to think that he is dead and that the chair and the house are now parts of the lives of some other. It is far more sobering to think of entire nations which have lived and died and passed away — almost out of remembrance of all mankind except for a few historians. Will that happen to us? Will strange people ever range over this continent, pointing out its landmarks, and say, 'This was a great city once, when the Americans lived here'?)

But the Etruscans did not altogether vanish. They left some traces in Roman religion, Roman art, Roman military and political organization, and even in the Latin language; and some of these traces have come down to us and are still alive. (Whenever we say that a speaker made a 'histrionic' gesture, we are using an Etruscan word which reached us through Latin.) They left some ruined cities, some large public works, and their tombs, hundreds and thousands of them. The Etruscan tombs remain in many areas in west- and north-central Italy, and wherever the tombs remain, the Etruscans still live. It is one of those paradoxes which distort and yet decorate the historical process, and keep us, if we have any brains, from calling history a 'science.' The Etruscans were one of several peoples who were important in their own time, and who affected history, and who would nevertheless be very imperfectly known if they had not taken such care to bury themselves in handsome, well-furnished tombs.

When you visit a group of Etruscan tombs, all that you see to begin with is an ordinary field. Sometimes it is a pasture with some hillocks in it. Sometimes it is a cornfield on which the stubble of high summer undulates gently over certain hemispherical bulges placed more or less at random. These hillocks and bulges, your guide tells you, are the tombs of the old people. You leave the little footpath along the edge of the field, and step across the stubble toward one of them. It looks like a mere accident of the earth, covered with grass or cornstalks. On one side there is a narrow gap and a trace of a footpath leading downward. The guide leads the way into a cleft beneath the surface of the field. Spiders hang around and above you as you descend among the bushes which almost hide the cleft; lizards look at you with wary intelligence and then rush away. A few steps more, and you are walking down a narrow stone staircase. A few feet more, down below the sunlit surface, and you enter a narrow door, going down into the darkness below the mound. To meet you, there rises up a faint but penetrating smell, something between a wine cellar, a springhouse, and a crypt. You shudder, and almost turn back, repressing a cry of protest. It is as though you were asked to die before your time.

But as soon as you enter the tomb, you are relieved, encouraged, even delighted by the atmosphere of charm and gaiety that surrounds you. A grave in Etruria, it appears, was not a place where dead people were hidden as corpses so that they could rot away in oblivion. It was a home, a home where they could live on with a life less fleeting but not less intense and delightful than the life they enjoyed in the flesh.

The guide switches on a light. You find that you are not in a gloomy sepulcher. You are in a room — about the size of a spacious modern living room — carved out of solid stone. This is the dead man's grave — or rather it is his house, and it is as gay as it can be. Its walls are elegantly painted with pictures in bright daylight colors, pale yellow and blue and green and rich red, which have survived seventy generations underground, and are only in danger of perishing nowadays if people leave the owner's door open so that the wind and the rain come in to spoil them, or crack the roof so that the water seeps in from above. In nearly every grave the pictures on the walls are different; but in nearly every one they are gay, charming, spontaneous, and sensitive. They nearly always show the dead man or his friends or all together, enjoying life. There are pretty girls dancing with handsome sunburned young men. There are athletes wrestling for a prize. There are men fishing and men diving into the sea, men hunting and men chasing birds. And most frequently of all there are parties where gracefully dressed couples listen to music, drink wine, watch dancers. The men and women at these parties are painted in such lively detail that you could recognize them at once if they walked into the room (and, indeed, when you come out you will see many of them imaged in their descendants on the streets of the Tuscan towns).

Emerging into the sunlight, you find the world curiously trivial. It was a grave which you left, a subterranean tomb dedicated to death and lit by artificial light; but it was also a projection of a gracious and intense life. Above, the grass squeaks under your feet, and the cicadas work their little adding machines, and the sun clangs like a gong; people look, and feel, unimportant. It might be any field in late summer. Following the guide, you stump across the clods and go down another little staircase into the ominous darkness. The same strange air — the air of the underworld, you think — drifts frigidly up to meet you. Within the tomb, the guide once more turns on a light; and once more you are enraptured with a vivid and cheerful impression of vitality. On the walls, a group of the dead man's friends are carousing at his funeral party; they have hung up their garlands and their mourning scarves; and look, at the end of the tomb they are saying good-by to him, beside a door which has just closed.

When you see these tombs they are empty — except for the paintings, and the occasional wall carvings, and the gracious presence of the dead. That is because they have been opened and stripped bare, long ago. If you could enter a new one, you would find not only the dead man's room neatly disposed, or all his house reproduced underground, not only his amusements and his friends painted around the walls, but all his finest possessions lying on the shelves and benches: the gold cup he used to drink out of, his shield and helmet, even his chariot, the gold pins for his robes, the plates for his food and the mixing bowl for his wine — everything he loved and felt to be precious. He himself would have been there for many centuries, lying on his bed of bronze or stone, with perhaps his wife on the bed opposite; but they would have fallen into dust long ago, leaving only remnants of their clothes and their metal ornaments, to show where the human forms had lain. All this would interest only antiquarians, were it not for one important quality: the Etruscans had beautiful taste. The things which they loved were not only valuable, because rich with gold; not only quaint, because so old; but very lovely. The ornaments which have been taken from their graves are almost always so delicate and charming that they make the average modern jeweler's shop look like a collection of prizes from a fun fair. The paintings on the walls are truly delightful — in economy, in mastery of movement and form, in grace of color, and in suavity of composition. And the occasional pieces of sculpture are nearly as good as all but the finest sculpture from Greece, with a peculiar vigor and toughness, a combination of powerful individuality and easy sensuality, which are quite unmistakable.

There is one tremendous example of Etruscan sculpture in the Metropolitan Museum of New York: a warrior, or a god of war. He is much bigger than life. His body is red, with the sunburn-red which all Etruscan men possessed; his eyes glow white from his red face. He wears strong body armor; his legs are bare and agile; he has a mighty helmet on his head; and he stands in a formidable posture of attack, with a spear ready to transfix his enemy. Whenever I look at him, I hear the steady 5/4 beat of the first movement of Holst's *Planets,* the evocation in sound of the elemental crudity and relentlessness of war. I think he is the finest male statue of a pagan divinity I have ever seen. It is risky to prefer any Western sculpture to the statuary of the Greeks. And yet this piece has something — call it primitive, call it semibarbarous if you will — which we rarely see in Greek sculpture. It has the ruthless masculinity which the Greeks in their art often idealized away into something handsomer, but weaker. The Etruscan warrior looks as Homer describes the warriors of the *Iliad* who sacked Troy.

But in many of the Etruscan tombs there was another kind of statuary, which shows us a different side of the character of that curious people. The dead men and women who inhabited the graves were portrayed in sculpture, sometimes as though asleep, often as though they were awake — half reclining on a couch, as though they were banqueting or resting, and might rise at any moment. There are many such coffins. On them lies sometimes a noble lady with her best dress and her jewels reproduced in stone, regarding us with dignity and detachment; sometimes an elderly man with his face shadowed by thought; sometimes a young man who died too early. On one such coffin lies a man of about thirty, propped up on one elbow as though at a meal, while at his feet there sits a quiet young woman with her eyes fixed upon him. Although human in shape, she is a little smaller than human size, with something unearthly about her face and manner: she is a spirit of death, come to join the young man's feast, and to terminate it.

That is a little sad, but there are many gay coffins. One of these, among the most beautiful of all, is a double coffin made for a husband and wife. It looks like a banqueting couch, or even a marriage bed. On it are statues — not in stone but in pottery, colored pottery — of a young couple, wearing graceful robes and jewels, and half lying, half sitting. They are not more than thirty years old, probably younger. The girl's hair is very carefully and beautifully done in long tresses, each separately plaited and brought over her shoulder to fall on her round breasts; she has little shoes with curving toes, and a charming dress in sheer material with elegant Egyptian pleats. The young man has a small pointed beard, and hair quite as carefully arranged. They have long, slanting eyes, and the hint of a smile dawning on their lips. One of his arms is round his wife, and the other holds a wine cup. And there they recline, as they reclined in their tomb for 2000 years and more, looking out with luxurious calm. They cheer me, that young couple; they cheer me and they calm me. Sometimes I am saddened to think that I shall never be an archaeologist, and never have the delightful experience of digging my way, with a few fellow workers, down through the root-matted soil toward the entrance of one of the many Etruscan tombs which are still unexplored, and clearing away the earth from the door, and gently forcing it open, and feeling the cool air of 500 B.C. rush out on my face; and then, taking in a powerful lamp, of looking for the first time into the cheerful house of the dead, of greeting the gay dancers or banqueters around the walls, and saluting the host and hostess, who raise their cups as though to welcome, newly arrived at a feast which has lasted for twenty-five centuries, a guest from the outer world.

A symbolic picture

NOT many of us believe that it is possible to tell *all* the truth about this world and our lives, simply by using clear, straightforward, logical language. We recognize that poetry which is obscure though beautiful, music which communicates without words, painting and sculpture which may be clear representations of recognizable things or may depict beings and events that were never seen by mortal eye — all these are methods of making statements about human experience, statements that may well convey truths otherwise unintelligible and inexpressible. An etching of a tree torn by stormy winds, a statue of a beautiful woman, a painting of a tired old man, each says something important about the world. A fugue by Bach exemplifies the order of the universe and the ordering power of the human mind. The shape of a Chinese vase and its color — these are not only decorations: they are messages.

The arts are languages. True; but why do the artists sometimes make these languages even *more* difficult to understand? It is hard for us to realize their full meaning when they speak those languages plainly. Why should they use them to utter enigmas, to describe what is frankly incredible, to paint impossibilities? What on earth does a poet mean by saying

> Love did make the bloody spear
> Once a leafy coat to wear?

Why should a painter spend months and months on a picture whose central figure is a man with his body changed into an enormous hollow egg, his legs turning into withered trees, and his feet transformed to sailboats? And, when the poet writes such words and the painter paints such figures, why do we often remember them — not necessarily enjoy them, but remember them, as though they haunted us, far more vividly than a simple poetic utterance or a picture representing what we have often seen? Why are they both vivid and obscure?

This is the mystery of symbolism. Statements which are too difficult to make in logical words can be put into some of the other media of art. Statements which are too difficult to make through clear poetry and immediately intelligible pictures must be conveyed through symbolic poems and symbolic paintings and symbolic sculptures. To understand such doubly difficult statements requires great patience, great knowledge (greater, usually, than most of us possess), and, first and foremost, a willingness to believe that symbols are worth trying to penetrate. If we do manage to penetrate them, we shall usually have a double satisfaction, a double revelation — although we may never be able to explain our revelation to anyone else, unless by merely pointing to the picture or repeating the enigmatic poem. Yet sometimes we can explain some of the central meanings which the critics and historians have enucleated: we can translate the body of the message; and then leave our friends to interpret the individual symbols for themselves. That is what the symbolic artists want us to do. They will not tell us their secret, unless we prove worthy of hearing it.

Several of the world's greatest painters are symbolists. Their best symbolic works cannot possibly be understood at first sight. When I first saw them, I turned away in perplexity and disgust. What converted me was the fact that their other works, their straightforward pictures, were so wonderful. It seemed clear that a man who could create strong, bold, memorable pictures of historical events or everyday life would not waste his time when he turned to symbolism, and spend months on constructing meaningless puzzles to throw dust in the eyes of the public. He must have had other purposes and sound ones, although perhaps he may have felt some of them to be purely instinctive.

Symbolism is the central artistic ideal of Salvador Dali and of Pavel Tchelitchev today; of Paul Klee and Yves Tanguy yesterday; and before that, of Odilon Redon and William Blake; some of the finest etchings of Goya and of Dürer are symbolic. Symbolism was one of the main inspirations of architecture and sculpture in the Middle Ages; it runs through much Oriental art, and far back into the art of prehistoric times. It has produced a remarkable, a bewildering body of work, some of it trivial, much of it majestic and disquieting. The two symbolic painters in the western world who seem to me to be the finest artists and to have left the most unforgettable pictures are two Dutchmen: Hieronymus Bosch and Pieter Bruegel. Bosch died in 1516. Bruegel was born a few years later, so that he never knew Bosch directly; but he modeled much of his work on that of Bosch, and used many of his symbols as though he knew what they meant, or at least felt their tremendous force.

Dutchmen are very sane people. They enjoy the ordinary. They love the obvious. They can even make imaginative poetry out of an everyday scene. These two painters, Bosch and Bruegel, are perfectly sane much of the time. They paint pictures in which everything is real, almost too real, even coarsely real; but, when they turn away, and enter the world of symbols . . .

One of the strangest pictures ever painted is a huge panorama by Hieronymus Bosch, now in the Prado Museum in Madrid. It is a triptych — a picture made up of three panels: it was meant to be folded up tight, and to be revealed, like a religious mystery, only after due preparation. On the outside of the triptych is a perfect sphere, showing the world just after its creation. When opened out, the whole thing is very large; the center panel is seven feet high by six feet broad, the two side panels the same height and half the breadth. Your eye moves naturally from left to right. In looking at the three panels, it passes from calm light through warm confusion into flaming darkness; from peace through organized excitement into impossible, incredible fury; from sanity through silliness into mania.

The left-hand panel, tall, graceful, almost empty, shows a weird but beautiful garden, with birds and animals and trees and flowers and water: cool colors, calm lines; only three figures, two naked and one clothed. The naked figures, thin, almost ascetic, but naïvely charming, are Adam and Eve. The clothed figure is God, giving Adam his newly made wife. Adam, just recovered from the first anaesthetic, is sitting up on the ground looking at God with wonder and gratitude. Eve, half kneeling and half standing, with her eyes modestly cast down and her long wavy hair flowing behind her, contrives to look like a princess, and also like the first and simplest of beloved women. There is no hint of the temptation, although we see the trees of life and of knowledge. But the animals and the birds of the Garden are not quite peaceful, not quite uncorrupted. A cat is walking complacently across the foreground with a doomed rat in her mouth, and a broadbilled bird is swallowing a frog, head first. Perhaps Bosch did not know the tradition that before the Fall of Adam, the animals did not eat one another; or perhaps he did know it, and wished to show that the first hints of corruption were already appearing.

The second picture, the big central panel, is not part of Biblical tradition at all. It shows a huge landscape full of naked figures: none of them indecent, but naked every one. In the middle is a pool full of women bathing; around them, on unicorns, bears, oxen, pigs, and other animals, rides a procession of young men. In the background is a large lake surrounded by grotesque buildings made of tree roots and glass rods and fragments of natural objects unnaturally joined together. In this lake floats a dark metallic sphere, or bubble, upon which naked figures are climbing and gamboling. Above, high in the air, appear weird groups, wonderful but apparently meaningless and purposeless: a flying fish carrying an armored figure with a long lizard tail, a griffin bearing a naked rider who brandishes a tree. The landscape stretches far into the remote distance, punctuated with fantastic figures like the inhabitants of a dream. The foreground is filled with other impossible groups: giant birds bestridden by tiny little men, girls and youths eating fruits far bigger than themselves, a pair of dancers interlinked, wearing a huge owl as a headdress. Everyone is active, even gay; but the whole picture looks like the garden of an asylum.

The third panel is quite obviously hell, but it is not hell as conceived in Christian religious thought. The center figure is a human being with nothing human left but his face, which looks like that of a catatonic. His body has become an enormous empty eggshell, inhabited by little figures drinking and carousing; his legs have become hollow trees, his feet are shaky boats in a sea full of drowning figures; his skull has turned into a dance floor, where a bishop in full robes, a bird-faced demon, and other strange characters move in a circle around a giant bagpipe. Who is this monstrous being? Is he, perhaps, Humanity? degenerate Humanity? Before him there are confused phantasmagorial scenes in which men and women are tortured by instruments or shapes of pleasure: a man crucified upon a harp, a gambler crushed beneath an overthrown gaming table, a poet or a scribe shrinking before the caresses of an amorous pig. Far in the background, flames, and buildings lit by conflagrations, and marching soldiers, and rivers of lurid fire.

This extraordinary picture, which must have taken many years of meditation to conceive and many months of work to paint, is sometimes called *The Garden of Delights,* because of the subject of its central panel; but surely it should have a more expressive title. Many different explanations of it have been put forward. One scholar believes it is the manifesto of a secret society of heretics who were sensualists and nudists. Another believes it is a collection of images drawn from the works of the early church Fathers, especially St. Augustine and St. Gregory, who loved to discourse upon the imagery of the Bible. The first explanation is improbable, the second unproved as yet. The several symbols in the picture are very hard to interpret; yet we can see the meaning of the entire work.

It is a bitter satire on the life of mankind — both the life of individual men and the life of the race. It opens with creation — or birth, lonely and innocent. It moves on to naked pleasure and simple animal folly: men and women closely associated with beasts (symbols of their various instinctive drives), all engaged in doing absurd things which delight them, but never thinking, never creating anything real or durable, their proudest monuments being frail monstrosities of fiber and glass, ready at any instant to collapse. It ends in hell — not the hell of Dante, which was built by eternal law and constructed on a perfectly orderly moral and philosophical system, so that, even through its torments and agonies, we perceive the constant pervasive power of wisdom: not that, but the hell of sheer lunacy, in which follies have become vices and vices have developed into manias, so that men and women are less important and powerful than beasts, or the beastly parts of themselves. In this hell, nothing happens for any reason. It is the end of the world, as Bosch sees it. Life begins in simplicity, corrupts into silliness, and collapses into incurable madness.

So then this is scarcely a religious picture. It is a moral satire, almost irreligious in its utter pessimism; and we can see why Father Siguenza, the historian of the Escorial, felt it necessary to defend Bosch against the charge of heresy. God appears in one panel of the triptych as the Creator, but the life of mankind is shown without a teacher, without a savior, and without repentance. At the end there is hell, without a judgment, without even a mention of heaven. The symbols in it are drawn from the darker depths of the subconscious mind, and reflect those which psychologists have found in the spirits of disturbed and desperate patients. Like all great satires, it teaches and preaches by omission. It portrays the life of man as a long fool's errand to the grave, the primrose way to the everlasting bonfire. What it lacks, what the age in which Hieronymus Bosch lived was felt to lack most painfully, what our own age also seems disastrously to lack, is the calm, pure, cohesive spirit of Reason.

That is only one of many wonderful symbolic pictures painted by Bosch. On each of them one could spend long hours of thought and admiration. Each of them is full of symbols which, though we may not fully comprehend them, are somehow more permanent than many an economic treatise, many a sociological analysis, many a pious sermon. Symbolist art is sometimes merely light and frivolous; but pictures such as this are grave and troublous. They remind us that the entire visible universe, which we see and hear and try to measure and comprehend, may be a symbol of some enormous truth, too great or too terrible for our minds to grasp.

The bird on the gibbet

ONE of the most remarkable painters in Europe died at the height of his powers, when he was about forty years old.

When I was at college, I frankly never cared very much about the dates and ages of distinguished artists and writers, except that I had to learn them off by heart for examinations. But nowadays I have come to see the importance of such facts. When a good poet like Keats dies at the age of twenty-five, when a good musician like Mozart dies at thirty-five, when a good painter dies at forty, it means that you and I and our forefathers and our children and successors have all lost something absolutely irreplaceable. We shall never have the delight of reading the magnificent poetic dramas which Keats was preparing to write; of hearing the many operas which disappeared into nothingness when Mozart closed his eyes; of seeing the pictures of life and death, gaiety and suffering and grotesquerie which were still to be painted by the Flemish painter Pieter Bruegel. He died just about four hundred years ago, in 1569. His pictures, even when they are enigmatic, are still vividly alive, and speak to us.

What they say to us — ah, that is what is most important. Colors brilliant or muted, forms exquisite or gross, composition as intricate as a fugue or as simple as a folk song — all these are means of communication. If there is no thought behind them, they are still pleasant enough because they exercise the most subtle of our senses, but they lack one of the essential powers of art, the power not only to decorate but to communicate. And yet, good artists often seem to be interested in making their utterance difficult. They want to communicate, but not easily, not immediately, and certainly not in simple affirmative or negative statements. They would feel they had failed if their entire message could be assimilated by a high-school class which had looked at their pictures for one afternoon; they would feel humiliated if anyone could take a course in Art Appreciation and forthwith grasp the entire significance of their lifework. In art, as in personal life, brief superficial contacts are usually worthless. This was certainly the artistic creed of Pieter Bruegel.

He is almost unknown, except through his pictures. He was born in Holland about 1530 (a generation before Shakespeare). He registered as a professional artist in Antwerp in 1551, went to Rome to study during his early twenties, returned to the Low Countries and painted large ambitious pictures, married, had two sons, died in 1569 and was buried in Brussels. Some of his best pictures are in the Metropolitan Museum in New York; there are several in Madrid; others are scattered throughout Europe and America. Taken all together, they show him as a brilliantly versatile, technically masterful, and provocatively original painter.

He is said to have left one of his pictures to his young widow — one of his best, painted the year before he died. We can look through it into Bruegel's world.

We are on top of a hill, a hill about 2000 feet high, looking over a large fertile plain. The country is interesting and varied. Crags and cliffs appear in the distance, faintly blue and brown, with traces of light mist. It is springtime. On each side of us there rise young happy trees, putting on their first leaves, bending and swaying and shimmering like bridesmaids. A bird is flying off through the clear air to the left, with that purposeful look which means it is getting material to build a nest. Right in the center, foreground, on a bare rocky outcrop from the hillside, there stands a sort of scaffolding or framework: two wooden props about twelve feet high, fitted into the rock, with a wooden crossbar at the top. It might be a swing for children, but there are no ropes and no little seat hanging from it. It is a gallows, a gibbet, on which men are executed by hanging and then left until their bodies rot away or are picked to pieces by animals and birds of prey. On the crossbar at this moment sits a solitary bird — a magpie — waiting, or looking for something, or perhaps remembering.

But this is not all the picture. On our left, far below, we see a castle set on a hill, and beneath it, under its authority and protection, a cheerful little town. It must be a holiday, for there, along the path between the young trees up our hillside, come the villagers. They are not walking as though it were a Sunday stroll. They are dancing round and round in little groups as they move up the hillside;

and they have a bagpiper to set the time and cheer them on. Just at the top of the hill, beside the gallows, are two men watching them. One of the men is gesturing with his right arm — either to welcome the dancers, or perhaps to remind them that the gibbet, although empty, still stands there. Our gaze falls away from the dancing villagers down the hillside to the right. There stands a cross, above some dead man who was obviously not buried in holy ground. Below, there is a mill, with the millstream running on and on like time.

Now, this is a beautiful painting. Most of it is landscape: sensitive and subtle, rich in delicate tints, pale greens and remote blues; suave with graceful curves, bending branches and burgeoning leaf clusters; full of contrasts — the hard rock at our feet and the dim crag five miles away, tiny sprays of foliage and distant groves of green merging into gray merging into blue. Even the gallows has something of the pathos of many wooden things made by men — like an old boat, or a rickety cabin in the woods: it looks so awkward among the living trees that we are almost sorry for it, and almost forget its sinister purpose. Even the men and women in the picture, though not beautiful, are cheerful. They are doing what comes naturally — taking a day off, dancing and cutting up, enjoying a holiday in the pleasant spring sunshine. No one is reproaching them; even the man with his arm up may simply be welcoming them. They have chosen a lovely spot for a picnic, this high hilltop overlooking the little town, with the marvelous view and the fresh air and the birds. Yes . . . if it were not for the gibbet; and yet the gibbet is empty. There is no body swinging there. No chains creak in the spring breeze. The gallows does not even seem to have been used for quite a long time.

That is certainly how the people in the picture think,

or else they would not be dancing — probably. It might be how some of the people who enjoy the picture as a scene of country life think. But it is not how we think: and, more important, it is not how the painter himself, Pieter Bruegel, thought. For this is only one of several such paintings of his, which are all at first sight cheerful or at least energetic and positive, but which, when we look into them, contain a bitter and painful contrast.

There is another painting by Bruegel which no one likes, but which is filled with the same painful truth. It shows a dry yellow landscape, full of figures all hurrying in the same direction, toward a little hill. They are all eager and excited. (At the extreme edge of the picture we see a pole with a cartwheel on the top of it: this is where a body has been broken and then exposed to die and to be picked to pieces by birds; and indeed a bird is sitting reflectively upon it now.) In the center of the picture, so small that he is obscure at first glance, is a man surrounded by mounted troopers in red tunics. He has been trying to carry a cross toward the hill, and has just fallen down under its weight. He still has about half a mile to go, and some people are trying to help him up and lift the cross back on to his shoulders. And then we see that in the right foreground there is at least *one* group which is not enjoying the occasion: a woman dressed in blue, with three or four friends, all weeping, or else in an extremity of grief too harsh for tears. The general impression of the picture is — I will not say cheerful, but at least active, purposeful, dynamic. It is with a considerable effort that we distinguish, at the heart of the hurrying crowd, one figure faltering; and realize that this is Jesus, who is about to be executed, and that the figure of anguish in the foreground is his mother. This dynamic festival is in fact the crucifixion of Jesus; this lively public demonstration contains a tragedy.

Most religious painters do not paint in this way. Most painters generally do not paint in this way. They prefer to see life simply. A pretty woman drying her hair after the bath; a raft full of starving sailors; a battle between two heroic champions; a sunlit sea smiling up at sunlit cliffs; a martyr just about to soar up to heaven: these are subjects which most artists prefer, and most people who like painting seem to agree with them.

That is why Pieter Bruegel is still, after nearly four centuries, not fully known. His landscape and peasant pictures, showing dancers at a village party or haymakers grouped around a sunlit tree, are the most famous, because they are easy to understand: they are straightforward; they display one mood, and one alone. The mood is sometimes bitter, sometimes merely calm and observant, sometimes harshly realistic.

Yet the most characteristic pictures by Bruegel are those which contain a contrast, whose meaning has to be worked out by the beholder. For example, there is a huge seascape with ships and fishing boats in the background, and on a cliffside in the foreground, three human figures — a ploughman ploughing doggedly, a fisherman fishing eagerly, a shepherd standing placidly beside his sheep; all is quiet and delightful, except for a faint splash in the sea, with a pair of human legs protruding from the water. Only when we read the title do we realize that this is a satirical depiction of the Fall of Icarus, one of the first men who ever flew through the air; his astounding flight and his disastrous crash into the sea have produced absolutely no effect on the rest of the world. Carefully and deliberately, Bruegel has taken a sentence from the famous classical description of the fall of Icarus, describing the astonishment of fisherman, shepherd, and ploughman (Ovid, *Metamorphoses* 8.217–220) and inverted, abolished, denied it all. Such again is Bruegel's picture of the suicide of King Saul: we see over most of the picture a tremendous battle going on, with hundreds of mounted men fighting furiously; far away in one corner, almost alone, is the despairing monarch of the Hebrews taking his own life. Such is Bruegel's picture of the conversion of St. Paul on the road to Damascus: it shows a difficult mountain pass, which is being crossed by a large force of cavalry and infantry; in the center is a tiny and undramatic figure lying on the ground. It is the apostle who has just had a vision of Jesus Christ; for us he is the focus of interest, but for all the other characters, scores and scores of them, he is merely an annoying delay, an encumbrance.

These are by no means pleasant pictures; but they are beautiful pictures. They are beautiful, and pessimistic. The grass grows, the trees break into leaf, the birds and animals breed and increase, men go about their business and their pleasure, and in the midst of it all, undeniable and ineradicable, although perhaps to be seen only by the visionary, there are inexplicable suffering and omnipresent death. There are very few painters who have understood how to paint tragedy, and Pieter Bruegel is one of the greatest among them.

Bach

IT is not easy to appreciate great artists. It demands a kind of self-surrender which many of us are unwilling to make: we must allow ourselves to be dominated by another, a larger soul. Also, it takes time, much time, before we can visit and grow acquainted with all their important works. We could spend years on one composer alone; on one playwright; on one painter.

But there is another difficulty in such appreciation. This is the problem of historical sympathy. It is fairly easy to understand a creative artist who lives in our own spiritual climate, or in some atmosphere which more or less resembles it. Thus, we find it quite simple to read Dickens or Flaubert, because the world they inhabited is not so far away from us; much of it, indeed, is still with us in fact or in memory. But it is really hard to feel at home in the work of an artist who lived in an age very different from our own, with a different religion, a different social structure, and different psychological and artistic ideals. We may agree that he is a great artist — in so far as he speaks to, and for, all humanity — but we shall surely misinterpret much of his personality and overlook some of the work he himself thought most interesting and important, unless we think ourselves back into his particular spiritual world. This can be done, but it needs a considerable effort: fortunately, it is a fructifying and educative effort.

What do you see when you look at a range of mountains — the chain of the Rockies from Denver, or the Swiss Alps from Berne? What do you see when you look at a forest — the wooded Vermont hills, or the Big Horn forest in Wyoming? You see the mountains as grand, something more than beautiful, noble and magnificent, God's footstool. You see the forest as a sweep of rich and splendid color, an uprush of the earth's own energy, nature not yet spoiled and made petty by the inroads of man.

Yes, but two or three hundred years ago you would not have seen the mountains or the forest with those eyes and with that spirit. You *could* not have so seen them, without a tremendous and very exceptional effort. You would have looked at the forest with distaste and a little horror, seeing it very much as we nowadays would look at a tropical swamp full of crawling snakes and decaying vegetation; it would have seemed disorderly and barbarous, a senseless upsurge of meaningless fertility. At most you might, if you had been rich, have conjectured that it would be a good place for a hunting party, but normally you would have turned away with revulsion. As for the mountains, they would have filled you with real loathing: negative and hostile words would have come into your mind automatically: words like *barren* and *horrid,* words like *monstrous, chaotic, savage.* You would have felt about them as the visitor to Yellowstone feels about those sinister valleys filled with foul vapors and gulfs of boiling mud. If you had had to cross them, you would have done so with anxiety and alarm; as for the notion that anyone would wish to sit and contemplate them, or to feel his spirit enriched by wandering among them, or (most ridiculous of all) to *climb* then — that would have seemed to you either impossible or insane.

Two or three hundred years ago the spiritual atmosphere was widely different from ours. We can think ourselves back into it, but we must first realize that it was different, and then admit that it also was a valid way of looking at the world, with virtues and perceptions from which we are debarred. After that, we can try to define its ideals — and then, only then satisfactorily, appreciate the art it produced.

I speak from experience. For nearly forty years I have been playing the piano and listening to music. But it is only in the last twenty that I have come to understand the work of Johann Sebastian Bach. All through my teens and twenties I thought he was a dry old stick who had written some peculiarly difficult puzzles for the piano and organ, and some tediously monotonous religious utterances for the choir. Now I think he was the greatest composer who ever lived. This change in view was not simply a matter of growing up and getting more sense. No, it sprang from a new understanding of the age in which Bach lived. He worked in the seventeenth and early eighteenth centuries — the period which has been called the age of baroque. I never understood the ideals of that period until I traveled in France, Germany, and Austria, and — quite unexpectedly — found myself overwhelmed by the power and the magnificence of baroque architecture. The palace of Versailles, the Church of the Theatines in Munich, and scores of other noble and splendid buildings, struck me as creations of the human spirit far superior to anything that we can build today. From that I went on to the appreciation of baroque sculpture, and learned to admire the astonishing technique of Bernini — and not only his technique but the intensity of his feeling; both technique and feeling struck me as something beyond anything I had ever experienced. Thereafter it was easy to understand the great baroque painters and etchers — Rembrandt, Rubens, Callot, and a dozen more. And so, perhaps because visual impressions are more direct and powerful than aural impressions, I came the long way round toward an understanding of the baroque composers, and of their greatest master, Bach.

Suppose we try to hear Bach's music as he and his friends heard it, to elicit from it the ideals which governed him as he composed. These are the ideals, the dominant creative ideals, of the baroque age.

The first of these ideals was *tradition*. Bach and his contemporaries did not believe that anything new was likely to be good, or even interesting. They thought that the newer and stranger it was, the worse it would probably turn out to be. This does not mean that they cultivated laborious repetition and copying in the manner of so many Far Eastern artists: no, they felt that any creator would surely produce novelties and ought to strive for originality, *but* they held that the most satisfactory creator would build on the work of others and prolong his own apprenticeship. Steady development was their ideal, rather than explosive newness. Again and again Bach said so, in terms which surprise us so much that we might think them insincere: they are not. When he was asked about his music, he did not imply that he had a genius for it, or was possessed by the spirit of melody. Far from it. When Goethe heard a recital of Bach's organ works, he said, 'It is as though eternal harmony were conversing with itself, as it may have happened in God's bosom shortly before He created the world.' But when Bach was asked about his organ playing, he said, 'You have only to hit the right notes at the right time, and the instrument plays itself.' Many a music critic has looked at Bach's production with amazement, and spoken of it as something superhuman. What did Bach say himself? He said, *'Ich habe fleissig sein müssen: wer es gleichfalls ist, wird eben so weit kommen.* — I had to be diligent. Anyone who works as hard will get just as far.' If you had complimented Bach on the construction of one of his great organ fugues, he would have reacted like an architect who is praised because his buildings don't fall down and kill people.

Tradition means learning and teaching. So Bach learned, all through his early life, and taught, all through his later life. When he was young, he copied out in his own hand dozens and dozens of compositions by elder musicians in order to learn their art. When he was eighteen or so, he walked (or hitchhiked) two hundred and thirty miles to hear the famous organist Buxtehude; he had four weeks' leave from his church to do so, and he stayed four months. After his style had matured, he went on teaching others. He taught all his children, and made several of them into fine musicians. He taught his second wife. He taught many neighbors and younger colleagues. We are apt to think that music must be an outpouring of the solitary soul (as in Beethoven's last quartets), but the preludes and fugues of Bach are something else; they are works through which a great soul teaches innumerable lesser spirits.

The second ideal of Bach's epoch was *symmetry*. As I look out of my window, I see a large apartment building. It has a tower on one side, not on the other; its frontage is stepped back, its rear elevation is irregular, just off straight; it has two grotesque water tanks on the top, and a crowd of TV masts. It looks a little clumsy to me. It would have looked grotesque, almost obscene, to Bach. The buildings of that age were absolutely symmetrical, and their aim was to combine grandeur and richness with an all-ordering harmony. (Think of St. Peter's at Rome.) It is because of his passion for symmetry that Bach was able to express an enormous range of human emotions within a single ordered pattern, the fugue. We feel that, but nowadays we find it terribly hard to understand the connection in Bach's mind between music and mathematics. For instance he took his own name, and turned it into numbers: B, the second letter of the alphabet, means 2; A means 1; C, 3; H, 8; the total is 14. Invert 14, and you have 41, which is J.S. Bach, numerically converted. So, in the composition Bach dictated on his deathbed, 'Before Thy throne I now appear,' the first line contains 14 notes, and the whole melody, 41 notes. That is only one of many such symbolic utterances throughout Bach's works.

Something quite beyond the scope of any contemporary composer in orderly ingenuity is shown in Bach's *Goldberg Variations:* one single tune, with thirty variations. This problem 'did not seem difficult enough for Bach': although he kept the same bass line, he determined to show the divine variety of music by building every kind of transformation upon it. Apart from all the other variations, Bach produced nine different canons upon this single bass line, one in every third variation, working up the gamut from one to nine, and throwing in an inversion at the fifth. And, apart from its ingenuity, this is all music.

One further ideal of the baroque age was *control*. It was the era of decorum. It was the epoch of authority. Outbursts of emotion were indecent; laughter and tears were repressed or sublimated. Hence the heroines of Racine's tragedies, though flaming with passion and seething with rage, still speak in perfectly arranged sentences and rigidly ordered couplets. Hence Bach's preludes and toccatas are often boldly spontaneous and occasionally almost shapeless, soaring and plunging through every key and almost every rhythm, and then — not with a sense of loss, but with a sense of relief — the music returns to the control of the intellect and the will, as expressed by the fugue which follows and transcends the prelude. (Notice that although Chopin used to play Bach's preludes and fugues before each concert of his own, he himself, less disciplined, could compose only a set of preludes.)

In spite of his admiration for these ideals, Bach felt that, like all systems, they were too small for the soul of a great artist. In theory he observed them, and allowed them to dictate much of his work, but in practice, again and again, he moved beyond them. His predecessors and some of his followers — good composers too — did little more than what could have been predicted. But genius is unpredictable. Like Rembrandt, Bach is more than a baroque artist. After establishing the laws of his work, he went beyond them. His noblest composition, the B minor Mass, is neither Protestant nor Catholic; it is baroque and more than baroque. It is nearly universal. Through it, as through most of his greatest music, Bach tells us that the way from the individual to the universal is through the understanding of tradition, the path to freedom lies through the acceptance, then the transcendence, of law.

The fascination of what's difficult

$\mathbf{A}$ NUMBER of American artists have been badly misunderstood. During their working lifetime they were little appreciated, because practically nobody could grasp what they were saying, while after they retired or died comprehension gradually came — and, with it, admiration. Such was Edgar Allan Poe; such was Herman Melville; such was Walt Whitman. One more, quite as remarkable as any of these men, was the musician who died in 1954, the Connecticut Yankee, Charles Ives.

You may never have heard of Charles Ives. Unless you live in a large city, or make a special point of attending recitals of modern music, you have probably never heard any of his works performed 'alive.' And if you have heard a composition by Ives, you certainly did not understand it at first hearing: you probably found it weird and vague and slightly unsympathetic, not to say uncompromising. If you have a good ear and a sensitive appreciation of rhythm, you surely noticed that it was a curious mixture of crude melodies and corny sounds with extremely subtle and complex harmonic and rhythmical patterns. And it was very difficult for you to realize what Ives thought about the world, what he was trying through his music to express. Fortunately, there is an excellent book on Ives, by the composer Henry Cowell and his wife. Mr. Cowell is himself an experienced and original musician who knew Charles Ives personally, liked his music, and understood both music and man. This is a clear and sympathetic guide to the art of a remarkable composer — worth reading for its psychological interest even if you have not hitherto been particularly attracted by Ives or his compositions.

Two of the chief facts about Ives are arrestingly peculiar. The first is that during the early part of his life he composed a great deal of music which was far ahead of his time in subtlety, in daring, in technical skill — but stopped abruptly when he was about forty, because no one would perform his work. Even when he printed it at his own expense and gave it away, people laughed at it and used his scores to adjust piano benches. Walter Damrosch tried one of his symphonies in 1910 with the New York Symphony Orchestra, but abandoned it after one rehearsal as the work of a crazy eccentric, partly because it contained a device which Ives explored more thoroughly than any other composer — the crossing of different rhythms, 2 against 3. Expert soloists would try over his pieces and then complain that the sounds were so hideous as to give them earache. Nobody cared. Many sneered. Ives did not give up composition entirely, but he lost the initial impetus and wrote very little more after his fortieth year. It is hard to think of any other career which followed such a pattern, except perhaps that of Rossini, who stopped composing (except for trifles) when he was thirty-seven.

The other oddity about Charles Ives is that he made a success in another career, a career quite different from music. He did not, like many romantic young geniuses, say, 'My art is everything. The world owes me a living, and in return I shall dedicate to it my next wood-wind septet.' His father, also a Connecticut Yankee, had taught him that independence is essential. He would not write cheap, easily salable music. Therefore he had to find some other career which would enable him to support himself and his family while he continued to compose. He chose life insurance. Starting with the Mutual Life at five dollars a week, he founded his own insurance firm with a single partner in 1907 when he was thirty-three (always a climacteric age): it prospered enormously; and in 1930, when he finally retired, he could have sold his interest for many millions of dollars. But he would not do that either. He had gone into business to make a living and to compose; he had done both; he now bowed out, without wealth, but with his cherished independence secured, and with his music written — although as yet unheard.

This also is unusual. It may be unique. Some painters die rich. A few musicians have made money out of music. Novelists occasionally do well. But original composers of serious music have seldom embarked on external careers and made a success of them. There is no sign that Ives felt his career in business interfered with his music. When he was once asked about that, he replied, 'My business experience revealed life to me in many aspects that I might otherwise have missed. . . . You cannot set an art off in the corner and hope for it to have vitality, reality and substance. There can be nothing *exclusive* about a substantial art. It comes directly out of the heart of experience of life and thinking about life and living life. My work in music helped my business and work in business helped my music.'

Now, both Ives's music and Ives's business success can be explained by his character and his view of life.

But before we explore them, we might ask why the same man, using bold and original methods to advance in American music and in American business during the same period (1900–1920), should have been so rapidly successful in one, and for long such a dismal failure in the other. The answer is that American business was then, as it is now, courageous and unconventional. Ives put into it his own dauntless courage and healthy unconventionality, together with his strong moral sense: he was personally convinced, and he persuaded his agents and his clients, that buying life insurance was not simply a method of saving money, but an ethical duty. On the other hand, musicians in America about 1900 were not very original. They were terrified of novelty in form or content. Therefore when Ives's work was offered to soloists and orchestras, they compared it, not with the most advanced European compositions which were being written at the same time, but with the old-fashioned mid-nineteenth-century tradition in which they had been brought up. They were one generation behind their European contemporaries, while Ives was — not only in business but also in music — one generation ahead. American poetry and American novels also suffered from that time-lag.

Ives's music, like his character, is 100 per cent American in its energy, its novelty, and its blend of tradition and originality. It is both revolutionary and conservative; it clings to old melodies, but it decorates them with startling new harmonies. America is not a young country, not any more; but it is a fresh and original country, and these are fresh and original pieces of music.

They are based on simple melodies. Some of their material comes from familiar hymns, patriotic songs and marches, dance tunes and jollifications; there are occasional quotations from other composers; and there are many simple but pervasive themes invented by Ives himself. But these melodies are seldom played straight. Sometimes they are merely overheard, like a gust of music from a distant orchestra borne to us by the wind, or like a faint reminiscence crossing the surface of the mind; often they are decorated with new and complicated harmonies, like multiple overtones; and often several of them are played together, so that the orchestra must emit and the hearer must follow two or three or even four rhythmical patterns at once. Now, Ives's first hearers asked 'Does he think these chords are beautiful, so full of dissonances and combinations unresolved? Does he think anyone can enjoy these conflicting rhythms? Doesn't the whole thing sound like a traffic jam, or a riot? Isn't it simply aesthetic and spiritual chaos?'

In the answers to these questions lies the secret of Ives's music.

First of all, he does not think that beauty is peace and tranquillity. He hates Mozart, and even more he hates the minor composers who cultivate dulcet sweetness. He thinks the essence of beauty is difficulty. Anything worth having, he believes, is worth fighting for. Listening to music therefore ought to be an effort, rewarded by the sense of a challenge successfully accepted. He likes to give both the performers and the audience something to grapple with. He does not want to baffle them; but he thinks competition is exciting. In the words of W. B. Yeats, he feels 'the fascination of what's difficult.'

Then Ives is a New Englander. He admires individuality. He does not believe everyone ought to sing the same tune. If one member of the choir likes singing in E flat while the others prefer G, Ives holds that the result will be more interesting than perfect traditional harmony. The essential thing is that they should all be trying to do the same thing, each in his own way. Ives's music is not a traffic jam, still less a riot, but something like a town meeting or a Fourth of July celebration, full of dissonances which are more vital than harmony. By the way, was it in irony that he called his biggest piano work the *Concord* sonata?

Much of this is hereditary. Ives's father was the conductor of the brass band in Danbury, Connecticut, and used to practice astounding experiments in unconventional acoustics. He spent many years in trying to split the musical atom — that is, the conventional semitone; and sometimes he broke up his band into sections posted in different parts of the town, one on the church steeple, one on the village green, and one on the roof of the newspaper building — each to play its own variation on a simple tune, such as 'Greenland's Icy Mountains.' And Ives himself, while playing hymns as a church organist, loved adding extra notes to them: not to deform the melody, but to complete it, or even to set it off in more than its original beauty. He would play the first verse straight, then add overtones in playing the second, and in the third create a weird, dissonant accompaniment which was exciting to some of his congregations and infuriating to others.

One further principle in Charles Ives's view of life and of art: he does not believe in completeness; he does not think perfection is possible to human beings or their works. Therefore almost all his music, although elaborate and even sophisticated, was rapidly written down and seldom if ever reduced to a definitive form. When he died, he had been working for years on a symphony, the *Universe* symphony, which he never intended to finish. Even in performance, he was not a stickler for exactitude. He felt that no single concert could ever express all he had in mind, and he would be content if the orchestra played with good will and came out approximately correct.

Of course, when he came up against the traditional musicians with these attitudes, they concluded it was better for the orchestra not even to try to play his work.

Who was right? Who was wrong? The answer probably is that both were right in their way. What Ives wanted to express was the ideals of his America, the America of the late nineteenth and early twentieth centuries, and in particular the ideals of New England. One of his finest pieces is his sonata on New England, whose separate movements are named for Emerson, Hawthorne, the Alcotts, and Thoreau. That was an America which, although expanding and full of competition, was cohesive; there was room in it for the development of individuality without the growth of tyranny, or anarchism, or mania.

But perhaps some of the European-trained musicians rejected Ives's work not because they were short-sighted but because they were long-sighted. They had already, in Europe, felt the power of disruptive spiritual forces; they saw the dangers of prolonged dissonance; they had read Nietzsche, who hoped for the subjugation of all mankind to a few bold and strenuous heroes without consciences, and who thought that the harmony of many minds was little more than the simultaneous chatter of many monkeys. Perhaps they could hear the first thunder of the world war, and perhaps they were shrinking from it; while Ives, like Whitman, could hear only the remote echoes of the

American Civil War, from which he extracted a complicated music in which dissonance did not mean enmity, nor conflict destruction. That music was truly expressive of America. It was not the only America there has ever been or will be; but it was an ideal never before given musical form. Optimistic, genial, naïve and yet profound, noisily energetic and yet tenderly meditative, fertile and careless, believing that man is individual and therefore imperfect but none the less to be respected, that all art is necessarily incomplete but not therefore negligible, Charles Ives both embodied and expressed some of the best of the American spirit.

Pictures of war

D ID you ever try to compare the different ways in which artists, living at different times or in different countries, handle the same subject? It is well worth doing. Usually it tells us something new about each of the artists, and the ages they lived in — something we might have suspected, but never realized with such vividness.

Take one powerful subject, which has been much in all our minds in these last years: the sufferings of the civilian population during a war. In wartime — always, from the beginning of history — soldiers and sailors have been able to fight and defend themselves: they can act as well as endure. But the noncombatants must only suffer in a world which seems to have gone mad. As soon as I think of this, there leaps into my mind's eye a photograph taken during the Japanese invasion of China. It showed a street, or a highroad, or possibly even a railroad station, partly ruined and apparently still under bombardment. The background contained several dim figures running for shelter. The air was dark with smoke and dust. In the foreground was one human being which epitomized the whole madness and cruelty of war. It was a baby of about two, deserted and alone, its face blackened with earth from shell-bursts, its limbs too small to carry it more than a few yards away, its mind too tormented to understand anything of what was happening, its parents perhaps killed a few moments before. There it sat, with its eyes closed on the universe, weeping bitterly.

Now, the same subject — the horrors of war as felt by defenseless civilians — has interested a number of the world's finest painters.

The most eminent painter of our generation, Pablo Picasso, made it the subject of his most famous picture: *Guernica*. This was done in 1937, just after the Nazi air force, working for Franco, had carried out, as a tactical experiment, the first saturation bombing raid in history, and had virtually destroyed the ancient Basque city of Guernica. Picasso does not attempt to show us the flaming and exploding city, nor the raiding airplanes. The whole picture, although it is enormous in size, contains only five human beings and two animals.

On the extreme right is a man with his mouth gaping in a hideous shriek, and his head thrown back at an angle so impossible that only an ultimate agony could produce it. He stretches two ugly and helpless hands to the black sky; and around him are triangular forms which look like stylized flames. On the extreme left is a woman, also screaming madly in a long endless scream, with a dead baby in her arms. In the foreground are three figures. One is a woman, rushing wildly across the scene — but such a woman as we have never seen except in a nightmare (and such events as this are nightmares, which have become facts). Every one of her limbs is distorted with speed and effort; she seems to be trying to escape from everything, even from her body. Opposite her is the corpse of a man, still clutching the fragment of a weapon, but dead — not only dead, but dismembered. Between the two is a gigantic horse, wounded, and screaming in agony, as though it were calling for death. Near it are the impassive head and fore-quarter of a fighting bull. (These are the two symbols of death best known to the Spaniards: the helpless horse, and the ruthless bull which attacks and destroys it, long before it is itself sacrificed.) Above this entire picture there is one face, not calm, but at least sane: the idealized face of a spirit, holding a lamp at the center of the scene and gazing on it with grief-stricken amazement. The entire picture is executed in gloomy colors: black, glaring white, many shades of gray. Instead of looking like a normal three-dimensional scene taken from reality and transferred to two-dimensional canvas, it seems to vibrate, to stagger, to jerk abruptly into harsh projections which strike our horrified eyes with something like a physical shock.

Look back now for more than a century. Look back to the Napoleonic wars. Spain suffered in them also, and a Spanish artist recorded her sufferings then too. This was Goya. His finest painting on this subject is *The Executions of May Third 1808*. Picasso's *Guernica* is all distortion and symbolism. Goya's *Executions of May Third* is all realism.

The scene is a little valley outside a Spanish city. There are stately buildings in the background. On the left stand four or five defenseless men in civilian clothes, with expressions of terror in their rough Spanish faces. One of them, all in white, waves his hands as though appealing for mercy. On the right, only a few feet away, is a line of uniformed French soldiers, aiming their muskets at the hearts of the condemned men. In one minute, in one second, they will fire a volley. The line of muskets is steady and efficient, appearing all the more ruthless because all the bayonets are fixed; if the bullets fail, the soldiers will stab the men to death. The soldiers themselves are quite impersonal: resolute efficient figures in uniforms and heavy shakos, their faces almost invisible behind arms raised to fire. (Their steady line, contrasted with the broken group of civilians, reminds us of another essential horror of war —that the forces of destruction always seem to be more efficient and better organized than the forces which build civilization.) In the center of the picture, behind the bayonets, is a group of condemned men waiting for their turn to die; they are kneeling, and hiding their faces, or perhaps weeping. A few corpses are already lying on the ground.

Now turn back further yet, another two hundred years, to the age which we know best as the age of the Pilgrim Fathers. Just about the time the Pilgrims were building their earliest settlement, a young man in France was completing a set of pictures which he named *The Miseries and Misfortunes of War*. This was Jacques Callot. He was one of the greatest etchers who ever lived, and probably the first man to turn etching into an independent art. He was born about 1592 (a generation after Shakespeare). His father was (of all things) a herald; and he himself was intended for the church. But he ran away from home twice, because he wanted to be an artist. At last he was sent to Italy for training. It was there that he learned his astounding technique and formed his style. For years he served the Medici in Florence. Then he returned to France, and worked for Louis XIII and other potentates. He himself was not a Frenchman, strictly speaking, but a Burgundian from Lorraine; there is a story that he made a wonderful etching of King Louis's siege of La Rochelle, but refused point-blank to make another picture of the same king's armies besieging his own native city of Nancy.

Now, consider one of Callot's etchings of *The Miseries and Misfortunes of War*. When we look at it, our first impression is not of destruction and disintegration, but of order, balance, symmetry, and even grace. It is quite a small picture. Picasso's *Guernica* is an enormous mural, covering many square yards. Goya's *Executions* is eight feet by eleven. Callot's etching is not much bigger than a man's hand. It looks rather like an episode from a picturesque ballet, seen from a distant part of the theater. Then we look more closely into it. We examine the various groups which make up this neat symmetrical composition. We see that, though they are all carefully disposed, and form an over-all pattern which is both pleasing and intricate, they are not merely posed — like lay figures. There is a good deal of action in their arrangement, and there is a sinister logic.

The scene is a small village. In the foreground there is a cottage of two or maybe three rooms, only one story high. There are three or four more cottages visible at the right. Opposite them a large old tree frames the picture gracefully. In the background is a little church, which when full might hold sixty people: the whole population of the village and the surrounding farms. It is an elegiac scene. Immediately in front of us as we look at it, an old cart has stopped, and the horse is hanging its head as though in exhaustion. And then we begin to see that the village has been transformed by a life which is not its own. Figures are climbing all over the cart, figures with gay feathers on their heads, and swords sticking out prominently from their left sides; they are unloading the wine casks and whatever else the cart was carrying. Two groups of what might be dancers, at right and left, prove to contain more of these befeathered and sworded figures. One has grasped a woman by the hair as she runs from him; the other is running rapidly after a terrified girl with his sword in the air. The cottages are smoking, with smoke which does not come from their peaceful hearths. They are burning. And the church itself, the church as we look more closely is seen to be on fire; the steeple is already pouring out smoke which will soon change to flames. On the extreme left a purposeful group of soldiers has discharged a volley of shots from muskets at the church. Apparently the villagers have gathered on its steps and in its churchyard to make a concerted stand. Some of them have guns, and are firing back.

But the issue is not in doubt. There is a vicious energy about the organized soldiers which convinces us that they will take this village and loot it as they have taken many more already; they are experienced in this kind of amateur fighting. Some of them have already started looting and raping. Meanwhile, how long will the villagers continue to resist, with the church burning over their heads?

This is not a mere atrocity picture. Such events were common during the terrible wars of the seventeenth century — especially in the religious conflicts, when men fought more savagely over religious dogmas than they have ever done over politics. Still, its effect is supremely harrowing. And yet there is a paradox. As an artistic composition, the picture is graceful and harmonious. The lines are deft and delicate, the figures of both murderers and victims are skilfully and not grotesquely posed, the bitter conflicts of emotion are offset by the control and the balance of the design.

Powerful, these contrasts between artists — powerful and significant. Working in our own time and using many of the new devices of twentieth-century art, Picasso conveyed the effect of an air raid by using figures which were anatomically (though not spiritually) impossible; which were less real than symbolic. In the early nineteenth century, Goya combined realism with romance; his picture of the execution looks like an eye-witness sketch, but it is in fact a collection of carefully composed and heightened contrasts, meant to play on our emotions. Callot, working in the period when the aim of art was symmetry and control, produced something comparable to a Bach fugue, combining heart-rending pathos with supreme intellectual and aesthetic detachment. Callot lived in the era of authority; Goya in the era of passion and rebellion; Picasso in — what can we call it? — the era of disintegration?

The indescribable city

THERE are certain places in the world which have never been truly and completely described. Probably they never will be. The most obvious of these, for Americans, is surely the Grand Canyon; for Europeans, probably the Matterhorn. Many a poet, many an imaginative author, has sat for hours contemplating that pale spike of rock rising out of green fields toward the blue sky, and has turned away in silence; many an ambitious American essayist has walked beside the Canyon, day after day, gazing into its terrifying depths and across its mighty chasms, watching its colors change with the hours and the clouds, and has abandoned the attempt to report what he saw.

There are cities also which are indescribable. Oxford — not as it is now with all its grumbling traffic and banausic crowds, but as it was when unspoiled — has never been put into words, unless in a single sonnet by Gerard Manley Hopkins, a fantastic romance by Max Beerbohm, and a paragraph or two by Matthew Arnold. Paris — has Paris ever been set down on paper, in poetry or prose? And the most strangely beautiful city in the entire world, alluring as its exquisite courtesans, elusive as the sunlight reflected from its waters, remains a perpetual temptation to authors, and a perpetual bafflement. This is Venice.

The greatest of modern European writers set one entire play in Venice, and he appears to have known the city personally; but he never tried to describe it. Indeed, in the first drama he ever wrote, he quoted a proverb which amounted to saying that Venice could not be even imagined: *Venetia, Venetia, chi non te vede, non te pretia.** Lord Byron actually lived in Venice for three years, and evoked her past grandeur in an ode and an elegiac passage of *Childe Harold's Pilgrimage,* together with a fragment or two; but even he shrank from the task of picturing the lovely city in anything like completeness.

Many later writers have tried to describe it. The most ambitious attempt in recent years is *Venice Observed,* by Mary McCarthy (published in 1956 by Reynal), a huge and sumptuous volume, in which Miss McCarthy's feline prose glides above, below, around, and occasionally through the interstices of at least two hundred brilliant photographs of Venice and reproductions of Venetian paintings and works of art. It is a fine book, but a very odd book. Miss McCarthy is never a simple or straightforward writer; and sometimes, when one is trying to follow the sinuous movement of her thought and the supple gestures of her style from the top of one page to the middle of the next past two

---

* *Love's Labour's Lost,* IV. ii. 100.

photographs and one half-page color facsimile, one feels as bewildered as the new visitor to Venice whose gondolier, turning twice to the right and three times to the left past a decaying palace beneath two ancient bridges and through a cheerful little slum, may indeed be taking him to his hotel, but occasionally seems as though he were trying deliberately to bewilder and entrap him for some sinister purpose.

This is a charming book; if you have never seen Venice, it is fascinating, almost incredible; but if you have, it is inadequate. Venice outdoes it, as it has always outdone all writers bold enough to endeavor to describe its unique loveliness.

Why is Venice such a baffling place to write about? It seems as though there were several convergent reasons, two in particular. One is that it is predominantly a place to be *seen*. The other is that its people have for many centuries cultivated mystery.

For a painter, Venice must be either paradise or hell. Paradise, on the whole, since so many good painters have gone there and come away full of fresh inspiration, or spent many long and productive years there, painting without fatigue and almost without repetition. Even to the rest of us, who are not painters, it is a feast for the eyes. To begin with, the city is — and this to most men is perpetually incredible — built not on solid earth but among the waters of the sea. One result of this is that it becomes a constant contradiction. A city is a thing aiming at permanence, full of stately buildings and durable streets; but Venice, based on the shifting and restless water, combines power and stability with incessant movement and change. Again, most cities are monotones. They are all gray concrete, or all red brick, or all sandstone or limestone. A few, which are wisely built and maintained, with plenty of green grass and oases of trees, may be of two colors. But the water which sidles and whispers through every part of Venice is of all colors, never one: it reflects the sky, clear blue or whitely clouded, pink in the dawn, golden at sunset, black and silver in lashing rain, cool bluish green in calm weather; it reflects the walls, with their old grays and browns, and the fronts of palaces, white, golden yellow, dark green, multi-colored, and brilliantly variegated. Further, the play of light in most cities is uninteresting. Some are shrouded in rainy or foggy twilight, as London so often is; some are almost deliberately cramped and lightless, like Naples — where one can scarcely believe in the narrow, stinking streets that one of the loveliest skies in the world smiles its happy smile above; a few have bold contrasts of light and dark, like New York, which is oriented almost exactly north and south; but surely no other city in the world can show such a range of contrasting lights and shadows as Venice, where you can pass in ten minutes from the full blaze of sunlight reverberating from miles of shallow sea waves, on the Piazzetta facing the harbor, to a quiet little canal which the sun strikes directly for only an hour or so each day, and which, for the rest of the time, is a moving mass of sidelong sunrays, dancing reflections, uncanny iridescences, and ghostly obscurities.

Quite apart from the color, light, and motion of the water beneath and through Venice, but no doubt inspired by its fluid nature, the very shape, the texture of the city, is unlike that of nearly all other Western cities. They are simply planned, with straight, broad avenues and boulevards intersecting at plain, open spaces, usually square or circular in form, like the Place de la Concorde or Piccadilly Circus. More and more, as we become more and more addicted to motor transport instead of walking, the plan of modern cities is simplifying itself into a network of intersecting motor highways, planned to achieve (in theory at least) the maximum of cruising speed and the minimum of formal beauty. Much as I love New York, I must admit that the checkerboard pattern of most of its streets is disastrously boring to walk through, or even to drive through. But it is impossible to be bored while walking through Venice. Bewildered, yes, constantly; bored, no. No two streets are the same. No street is the same as itself for five blocks. No two squares are the same; no two churches or palaces. Being rowed through Venice in a gondola is even less monotonous, for in a very few minutes you can move from a tiny twisting *rio* scarcely wide enough for two gondolas to pass each other, to the Grand Canal, populous with barges and ferries, and so wide and deep that it might well be the estuary of a fair-sized river, and then out onto the open lagoon with its sea breezes and dancing waves. To wander through most cities nowadays is rather like touring a big, prosperous department store, with goods of all qualities laid out on neatly arranged counters separated by symmetrical aisles. To explore Venice on foot is like talking to a poet whose conversation is full of flowers and stars, or watching a beautiful woman whose charm and whose personality show new facets to every ray of light.

But beyond the physical character of Venice, its mutability and its intricacy, there lies its peculiar, its unique ethos as a city, once a sovereign state and head of a mighty empire. This ethos, although easy to feel, is hard to define; but near its center lies an inveterate custom of silence and secrecy. For centuries upon centuries the Venetians operated the finest intelligence service in Europe; their spies and their informants were everywhere from London to Istanbul; their foreign ministers were the founders of modern Western diplomacy, and the archives of their for-

eign service contained the distilled wisdom of many generations, never to be revealed to foreigners and competitors.
Their central government, proud, patient, aristocratic, and
aloof, was able to treat with monarchs and popes on an
equal footing, shunned the excitements and depressions of
democracy, kept its deepest plans and policies secret from
all the world except the innermost council of the Republic, and concealed its most important mysteries in a
darkness and silence which are still partially impenetrable.
And privately, Venice was above all others the city of disguise and masquerade, the center of secret feuds and secret
love affairs, the home of the hooded and cloaked assassin,
the somber stage of the dagger thrust and the body lowered
silently into the dark canal. Even the garrulous Casanova
had one love affair in Venice which involved a woman
whose name he will not reveal (he calls her 'ma chère
M.M.') and a foreign nobleman whose name he never knew
for certain. Nowadays Venice is openly governed and
effectively policed; yet, both in its tortuous streets and in
the cool politeness of its citizens, both in its populous loneliness and in the traffic-free conversational hush that makes
it the quietest of all contemporary cities, both in the slow,
deliberate pace of those who walk through it and in the
suave, almost noiseless movement of those elegant anachro-
nisms, the gondolas, there remain the engrained habit of
evasion, reserve, emotionless courtesy, and sotto voce conversation, the custom of passion governed by prudence (it
is impossible to be really imprudent if you cannot take ten
steps without the danger of falling into the water, it is
impossible to be daringly and ostentatiously passionate if
the horizon is bounded on all sides by vanishing vistas of
cool water and shuttered houses); further, there is a deep
sense of independence and uniqueness, and above all a
delicate epicureanism, which is determined — not to live

without effort, nor to live for the sake of working, but from the optimum expenditure of energy to extract the maximum quantity of physical, emotional, and aesthetic pleasure. Venice has never been a lotos-land, except perhaps in the eighteenth century, but it has always balanced work against reward more carefully and sensitively than most other cities of the world.

And therefore Venice has eluded all those who have attempted to write about it. Miss McCarthy — although (as one would expect) her book is brilliant — almost wholly fails to explain why and how Venice is so intensely beautiful, still so fundamentally dignified and aloof in spite of the cheap glass gondolas in its shops, in spite of the throngs of overweight French tourists and muscular German tourists and naïve American tourists and non-U British tourists, still so enchanting and so intensely itself. Her most industrious predecessor, John Ruskin, produced a book called *Stones of Venice* which, for all its extreme sensibility and serpentine eloquence, is so absurdly prejudiced as to be worse than useless. (Imagine a book on Venice which stops describing its architecture and art just at the period when the great palaces begin to be built and the great painters to start their work!) Ruskin's translator and successor, Marcel Proust, could not describe the city, but he could evoke it as a sort of vision (in Chapter III of *Albertine Disparue*):

> I had penetrated a mesh of little lanes, *calli,* which divided with their criss-cross grooves a section of Venice bounded between a canal and the lagoon, as though it had crystallized into a multitude of tiny slender shapes. Suddenly at the end of one of those little streets, the crystallized material seemed to be distended. A huge and sumptuous *campo* — whose size I could certainly never have guessed amid that mesh

of little streets, which I could never even have imagined as situated among them — stretched before me,
surrounded by charming moonlight-pale palaces. In
another city, the streets seem to move towards a scene
like this, they guide you to it and set it off in a frame.
Here, it seemed to be deliberately hidden in a laby-
rinth of alleys, like the Arabian Nights palaces to
which a man is brought at night, and which after
being taken home next morning he can never find
again, so that he believes they were nothing but a
dream.

For Proust it was a visionary city. For most visitors it
has always been a visionary city. Miss McCarthy does not
like to dream; she herself is always fully conscious. She is
in the minority. Whether the Venetians themselves dream
or not, I cannot tell; but surely all those who visit that
magical city are living in a dream. The only persons I have
ever known who are capable of looking around the Piazza
di S. Marco in the evening, with the three fine baroque
walls which make it (in Napoleon's words) 'the best drawing-room in Europe,' and on the fourth side the delicious
bubbles of gold and green which are the roof of a cathedral,
but which look like the emanation of the shallow green
and gold sea; of looking around this fantastic scene, and
listening to the gay chatter of the innumerable people —
free as nowhere else from business and traffic and the bonds
of pleasureless routine — while enjoying the music which
filters through the air from the *caffès* as effortlessly as, in
the gathering dusk, the gondolas slide through the twilit
canals; of seeing and hearing all that and still remaining
cool, impassive and critical, are Miss McCarthy herself, that
admirable intelligence, and the advertising man I once
overheard, gazing pensively at the view out over the mouth
of the Grand Canal toward the exquisite church of St.

George, and saying to his wife, 'What a wonderful place to put a big sky sign! TOPFLITE BISCUITS TOPFLITE BISCUITS — can't you see it, shining over the lagoon in three colors, switching on and off every ten seconds, day and night? That would add something. Trouble is, this place is too dreamy. It needs a touch of reality.'

Characters

Madam Cat

IN the summer of 1954 an old, a very old French lady died. She was buried with mighty pomp and circumstance: her body lay in state as though she had been a monarch; many of the great men of France paid personal tributes to her in speech and writing. On the other hand, the Roman Catholic church refused to allow her to be interred in consecrated ground. She had been famous — and sometimes notorious — in France for about half a century. Not many people in the United States knew much about her until two or three years before her death. Then she got into the news by discovering a beautiful and talented young actress and making her the star of one of her own plays. The play was *Gigi*. The actress was Audrey Hepburn. The old lady was the eminent writer who signed herself Colette: Sidonie-Gabrielle Colette.

You probably recall the pictures of Colette which appeared in the last few years of her life. Her curious personality came over in them very well — at least, as much of it as had survived eighty years of hard work, incessant publicity, and daring adventure. What you saw was apparently a heap of ashes, in which hot embers were still glowing. Her body was indistinguishable and shapeless: she suffered terribly from arthritis in the later years (sad for a woman who had been exquisitely slender and supple and who had actually enjoyed a career as a dancer); and she was evidently chilled by age, so that she had to huddle herself into many blankets and wraps and scarves and shawls. She also had that peculiarly dogged clutch on life which many old ladies possess: it is a passion for surrendering as little as possible to Time, for keeping hundreds of relics of long-vanished years, for immortalizing the past through memory and mementoes: so we should imagine from the photographs which showed her room (like her books) to be crowded with personal souvenirs. In the midst of the shawls and the cushions and the *reliquiae,* there was Colette's strange old face. It never smiled — at least, never for photographers. It usually looked sad. She was in frequent pain from her disease, and without a doubt she mourned bitterly for her lost youth. ('Youth, that wonderful thing,' said Bernard Shaw, 'what a crime that it should be wasted on the young!') Sad, Colette's face was, but it was exceedingly intelligent, and a little more than that. Large penetrating eyes; frizzy hair — a souvenir of a style which had once suited her and which even later she would not abandon, perhaps also insurance against being suspected of wearing a wig; a wilful mouth; a pointed chin; and an indescribably deep air of sophistication, wiliness, and fatigue. With her white make-up and her dark piercing eyes and her unquiet gaze, she looked like one of the less flattering portraits of bad old biddies drawn by her own contemporary, Henri de Toulouse-Lautrec.

There are other photographs of Colette, taken at much earlier stages of her life: in her twenties, when she was a young but not innocent wife; in her thirties, when she was a spectacular dancer, something between Isadora Duncan and Mistinguette. Yet neither these nor the portraits of Colette in her old age show much evidence of one quality which she assuredly possessed: her fascination. She was a charmer. I never met her, I never even saw her, but I have read numbers of her books, and from them I know that she, like her style, must have been unforgettably winning. Those who knew her personally all agree in saying that she was an enchanting creature: some called her a lovely witch.

Her life was simply extraordinary. Only a very brave, a very energetic, a very determined, and a very unusual woman could have made a success of it. She was born in 1873, down south in the Burgundy country. She was not purely French. Her mother was French, but her father was a quadroon — a tremendous fellow, an ex-officer of the Zouaves, with a ferocious temper, a bristling beard, and only one leg. Colette was brought up in a small village where they spoke a rich, old-fashioned dialect full of words and phrases never used in ordinary French; but her mother also taught her to read and re-read the French classics, so that even before she left school she acquired the essentials of a fine prose style. Once when she was a little girl of eight, her mother expressed great surprise that she was not reading the *Memoirs* of Saint-Simon. 'Strange,' she said, 'that at your age you should neglect such an interesting book!'

In her late teens Colette came to Paris. At twenty she was married — and to what a husband! He would have wrecked the lives of most women, and he did his very best to wreck hers. He was a fat, bearded, sensual, conscience-less, painfully stingy, and wildly extravagant fellow nearly twice her age. He made his money as a best-selling author. His name was Henri Gauthier-Villars, but he used to publish under the simple pseudonym 'Willy.' (This sounds pretty naïve to us, but perhaps it seemed foreign and sophisticated to the French.) Not only his own books were signed 'Willy,' but a stream of hack novels and ephemeral articles produced for him by ghost writers. Like Dumas before him, he ran a sort of factory for producing popular romances, and employed many young writers who might, if they had written independently, have made a distinguished name for themselves. Not long after marrying Colette, he put her also into the salt mines: not so much like a husband asking his wife to help him in an artistic project, as like an unscrupulous teacher with a gifted pupil, or a slaveowner with a brilliant new purchase. He told her to write her reminiscences of her rather naughty life at school, and then published the book under his own pseudonym. It is called *Claudine at School*. It is so unmistakably feminine and so charmingly youthful that it is difficult to see how any human being could ever have believed for a moment that it was written by a fat middle-aged man; but in spite of the apparent discrepancy it became an immediate best-seller, and has been popular ever since. Willy was both mean and wasteful. He would not even buy Colette a winter coat; and yet he sold this book outright to the publishers, and made her also sign the sale contract, so that apparently she never made another franc out of a novel which sold steadily for over fifty years.

She followed the story of her schooldays with another novel telling how she (or Claudine) came to Paris, fell in love with a middle-aged intellectual, and married him; then with another about Claudine's first years as a young wife; and finally with a book about the break-up of the marriage. These four made her initially famous: *Claudine at School* (1900), *Claudine in Paris* (1901), *Claudine Married* (1902), and *Claudine Goes Away* (1903). Years later, after she had left her husband and published some books of her own, the signature on these four was altered to 'Colette-Willy': the ex-husband and ex-wife added a note to explain that they now wished to share the credit of the authorship of the tetralogy. This seems extremely generous on Colette's part. Although she *might* never have written a line without pressure from her husband, and although he did give her some ideas and did take the trouble to discipline her prose, still, he got the kudos and the cash. Remarkable revolution: she started so immature, apparently so gentle and elusive and unknown, while Willy was one of the best-known writers in France. She ended as a world-famous author, and something like a classic, while he is entirely and utterly forgotten.

After leaving Willy, Colette went on the stage and had a spectacular career as a dancer, showing the maximum amount of flesh permitted under French law, which is almost the maximum amount possible. She acquired an even more spectacular experience of love. And she wrote a great deal — almost too much. Yet, as well as teaching her to write with variety and purity of style, Willy had evidently taught her one of the invaluable secrets every successful writer must know — the secret of establishing a creative harmony between the unconscious self, with all its fertile imaginings and unaccountable impulses, and the conscious mind, which shapes such material into the final form of art. For, although she wrote dozens of books and essays, they always sound quite spontaneous. This spontaneity was the center of her fascination. In essence, it is not a literary gift at all. Many good conversationalists are fascinating because they are (or appear) spontaneous. Every now and then one meets a Polish *émigrée,* or a lady from New Orleans, who talks on and on and on as freely as the wind playing over the water: what she says may be little more than water and wind, yet it is delightful to listen to the breeze and watch the ripples. I do not recall a single mechanical sentence in the whole of Colette's works. There are none of those tedious camera-eye passages where the author painstakingly explains details which the reader could have imagined for himself.

> Next evening John came home at six as usual, tired with his day's work in the accounting office and exasperated by the new burdens which Mr. Miller had placed upon his shoulders. Mary had his supper waiting for him, but he could not eat. He sat there in silence, toying gloomily with his food — although she had made the meat-balls specially round, and had spent many hours knotting the spaghetti into appetizing bundles.

Instead of that kind of thing, Colette's stories sound like the conversation of an extremely intelligent woman who assumes that her listener also is intelligent and interested, and would indeed stop talking if he were not.

Colette's style is exquisite. Her subjects are nearly always profoundly shocking. This is one reason why she is so unusual among novelists. She can describe the most outrageous actions and emotions in sentences that can be read aloud and admired sheerly for their melody, and scarcely questioned for their sinister meaning: so that in her books, as Burke said, 'vice loses half its evil by losing all its grossness.' In this antinomy lies one of the secrets of Colette's work, and probably of her own personal charm. In *Gigi* extreme innocence and disgusting vice are closely coupled, sometimes in competition, sometimes apparently in alliance. This is the main theme of much of Colette's writing: not the conflict between virtue and sin (indeed, I can scarcely remember a single truly virtuous man or woman in all her books), but the conflict between candor, which is strong, and sophistication, which is weak and devious; between honest simplicity which can defend itself, and the awful compulsions of neurotic viciousness. She is not a tragic writer. She is a romantic and comic writer — so sweetly, hopefully romantic, and so deftly, wittily comic that it is difficult to remember how sordid, and in fact how unnatural, most of her subjects are. What interested her most was what her eighteenth-century predecessor, Choderlos de Laclos, called 'dangerous liaisons': absurdly maladjusted couples who somehow got on better, or at least lived more intensely, than ordinary well-balanced couples: a tired, wise, aging woman with a young, handsome, amorous man; a young bride with an elderly husband, both equally sensual; or, as in *Gigi,* a hard mercenary mother with an innocent daughter who turns out to be much more worldly-wise.

At the time her books came out they were both shocking and attractive for another reason, which has now faded away. It was this: although her stories posed as fiction, they were awfully close to fact — so close that their readers could identify many of the people in them. No doubt the fictitious Claudine was not the real Sidonie-Gabrielle Colette. Yet she was described as looking like the real Sidonie-Gabrielle Colette, with a pointed chin, and unusual hair, and a Burgundian turn of speech, and so forth. That elderly roué, the husband of Claudine, looked nobler than Willy and had a more dignified career; yet, in age and manners, he closely resembled the real Willy. So there was a scandalous delight in reading about the outrageous sexual and emotional lives of a couple whom one might see in a *café* or meet at a party. In later books, Colette carried this even further, and inserted brief witty portraits of many recognizable characters, some of them world-famous — but in diabolically indecorous situations.

She loved to shock the public. Still, it is hard to say her books were wicked. They were full of acts which we describe as immoral, but the actors were usually almost devoid of any sense of morality. It was chiefly in this (apart from the style) that they differed from the novels of André Gide. Gide's characters are always doing wicked things quite consciously, and then gloating over them. Colette's characters are always quite single-minded.

The animals that people admire are often symbols of their own subconscious mind. Ernest Hemingway admires big, strong, combative animals. Jack London liked fierce dogs. Some people love birds — not caged birds, or half-tame poultry like pigeons, but wild birds, flying freely and living harmlessly and making their own music. Colette admired the only animal which will live with human beings and remain almost wholly self-centered; the pet animal which refuses to be disciplined like the horse or to demonstrate loyalty like the dog; the animal which smiles, but never laughs, which can be graceful even in impossibly embarrassing situations, which is habitually polite — except in sudden crises of passion; the animal which, by its very walk, seems to convert a garden into a clearing in the jungle, and a dark room into a cavern full of ghosts; the animal which, although fed by human beings, remains its own master and sometimes dominates the other inmates of the house: the most cunning, the most cruel, and the most beautiful of all domestic beasts: the cat. Horses can be mean; both dogs and men can be evil; but even when a cat is being fiendishly cruel or spectacularly sensual it cannot be called wicked. If you can imagine a series of novels written by an unusually intelligent cat, in a style varying from a silken purr to a melodious but occasionally threatening *meow,* and on subjects almost as remote from ordinary morality as feline ethics are from human ethics, you will have a very good notion of the books of that fluffy old thing with nine lives, Madame Colette.

Death of a poet

IN November 1953 at St. Vincent's Hospital in New York
City, the brilliant Welsh poet Dylan Thomas, after lying
for many hours in a coma, died. He had just passed his
thirty-ninth birthday. The doctors said his death was due
to alcoholic poisoning of the brain. On his deathbed he was
surrounded by men and women who loved him dearly.
They were grieved by the doom which had overtaken him;
and yet nearly all of them knew it was inevitable. They had
watched him killing himself for years.

One of them — a man who knew Dylan Thomas well
and admired both his work and his essentially lovable
character — wrote a book about those last years. It is *Dylan
Thomas in America,* by John Malcolm Brinnin (published
by Little, Brown). Well written, sympathetic, charmingly

modest — when one considers that Mr. Brinnin was Thomas's agent on his American tours and helped him to make thousands of badly needed dollars, it is remarkable that he says comparatively little of the many, many headaches the job must have given him — charmingly modest, and infused throughout with a sense of bitter sorrow for the loss of a difficult but charming friend and a difficult but marvelous poet, this is a book which is very hard to forget. It is full of stories which are almost unbelievable to anyone who did not know Dylan Thomas personally. He was not merely a terrific drinker; he was a rioter. He loved shocking people, the grander and more learned the better — he himself used to call it the Provincial Push, or the Up-Rimbaud-and-at-'em attack. And in his cups he used to make passes publicly at beautiful women, making his intentions perfectly clear by word and act. Some of the stories in this book sound as though they were imaginary, and yet there is reason to believe that they are true. They were invented by that perennial naughty boy with the wild and whirling imagination, Dylan Thomas himself; he not only invented these fantastic escapades, but in person performed them.

It must have been a difficult book to write. It must have been a painful book to write. Not only Dylan Thomas appears in it — in circumstances so degrading as to provoke acute embarrassment even in the minds of readers who never saw him close-to; but also several of his mistresses; and his beautiful and strange wife, whose last appearance is in a strait jacket, departing for a rest home. Both Thomas's life and his death were agony for her. The agony is apparently not yet over. At her request, the author and publisher of the book inserted a statement over her signature saying that, although she was 'not quarrelling with Brinnin's presentation of Dylan,' she still considered that

it was 'onesided' and did not 'do justice to the circumfer-
ence of the subject.' That is probably true; but after all,
Mr. Brinnin did not set out to write a complete life of
Thomas, which would be an enormously complicated and
absorbing task, half a life-work; he made his book center
on the poet's visits to the United States on reading tours,
adding only a few reminiscences of his own trips to see
Thomas in Wales and in London. Dylan Thomas's entire
life would be far richer, but it would also be even more
painful.

As we read this book, and realize that it is the story of a
man who was, in spite of his remarkable talents, busily and
almost incessantly engaged in killing himself with drink,
we have to ask, *Why?* Mr. Brinnin himself acknowledges
that he can scarcely answer the question. That part of
Thomas's life he could share only with an effort, and could
only partially understand. Women who knew Thomas even
better also found him a mystery if they attempted to penetrate his mind — a mind whose difficulty and complexity
were only partially reflected in his enigmatic poems. Those
who found him easiest to be with were apparently able to
accept him merely as a jolly, talkative, amorous, wildly
imaginative, outrageously violent tosspot, and to ask no
questions of, or about, the inner man. But if one loves
poetry, and his poetry in particular, one will be shocked
and saddened by this book about him, and compelled to
ask, again and again, *Why?*

The obvious reasons which have driven other artists to
drink and drugs were scarcely operative in his case. Baudelaire's troubles began with his upright but hard stepfather,
and continued with his absurd desire to live like a rich
nobleman and an extravagant dandy. De Quincey started
opium eating because of severe neuralgia. Poe was rootless
and poor and friendless. Dylan Thomas was physically very

sound, seems to have been fond of both his parents, had a handsome wife and children, and earned a lot of money; although he had perpetual financial troubles, they were rather a symptom than a cause of his central difficulty.

Perhaps it was not one difficulty but a combination of factors — each of them powerful, all of them together almost insuperable.

The first of them was that very physical strength. He had too much energy, and he did not use it up sanely. When he met Katherine Anne Porter, he suddenly lifted her in both his strong arms until her head was an inch from the ceiling, and kept her there. He could stay up drinking for hours and hours, when most men would simply have fallen asleep, or passed out. There have been other writers like this, notably Byron, who blazed with vitality; but Byron had the good sense to work it off in physical exercise — he boxed, he fenced, he went for long gallops on horseback, he swam for hours through dangerous seas, and in spite of many bouts of fever he remained fundamentally healthy until his last illness. It is one of the problems which every creative writer has to face and solve: what to do with himself between the rare moments in which literature comes into his mind. Thomas Wolfe, who was a regular giant, could not solve it either. Dylan Thomas's great readings of the best British poetry were one way, and a very fine way, of taxing his physical strength and restoring some sort of balance; but it would have been well for him if he had found other ways of pouring out his energy, if only by walking over the earth or swimming in the sea. As he said of himself,

> The force that drives the water through the rocks
> Drives my red blood.

In trying to understand his friend, Mr. Brinnin speaks several times of Dylan Thomas's 'load of guilt,' but he never makes it quite clear what kind of guilt. Certainly it was not a profound sense of sin. Something of it was the sense that, although a husband and a father, he was not providing regularly for his family, and that he could not undertake, he could not even endure without rebellion, the repeated effort to write something salable and to earn money by working on schedule.

More important than his guilt was his insecurity. He came from a respectable, middle-class Welsh family, but he himself called certain types of people 'the grand'; sometimes he would say anything to shock them; sometimes, with a big cigar and a lordly manner, he would try to persuade himself that he was one of them. Also, the United States, with all its wealth and power, is terribly impressive to most European visitors — whether they will admit it or not. (Most of them feel this impressiveness, but try by hostility or constant carping to defend themselves against it.) There is a rather touching story about Mrs. Thomas on her first day in America. She was given a drink in an ordinary mid-town hotel in New York. The first thing she said was 'Is this a posh bar?' — 'posh,' in non-U English slang, means 'extremely smart.' And Mr. Brinnin himself says that Thomas at first thought of himself as 'a mendicant poet come to America in a fear that he might lose everything, including his identity.' That would explain the peculiar fact that he had to steal some shirts from Mr. Francis Biddle's house; compulsive and unnecessary stealing is always a sign of profound envy. Then again, although Thomas wrote beautifully both in prose and in poetry and was widely read in English and American literature at least, he was not a trained critic, was embarrassed by professors and people who asked him technical questions about the aesthetic side of literature, was never at home with the jargon of the little magazines, and was apt to reply to any such question with a vague remark, a Welsh evasion, glum silence, or a dirty epigram. And, worst of all, he suffered from the insecurity that besets nearly every creative artist: the feeling that he had already done all he could, that he had written himself out by the mid-thirties, and that even his previous success was a fraud and he himself an imposter. That is a bitter agony to every artist. There are ways, through discipline and long preparation and thoughtful application, to overcome it, but he never seems to have discovered them or been able to use them.

One further aspect of his insecurity — whether it was a cause or a symptom we cannot tell — was his wife trouble. His wife Caitlin was handsome, and he loved her as much as he could love anyone except himself, but they had terrible rows in private and in public, accompanied by physical violence. Mr. Brinnin speaks of one evening party which was broken up by a fight between them, 'rooms littered with smashed glasses, overturned tables and broken *objets d'art*.' In fact, they fought like Cait and Dog.

Quite apart from all that, there was another cause for his love of the bottle; and this is one which might not occur to most people. It is that he was a Welsh visionary. In Wales, poets and preachers have long been respected for their ability to enter another world, to be rapt away into a state of wild excitement in which they see sights no ordinary mortal can see, and describe them in a frenzy of eloquence, pouring out words which are almost incomprehensible and yet convey, in their very richness and rapidity and fantastic strangeness, something of the ecstasy of inhabiting a dream. The Welsh call this rapture the *hwyl*. Mr. Brinnin once at least saw Thomas — in the company of the musician John Cage — spend a long time, quite sober, talking incessantly and ecstatically, in a state of wild and fanciful and uninhibited gaiety. Yet all the time he was perfectly sober. It was in such a mood of sober excitement that he conceived his poems and worked some of them out. Only, we may suspect that, like drug-addicts, when the *hwyl* did not visit him of its own accord, he would try to summon it through drink; and he usually failed.

Stronger than his hope of the *hwyl,* much stronger than his social and intellectual insecurity, was one other impulse in him, perhaps the most central of all. It was recognized by many of those who knew him. Mr. Brinnin again and again — although he is speaking of a man in his late thirties — uses phrases such as 'babyish,' 'boyish,' 'unhappy child,' and even 'pouting.' Thomas felt that his thirty-ninth birthday, which he passed in New York, was an occasion not for rejoicing and congratulation, but for gloom. It was a sort of death for him. He wrote most of his poetry about childhood and adolescence, and, if he could, he would have remained a child all his life. My guess is (though I do not know) that his realization of the loss of childhood hit him hardest in his early thirties. At thirty, he was still happy, as we can see from his 'Poem in October.' This is only a guess, but I venture to make it because the same trouble overtook at least two other British poets at that same age. Wordsworth and Coleridge, both visionaries, both traversed a crisis of great gloom in 1802. They both felt that there had 'past away a glory from the earth'; that custom, routine, encroaching age, lay upon them 'with a weight heavy as frost and deep almost as life.' They realized that they had been poets and had seen nature with visionary eyes because they were still children; and now they had left childhood behind, forever. They saw ahead of them that which Dylan Thomas tried constantly to escape: a world of prosaic routine and of inevitable responsibility. Coleridge tried to take refuge from his realization in opium and German philosophy. Wordsworth faced his own, and, in the magnificent 'Ode, Intimations of Immortality,' he accepted it. Dylan Thomas would never accept it; and the central reason why he drank was that he wished to defy

> time, the quiet gentleman
> Whose beard wags in Egyptian wind.

He wished to

> rage, rage against the dying of the light.

Both his chief intoxications, poetry and liquor, were assertions of the impossible. They were the search for eternal youth, the simple paradise of playing ball with the other boys in a park. (For more than twenty years he kept in his wallet a newspaper photograph of himself at the age of twelve, taken just after he had won a race in the school sports; a very thin, small, frightened boy, he was the essential Dylan Thomas.) In fact he refused to grow up. He killed himself rather than grow old, and, in the words of his best poem,

> Time held him green and dying
> Though he sang in his chains like the sea.

The decadent

I HAVE been traveling on the New York subway system for nearly twenty years. Probably by this time I look just as benumbed as all my fellow-sufferers. Yet the other day I had a strange mystical experience on the subway, which changed the place, and changed me, and illuminated for me the transforming power of the spirit.

Standing in a subway station, I began to appreciate the place — almost to enjoy it. First of all, I looked at the lighting: a row of meager electric bulbs, unscreened, yellow, and coated with filth, stretched away toward the black mouth of the tunnel, as though it were a bolt hole in an abandoned coal mine. Then I lingered, with zest, on the walls and ceiling: lavatory tiles which had been white about fifty years ago, and were now encrusted with soot, coated with the remains of a dirty liquid which might be either atmospheric humidity mingled with smog or the result of a perfunctory attempt to clean them with cold water; and, above them, gloomy vaulting from which dingy paint was peeling off like scabs from an old wound, sick black paint leaving a leprous white undersurface. Beneath my feet, the floor was a nauseating dark brown with black stains upon it which might be stale oil or dry chewing gum or some worse defilement; it looked like the hallway of a condemned slum building. Then my eye traveled to the tracks, where two lines of glittering steel — the only positively clean objects in the whole place — ran out of darkness into darkness above an unspeakable mass of congealed oil, puddles of dubious liquid, and a mishmash of old cigarette packets, mutilated and filthy newspapers, and the débris that filtered down from the street above through a barred grating in the roof. As I looked up toward the sunlight, I could see more débris sifting slowly downward, and making an abominable pattern in the slanting beam of dirt-laden sunlight. I was going on to relish more features of this unique scene: such as the advertisement posters on the walls — here a text from the Bible, there a half-naked girl, here a woman wearing a hat consisting of a hen sitting on a nest full of eggs, and there a pair of girl's legs walking up the keys of a cash register — all scribbled over with unknown names and well-known obscenities in black crayon and red lipstick; but then my train came in at last, I boarded it, and began to read. The experience was over for the time.

Still, it lingered in my mind. It had been very peculiar. For me it had been unique. But since then I have been able to repeat it, almost at will. Now I find it possible to extract a certain stimulus, an unusual type of aesthetic awareness, from many situations to which I was once oblivious: for example, from walking along certain streets in the center of New York City, picking my way among the filth left by pet dogs on the sidewalk, breathing in the effluvia of hundreds of car engines, feeling the hot blast from the exhausts of buses as they lurch giddily forward, dodging the flying pieces of newspaper and the showers of gritty dust churned up by the ascending stream of gas fumes, drinking in the insane chatter of pneumatic paving breakers from a nearby street, and listening to the symphony of fifty motor horns all blowing with a fury which appears even in their excited rhythm, and which is punctuated by the scream of brakes as another accident is avoided by a hairbreadth, but dominated by the penetrating roar of a big airliner hacking its way through the turbulence a few thousand feet above the ground. With a slight adaptation of my sensibility, I find that I can actually relish this experience.

This kind of sensibility is painful, but it has its value. Some artists, both ancient and modern, have made much use of it (for instance, Hogarth and Reginald Marsh). It appears quite often in poetry — there is something of it in Eliot and much in Rimbaud. In prose it has produced a few minor masterpieces, and one author of great distinction.

He was a Frenchman of Dutch descent, called Joris-Karl Huysmans. He was born in Paris in 1848, and died there, very painfully, in 1907. His novels are stranger and more intense than any other works of modern fiction known to me; they have had a strong, though limited, influence, and I imagine that, if people come to think more and more about topics which were once left to orthodox religious believers — such as the problem of suffering, the mystery of evil, and the consciousness of sin — the books of Huysmans will find more and more readers. Do you remember the most remarkable of the fantasies of Oscar Wilde, *The Picture of Dorian Gray* — the romance in which Wilde himself admits that vice, however carefully and magically concealed, still acts on the soul as cancer does on the body, perverting all its energies and ultimately destroying it? This book was partly modeled on Huysmans' novel *A Rebours,* or (in English) *Against the Grain;* and in it, Huysmans' novel plays a strong and symbolic part, becoming almost the testament of the evil selfish will of Dorian Gray. Other novelists also, and many readers, have been moved by his work.

His novels are not for weak stomachs; in fact, they are not for ordinary readers at all. They are too intense and usually too horrible. The most frightful book of fiction I have ever read is Huysmans' *Là-Bas;* part of it is devoted to a close and sympathetic analysis of the atrocious life of the legendary monster Bluebeard, or Gilles de Rais, and part to an account of a modern society of devil-worshipers who celebrate a Black Mass with every circumstance of horror. Yet it is not quite true to say that this is the most frightful book of fiction I have ever read. The novels of the Marquis de Sade are far worse; but Sade was really insane, and his books are equivalent to criminal assaults, while Huysmans — although hypersensitive — was perfectly sane, had very strong, and indeed noble, moral standards, and died as a devout and practicing Christian. In English, the books which correspond to them most closely are the novels of William Faulkner, which go almost as deeply into problems of sin and suffering, but whose characters (unlike those of Huysmans) have very little perception of the beauties of art, and apparently no idea of the existence and nature of God. The two authors even look like each other: Mr. Faulkner is a small, thin, dry man with an expression of quizzical dignity, of intelligence and rebellion half-veiled behind a screen of conventional manners, and of humility mingled with enormous pride. So was Huysmans, with the minor difference that he wore a beard (which was at first satyric and then became monkish). But Mr. Faulkner cannot or will not say clearly all that is in his tormented mind, while one of the chief merits of Huysmans' novels is that, even when he is describing a scene of appalling vice or of half-comical, half-macabre horror, he is as precise, as accurate, and as conscientiously clear as the Dutch artists who were his ancestors.

Almost all the novels of Huysmans are based on powerful episodes in his own life. Taken all together, they tell how he began by being an aesthete who tried to live wholly for himself, with no belief in the accepted rules of morality and no faith in God; later struggled through many sins, which both repelled and attracted him, toward the realization that virtue, *even if* the middle class approved it and *even if* the church taught it, was still necessary to a satisfactory life on this earth and the only way of approach to certain higher activities of the spirit; and at last, after much suffering, was converted to Christianity.

The plots of his novels are their least important and usually their least absorbing part, except in so far as (taken all together) they tell a moving and unusual story. The characters are sometimes interesting, sometimes (although copied directly from life) fantastic, and sometimes merely mouthpieces for his own ideas. The great merits of his work are, first, his extraordinarily vivid style, with its very complex and carefully varied sentence structure and its enormous vocabulary, ranging all the way from remote and pedantic dictionary words to vulgar slang; and, second, his uncanny power to appreciate and evoke sights, sounds, smells, colors, physical feelings both external and internal, and spiritual states, particularly those which are associated with revulsion and pain.

In fact, Huysmans was a mystic of suffering. In the Middle Ages, instead of working as a civil servant and writing novels in his spare time, he would have been an ascetic in a lonely monastery, perhaps with one manual of penitential devotions to his credit.

His life revolved around two central ideas, both of which are strange to many of us. One was that it is possible and in fact desirable for the human spirit to pay the same kind of attention to ugliness as it does to beauty — that the aesthetic sense can be exercised both by a painting of the grave, calm, majestic river Seine at sunrise, and by an etching of a miserable, degraded little stream, half canal and half sewer, full of dead cats and floating abominations, winding its slow way between the backs of slum houses and the noisome yards of tanneries; both by the contemplation of the cathedral of Notre Dame, superb and saintly, and by the spectacle of a cheap saloon, garishly lit, hideously noisy, full of vulgar decorations, repulsive smells, and the faces of coarse and swinish men and women.

His other idea (allied to the first) was the conception that a truly sensitive soul can be as happy in suffering pain as in enjoying perfect physical and spiritual bliss, simply because the two intensities approach one another, and both are far clearer and far nobler than any mild, half-numb, half-blind perception of the commonplace. He was a man of really exceptional sensibility. One of his friends said he had been born 'with one skin too few.' It was not an accident of birth, but rather poverty and early squalor that flayed him alive. Until you read Huysmans' own works you cannot credit how far his masochistic sensibility can go. For instance, one of the most individual qualities of the French people is their economy in soap and water; even apart from the garlic breaths, the smell of a Parisian crowd in a hot music hall or in the stifling Métro is quite unforgettable. Well, Huysmans (unlike most Frenchmen) perceived this; he saw it was inescapable, and he rhapsodized on it. He wrote a prose poem about the sweaty odor of imperfectly bathed Parisian girls, and he claimed to be able to distinguish, with his eyes shut, between brunettes, blondes, and redheads. And Huysmans on the restaurants of nineteenth-century Paris, where Algerian wine adulterated with turpentine and dubious meat cooked in stale oil were served in cracked glasses and plates (with dirt lurking in each crack) by waiters with black fingernails, who emerged from unspeakable roach- and rat-infested kitchens — ah, he is vivid, but nauseating, and makes the reader resolve never to order anything in Paris except a soft-boiled egg.

But Huysmans soon passed beyond this, to the polarity of suffering and bliss which can be found in religion. He wrote a detailed study of Blessed Lydwine of Schiedam, a bedridden medieval mystic who suffered almost every possible physical disease except leprosy, and underwent agonies almost beyond imagination, while taking no food except the Eucharist. Through that book, and through the sufferings he himself underwent toward the end, he explained the strange doctrine, known in other creeds besides Christianity, that extreme suffering and perfect bliss are not only akin but may almost be identified through religion, and may both be regarded as proofs of sanctity. Many Christians approved of this. But it was hard for them to stomach his declaration, after a visit to Lourdes, that much Catholic art of the nineteenth century had obviously been created at the instigation of the devil as an insult to the Virgin Mary; and it was equally hard for them to endure his insistence on the idea that the more naïve aspects of religion, the noisy processions and the mass-produced pictures of sacred themes, were additional sufferings which the truly religious soul had to steel itself to accept. He was a wonderful writer, Huysmans; toward the end he was a truly religious soul; but he lacked the one thing which St. Paul insisted on, saying that any eloquence and any learning in language without it was only sounding brass and a tinkling cymbal: he lacked love.

By the way, how did Huysmans live, apart from his writing? He was an executive in the French FBI, the Sureté Nationale; his chief job was following up anarchists and expelling undesirable aliens. He never took the slightest particle of interest in his work.

Inside Aubrey

———————————

ONE of the pleasures of reading is that it makes friends for you. Not social friends, but intellectual friends: the authors whose works you know best. To become friendly with a writer, you ought to read his books again and again — so that, when you reopen one of them, you seem not to be reading printed words on a page, but rather to be hearing a familiar voice speaking to you.

Such a writer need not necessarily be great, nor his works masterpieces. It is enough if he appeals to you, and if — even after ten or fifteen years — he still seems likable. I have several such friends who are not terribly important, and yet I love them, because their work gives me a special kind of pleasure, because they are individuals and not types, and perhaps because they do not try too hard to be great.

One of them is an antiquarian who lived in southern England about three hundred years ago. His name was John Aubrey. He was a tremendously hard worker, but most of his work never got beyond the manuscript stage. (I have known quite a number of scholars who were like that; they could scarcely bring themselves to publish a book — that is, actually to stop revising it and send it to the printer — because they always thought they could find out something more and alter a couple of chapters.) When Aubrey died he left huge quantities of notes in his own handwriting, covering biography, church history, surveys of English counties, and so forth. Ever since his death scholars have been going over these notes and publishing them, sometimes by incorporating them into other books, sometimes by printing them as they stand. They are extremely useful and interesting, even though they are rather higgledy-piggledy: for Aubrey was no fool. He was well educated (Oxford and the Middle Temple); he was a Fellow of the Royal Society; he had a huge number of friends among the intelligentsia; he had the reporter's art of extracting valuable information from the most unlikely people; and he had a most active mind. As he says of himself, his 'head was alwaies working; never idle, and even travelling . . . did gleane som observations.' In our own time, he might have been a super-reporter like John Gunther, or else a professor of some odd but valuable subject such as prehistoric archaeology, spending much of his time burrowing into caverns in search of the art and the tools of the Stone Age men. He does in fact tell how, when staying at a country house at the age of twenty-three, he went out hunting with the other members of the party, but, seeing the great megalithic stone circles at the village of Avebury, he left hounds and huntsmen to take care of themselves and spent his time examining these formidable prehistoric relics, 'entertaining [himself] with a more de·lightful indagation [i.e. hunting].'

In his own time he might have done more solid work and become more famous, but for two pieces of evil fortune. One was that he lived during the period of the English Civil War and the troubles that followed it, and he kept being embarrassed by extremists who suspected him of belonging to the wrong party. The other was money. His father had independent means, but was a poor businessman and died leaving his affairs in disorder. Aubrey spent the first part of his life engaged in interminable lawsuits, selling off estates to pay current expenses, and dodging the 'crocodiles' (bill collectors). By the time he was about forty-five, his lawsuits were over, and he had lost every penny. Since it relieved him of anxiety, it was in a way a blessing.

For the rest of his life, Aubrey lived on his friends, not by cadging, but by staying in their houses for long periods (his conversation must have been ample reward for their hospitality) and by getting gifts from those who were more fortunate than he. William Penn, for instance, gave him six hundred acres in Pennsylvania. And once, when he was dreaming, he thought of emigrating to the New World, and becoming rich. 'I could goe into Maryland, which is one of the finest countrys of the world; same climate with France; between Virginia and New England. I can have all the favour of my lord Baltemore I could wish. His brother is his lieutenant there; and a very good natured gentleman. Plenty of all things: ground there is 2000 miles westwards. I could be able I believe to carry a colony of rogues; another, of ingeniose artificers; and I doubt not one might make shift to have five or six ingeniose companions, which is enough.' Much of his later life was spent collaborating with Anthony Wood on an important history of Oxford University, the *Athenae Oxonienses*. Wood thanked him by describing him as 'a shiftless person, roving and magotie-headed,' but Wood was like that to everyone. Aubrey died at the age of seventy-one, of a cerebral hemorrhage.

The book which makes me call Aubrey my friend is a collection of *Brief Lives* of people he had known at first- or second-hand. (It was first published from his manuscript notes, exactly two hundred years after his death, and often reprinted.) They are not systematic biographies, but sketches put down just as Aubrey happened to remember them; but when you read four or five pages, you can almost hear the old fellow chatting to you.

He begins his life of the mathematician Sir Jonas Moore with one splendid sentence: 'Sciatica he cured it, by boyling his buttock.'

His life of Sir Thomas Badd consists of only three sentences. Two of them are irrelevant, but delicious. 'Sir Thomas Bad's father, a shoemaker, married the brewer's widow of Portsmouth, worth 20,000 *li*. The happinesse a shoemaker haz in drawing on a fair lady's shoe. I know one that it was the hight of his ambition to be prentice to his mistress's shoemaker upon that condicion.'

His life of someone called Yarrington is even shorter. 'Capt. Yarrington dyed at London about March last. The cause of his death was a beating and throwne into a tub of water.'

Mr. Gwyn, otherwise unknown to fame, has been immortalized in three sentences.

> Surliness and inurbanitie too common in England: chastise these very severely. [This is Aubrey reminding himself of one of the books he intends to write.] A better instance of a squeamish and disobligeing,

slighting, insolent, proud, fellow, perhaps cant be found then in Gwin, the earl of Oxford's secretary. No reason satisfies him, but he overweenes, and cutts some sower faces that would turn the milke in a faire ladie's breast.

Some of his stories are delightfully vivid and old-fashioned at the same time. Once, he says, the mathematician Thomas Allen was staying in the country with a friend. In those days the common people thought mathematics and magic were the same (perhaps they may have been right). 'He happened to leave his watch in the chamber windowe — (watches were then rarities) — The maydes came in to make the bed, and hearing a thing in a case cry *Tick, Tick, Tick,* presently concluded that that was his Devill, and tooke it by the string with the tongues, and threw it out of the windowe into the mote (to drowne the Devill).'

And so at the end of his life of the Duke of Buckingham, he suddenly puts in a short but charming ghost story. '*Anno* 1670, not far from Cirencester, was an apparition: being demanded, whether a good spirit or a bad? returned no answer, but disappeared with a curious perfume and most melodious twang.'

One of the things that makes old Aubrey important as well as interesting is that he reports facts about famous people which would otherwise have been lost. (Once he himself reflected, 'How these curiosities would be quite forgott, did not such idle fellowes as I am putt them downe!') For instance, he got a first-hand account of the death of Francis Bacon.

> Mr. Hobbs told me that the cause of his lordship's death was trying an experiment: *viz.,* as he was taking the aire in a coach with Dr. Witherborne (a Scotchman, Physitian to the King) towards High-gate,

snow lay on the ground, and it came into my lord's thoughts, why flesh might not be preserved in snow, as in salt. They were resolved they would try the experiment presently. They alighted out of the coach, and went into a poore woman's howse at the bottome of Highgate hill, and bought a hen, and made the woman exenterate it, and then stuffed the bodie with snow, and my lord did help to doe it himselfe. The snow so chilled him, that he immediately fell so extremely ill, that he could not returne to his lodgings (I suppose then at Graye's Inne), but went to the earle of Arundell's house at High-gate, where they putt him into a good bed warmed with a panne, but it was a damp bed that had not been layn-in in about a yeare before, which gave him such a cold that in two or three dayes, as I remember he [Hobbes] told me, he dyed of suffocation.

Remarkable how things survive. Bacon was making an experiment in refrigeration, which is now a highly developed branch of technology. The leaders of the industry have gone far beyond stuffing a dead chicken with snow; but it is still possible to be refrigerated and to contract pneumonia in a cold English bedroom and a damp English bed.

His life of Sir Walter Raleigh is one of the most vivid of all his brief biographies: it makes us hear Raleigh's very voice (with its broad Devonshire accent), see his very face ('long-faced, and sour eie-lidded, a kind of pigge-eie') with its strong beard which turned up naturally, and savor his wit and his energy. Aubrey gives a delightful account of one of his escapades in the court of the Virgin Queen.

He loved a wench well: and one time getting up one of the mayds of honor against a tree in a wood ('twas his first lady) who seemed at first boarding to be something fearful of her Honour, and modest, she cryed Sweet Sir Walter, what do you me ask? Will you undoe me? Nay, sweet Sir Walter! Sir Walter!

At last, as the danger and the pleasure at the same time grew higher, she cried in the extacey Swisser Swatter! Swisser Swatter!

With obvious admiration, Aubrey adds:

She proved with child and I doubt not but this hero tooke care of them both, as also that the product was more then an ordinary mortall.

Aubrey was also one of the first to record anything about the life of William Shakespeare. He went to Stratford and talked to people who had actually known Shakespeare in his boyhood, and he looked up an actor who was the son of a member of Shakespeare's company. He got a few details wrong (as when he says Shakespeare's father was a butcher, instead of a leather merchant) but not far wrong; and he found out valuable details about his early career and his gifts. We admire Shakespeare's genius for making his characters seem vividly alive — more alive, often, than the people in the audience. Aubrey tells us that (along with Ben Jonson) Shakespeare used to memorize the characteristics of real men and women, their odd ways of speaking, their quirks and complexes. 'Ben Johnson and he did gather humours of men dayly where ever they came.' And he adds that the model of one of Shakespeare's characters (probably Dogberry in *Much Ado*) was still alive in 1642, when Aubrey himself went up to Oxford. There are other ways of writing good drama, but this has always been one of the best; and Aubrey realized that, for he wrote of Shakespeare: 'His comoedies will remaine witt as long as the English tongue is understood, for that he handles *mores hominum*. Now our present writers reflect so much upon particular persons and coxcombeities, that twenty years hence they will not be understood.'

Aubrey was always interested in the workings of the human mind. This started, with him, at a very early period. (He tells us that he began Latin when he was eight years old, and had a good, gentle, intelligent Latin teacher. One of the methods this clever young man employed was quite simple, and yet unforgettable. Every time one of the little boys asked leave to go to the bathroom, he gave them it, and told them to remember a Latin word and tell it to him when they came back to the classroom: 'Now, remember, *imperium* means command'; and so, as Aubrey says, 'in a little while this amounted to a good number of words.')

He tells us what few other authors ever care to report — *how* distinguished thinkers actually meditated and what stages of thought they passed through. For example, he says the philosopher Hobbes was forty years old before he knew anything about geometry, and then it was an accident. Hobbes happened to be in a friend's library, where he saw a copy of Euclid, lying open at the 47th theorem of the first book. 'He read the proposition. "By G — ," sayd he, (He would now and then sweare, by way of emphasis), "this is impossible!" So he reads the demonstration of it, which referred him back to such a proposition; which proposition he read. That referred him back to another, which he also read. *Et sic deinceps* [and so in succession] back to the first, that at last he was demonstratively convinced of that trueth. This made him in love with geometry.'

So also he tells us how the poet Milton composed his great poem, after becoming blind, and even reports his daily routine.

He was a early riser (*scil.* at 4 a clock *manè*); yea, after he lost his sight. He had a man read to him. The first thing he read was the Hebrew Bible, and that was at 4 h. *manè* ½ h. or so. Then he contemplated. At 7 his man came to him again, and then read to him again, and wrote till dinner: the writing was as much [took up as much time] as the reading. His daughter, Deborah, could read to him Latin, Italian and French, and Greeke. . . . After dinner he used to walke three or four houres at a time (he alwayes had a garden where he lived); went to bed about 9. Temperate man, rarely dranke between meales.

Charming, all this; and gives us a milder, kindlier view of Milton than we might get from his tremendous epic. Aubrey is always frank, and if there were anything really discreditable to relate about Milton, he would have written it down. He tells us, in two surprising sentences, that a famous cavalier poet was a professional crook. 'Sir John Suckling invented the game of cribbidge. He sent his cards to all gameing places in the country, which were marked with private markes of his: he gott 20,000 *li.* by this way.' Some of the scandalous tales in Aubrey's *Lives* are even more surprising and even funnier than these; most of them were never recorded by anyone else. Aubrey was one of those rare writers who make history, not out of books, but out of people. Like Proust, he was more interested in the lives of others, and of past generations, than in his own personal career. He says that he, 'when a boy, did ever love to converse with old men, as living histories'; and it is exactly for that reason that I love, not to read his book, but rather to hear him, in his own giddy and magotie-headed utterance, converse, as a living history.

The Vergil of the insects

LET us take a trip into the past. Suppose we go back about sixty years, and visit a small house in the south of France, owned by a quiet retired schoolmaster with a passionate interest in natural history. (Although he knew the name and the appearance of every flower, every plant and every insect in his neighborhood, he often said that he did not fully understand them; he did not know in every detail how they lived; he was constantly surprised by their behavior; and he never lost the greatest gift of any scientist, the gift of wonder. Although he collected his subjects year after year and studied them with patient and unhasting, unresting energy, he found that nature, with its infinite intricacy and variety, was constantly putting questions to him, questions which he himself might never have devised, but felt bound to answer.)

One spring evening in the 1890s, the schoolmaster-naturalist and his family were in a great state of excitement. Nature had once more got ahead of them, and they could not understand exactly how.

That morning a moth had hatched from a cocoon in the laboratory: a fine female moth, still moist and quivering from the effort of metamorphosis. It was a specimen of the big beautiful emperor moth, with a coat of dark brown velvet fringed with smoky white, wearing on each wing a huge eye like the markings on a peacock's tail. When it was born, the naturalist popped it under a cover of fine wire netting; he studied it for a while, then turned to something else, and after dark started for bed.

While he was undressing, he heard his little son next door, shouting and banging things and running about. 'Come quick, daddy!' he was calling; 'the room's full of big moths, as big as birds!' And so it was. The boy's bedroom had been invaded by emperor moths; they were cruising along the ceiling and flying wildly round the lamp. 'Aha!' said the naturalist, and he told the boy to get dressed again and come upstairs to the laboratory. On the way, they saw the maid running about the kitchen, flapping with her apron at more emperor moths; she thought they were bats. Then, candle in hand, the father and son entered the laboratory. It was alive with enormous emperor moths. In the flickering light, it looked like the cave of a magician, and little Paul clung tightly to his father's hand. A moment later one of the huge quiet creatures flew into the flame of the candle and dashed it out; they felt others settling on their shoulders and grazing their faces, all in silence and in darkness. When they relit the candle, they saw that most of the moths were circling round and round the wire cage where the female moth, born only that morning, was resting motionless and silent. But soon the candle flame attracted them again, it became impossible to observe any further, and the naturalist closed the door on the strange midnight orgy.

All these visitors, nearly forty altogether, were male moths; and they were all attracted to the house by the presence of one newly born female moth, in a cage inside a dark room. Next night, the naturalist was on the watch; next night, more moths arrived, and so the next and the next, for over a week.

At once he was faced with the central question: how did the lovers know that their beloved was there? Although it was early in May, the sky was overcast, the weather was stormy, and the nights were profoundly, almost impenetrably, dark. In addition, the house was surrounded by heavy plantings of bushes and trees, so that the moths had to make their way past screens of leaves and branches. During the eight nights of his experiments, he recorded a total of one hundred and fifty male emperor moths in his house — and that although the emperor is a fairly rare insect, and he himself had found it difficult to locate its cocoons.

By moving the cage in which the young princess lived, and by changing its material and its accessibility, the naturalist gradually eliminated various possibilities. First of all, her suitors did not locate her by the sense of sight. They could scarcely have seen several yards into the upstairs room of an unknown house, to begin with; and later, when she was hidden in a closet, lovers still flew into the windows, went straight to the closet doors, and beat upon them with their wings.

Or perhaps the female moth sent out some kind of signal? The emperor moths have sensitive antennae, which might very well be used for receiving microwaves — either of sound, so shrill that our ears can never hear it, or of electrical impulses too subtle to be picked up by our receivers. The naturalist thought of this possibility. So he put the princess in hermetically sealed boxes of various kinds: metal, glass, wood and cardboard. Through some of these she could certainly have transmitted either sound or electricity. As long as they were sealed, no lovers appeared. Yet when any one of them was opened so as to produce communication with the outer air, even through a tiny crack, it was soon surrounded by eager suitors.

It was not sight, it was not hearing, it was not electrical impulses that brought them to visit her. It might therefore be the sense of smell. The naturalist determined to find out. But it was too difficult to continue the experiments with the emperor moths, because they are active only at night; he had to use a lamp, which distracted them and sometimes killed them. Therefore he got the cocoon of a day moth, the oak egger, hatched it carefully, and put it in a similar wire cage. Although this was a very rare moth in his neighborhood, it attracted not less than sixty males, which flew in from all directions, circled over the cage, and clambered up and down the wire netting while the princess remained immovable within it. Every day they found the room and the cage, exactly as the emperor moths had found their princess every night. But mark this: whenever she was enclosed in a sealed vessel, not a single lover arrived. Surely it had to be her scent which attracted them? And yet no scent was perceptible to human nostrils.

The naturalist surrounded the princess with saucers full of powerful smells: oil of lavender, gasoline, naphthaline, sulphuretted hydrogen. By the usual visiting hour (3 p.m.) the laboratory was full of an abominable mixture of odors; and, just to make things more difficult, the naturalist covered the cage with a thick cloth. He opened the window. Without hesitation, the male moths flew in, ignoring the stenches, made straight for the cloth-covered cage, and tried to burrow through the cloth to reach the expectant female.

This was almost too much. Surely the lovers could not perceive the lady's scent through all that wild mixture of extreme smells? The naturalist was thinking he ought to abandon the theory and look for some other explanation, when an accident came to his assistance. Making one more experiment to determine whether the male moths came to the female because they *saw* her, he took her out of the wire cage and put her into a bell-glass cover, and then stood it on a table facing the window. As for the empty cage with the tray of sand on which she had slept during the night, he placed it at the dark end of the room and thought no more about it. Visiting hour came round. The first male moths arrived. They flew in through the open window. They passed the princess in her glass case without even glancing at her. They went straight to the empty cage where she had spent the night, and all afternoon they flew and danced about the little prison, not where the princess now was, but where she had been.

That proved the point. That solved the question. The male moths were attracted only by the scent of the female. The scent could be attached to anything — an empty cage, a twig, a piece of paper, a rag. They would ignore the lady even if she was in plain view, to seek out the place where she had been lying for some time. They would pass her by even when she was accessible — if the naturalist had just moved her from an earlier position which had been thoroughly impregnated with her scent. And yet no human being, not even the naturalist's little boy with the keen senses of youth, could smell anything whatever of that odor, though it was so powerful that it could bring moths from a distance of a mile or more into a strange house, so dominant that it would attach itself to anything that the princess herself had merely touched. Truly the insects live in a world remote from our own.

This, very briefly told, is only one of the many beautiful experiments carried out by one of the greatest of French scientists, Jean-Henri Fabre. He died in 1915, after a very unusual life — most of it spent in bitter poverty (he called it *'la misère en habit noir'*), relieved by the economical French authorities only in the few final years. Hard as it was, his life was exemplary. He was born of poor parents in Aveyron, one of the poorest regions of southern France. He put himself through school by working and by winning scholarships, and became a schoolmaster at the age of nineteen. Although he had to teach pretty well everything (including reading and writing), he went on studying at home and taking more degrees, finishing with a doctorate in natural science from the University of Paris. (Nevertheless, he knew Greek and was excellent in Latin, illustrating his writings with beautiful quotations from Vergil.) In middle life he got a good school position in Avignon; he was befriended by the great Minister of Education, Victor Duruy; he began to give public lectures on science; his fame and his influence were growing — and then opposition to his work began, and was fomented by certain elements in the church, which saw his work as materialistic and tending toward blasphemy. He was forced out of Avignon. At the age of forty-eight, he retired.

Thenceforward he supported himself and his large family mainly by writing popular science textbooks; and, day after day, month after month, year after year, with only the most primitive instruments and with scarcely any access to scientific periodicals, he carried out a long and arduous series of investigations into the life history and social habits of many different kinds of insects. It took him nearly forty years to complete his researches on one particular beetle, and some of the most obscure phenomena (such as the praying mantis's construction of a nest) he saw only once in his lifetime. But he was, as Charles Darwin said, a 'matchless observer,' and he commanded what is beyond the range of most scientists, a beautiful prose style. When he was about sixty, he began to set down his observations and publish them in a series of ten volumes called *Souvenirs entomologiques*. These, both for scientists and for non-scientists, are for the insect world what Audubon's exquisite pictures are for the world of birds.

Translations of his works are still in many libraries. You may not like insects much (most of us don't), but you will almost certainly be fascinated by the weirdness of their manners, stimulated by the patience and minuteness of Fabre's observations, and charmed by the humor and grace of his prose style. You will read several chapters on the harmless but slightly disgusting dung beetle which are worthy both of Rabelais and of Anatole France; you will see Fabre carefully dissecting the cicada to see how it makes its music, that shrill incessant chirp, and yet acknowledging that he cannot tell *why* it sings; you will watch, in his company, the incredibly delicate workmanship of many different types of spider, calculating the architecture of their slender webs and traps more accurately than any human workman operating without fine machinery; and gradually you will realize why Fabre was not popular throughout most of his life. Although Darwin praised him, Fabre did not admire Darwin, and he thought the theory of evolution was a crude overstatement. At the same time it was impossible for naïvely religious people to use Fabre's work to prove the omnipotence of a benevolent Creator, for the world of insects which he revealed was a world riddled with the most fearful and essential cruelty: it was a world in which almost every living being preyed upon some other being, and even upon its own brothers and mates, ambushing them, stabbing them, poisoning them, devouring them alive. And, in spite of all the wisdom which the insects appeared to display, Fabre's researches seemed to show that they had no intelligence whatever, only a mindless set of instincts, totally insufficient to cope with even a tiny alteration in their customary routine. Perhaps we ought to be grateful to him for this. When you read the chapter in which he describes the wedding of that grotesque demon, the praying mantis, and shows us the female of the species finishing the ceremony by eating the bridegroom even while he is clasped in her loving arms — and then opening her arms to receive still another and another bridegroom, each to go the same way — you are struck with wonder at the world which contains such creatures, with admiration for the delicacy of Fabre's style, and with gratitude to the Providence which has made the insects so small, and, since they are even more cruel and ruthless than man, deprived them of reason.

The trial of Socrates

ONE of the most famous trials in human history took place nearly twenty-four centuries ago. I suppose it was one of the most important. It was the trial of the old Athenian philosopher Socrates. Nearly all trials of important men and women accused on serious charges are interesting: it is possible to travel backward through time and to sympathize with the accused or the prosecutors or the bewildered witnesses, to feel as though one were present in the courtroom, or even serving on the jury. The trial of Socrates is particularly moving because we know something of what was said: we seem to hear his very voice raised in his defense. It is moving for another reason also. This is the fact that he was condemned to death, but (because of a religious and legal technicality) not executed at once.

Therefore we have two books which show him in the condemned cell after the trial was over, talking calmly and graciously to his friends, and finally facing his death with unflinching courage, even with something like his old ironic humor. These are Plato's dialogues, the *Crito* and the *Phaedo*.

Interesting, and sometimes profoundly touching — that the trial of Socrates is; but also it is quite confusing, quite difficult to understand. Modern men trying to grapple with it must start with a short book by Socrates' pupil Plato. (It was the first book I ever read in classical Greek, I remember, and I have respected it for something like thirty-five years.) The book suffers — like so many classical works — from having a stupidly translated title. Usually it is given in English as *The Apology of Socrates*. In fact, it ought to be called *The Defense of Socrates*. It is supposed to be three speeches delivered by Socrates at his trial. Their tone is confident, easy, even combative; there is nothing apologetic about them. The Greek word *apologia* does mean 'defense,' but it was silly of the translators to take it straight over into English, without considering its different implications in our language.

Socrates was over seventy when he was indicted and brought to trial. He had lived in Athens all his long life, and knew almost every Athenian worth talking to. He had served in the army (with considerable courage) and had taken part in the government of the city by sitting on its executive board. But his chief occupation, indeed, his only important occupation throughout his career, was thinking and talking about problems of ethics, religion, metaphysics, art, and society, which he discussed with literally anyone who would listen and/or join in the discussion. Unlike the professors (called 'sophists') he did not give prepared lectures, but merely engaged in conversations — usually through question and answer, and apparently quite un-studied and improvised. Apparently: though, like any skil-ful lawyer conducting a cross-examination, or like any skilful teacher following Socrates' own example, he clearly had a very good idea of the course which he wanted the conversation to follow. The dialogues, or 'conversations,' of Plato show us how Socrates applied this technique to the discussion of many problems, sometimes in interviews which can scarcely have lasted more than a few minutes, sometimes, as in *The Republic,* in an extended argument which continued for hours on end.

Not everyone who knew Socrates liked him. Some peo-ple thought he was a crackpot, fascinating or mildly annoy-ing. Others hated him like poison, being convinced that he was a calculating and malevolent destroyer of the moral code, the religious beliefs, and the social solidarity of his own country. They believed, in fact, that he was not merely an unprejudiced searcher after truth (as he claimed to be); that he was asking questions not (as he often said) merely in order to remedy his own ignorance and to discover the real facts, but in order to trap all the leading figures of Athenian life into contradicting themselves or making fools of themselves by confessing bewilderment; that his questions really constituted a long campaign of negative criticism, whose cumulative effect was to discredit the genuine achievements of his fellow countrymen — the men who built the Parthenon, who constructed the Athe-nian democracy, who wrote the immortal tragedies and comedies of the Athenian stage — and to lead the younger generation into a hopeless intellectual anarchy, where they were left with nothing to admire as truly wise or beautiful, no vision of life except as dominated by almost universal vanity and ignorance, opposed by the slender sword of reason. It was by men who thought of Socrates not as a crank but as a destroyer of what had once been a liberal and flourishing state, that he was brought to trial.

The charges were rather vague. There were two. The first was the charge that he did not believe in the gods of Athens. The second was the charge that he corrupted the young men of Athens. There were no professional lawyers and no presiding judge. The case was heard by a large jury picked from among the ordinary public, which both the prosecutors and the accused man addressed directly. Both sides could cross-examine each other and call witnesses. In the event of a verdict of guilty, both sides were expected to suggest a penalty, and the jury then voted once again to decide whether it would accept the suggestion of the prosecutor or of the defendant.

In Plato's work, *The Defense of Socrates,* there are three speeches, all supposed to be made by Socrates. The speeches of the prosecutors are not given, nor is the evidence for the prosecution. The text of the speeches is probably fairly close to Socrates' own words, and it seems to reproduce his manner fairly accurately. (Plato was in court during the trial; he was about thirty when it took place, he had known and loved Socrates for many years, and he published the book in Athens among people who had known Socrates and attended the trial. It cannot therefore have been too far from the truth.)

Only the first speech is the reply of Socrates to the charges laid against him. He was found guilty, by a sizable plurality vote. After that he spoke again. The prosecution had suggested the death penalty. Socrates countered by making a short speech which obviously had a bad effect. He proposed that he should be maintained for the rest of his life, at the state's expense, as a public benefactor; then he withdrew that and offered (with the assistance of Plato and other friends) to pay a fine. The jury apparently took this as showing something like contempt of its verdict, and voted by an increased majority to inflict the death penalty. The last of the three speeches is a short but noble comment on the verdict, with a farewell both to Socrates' enemies and to his friends.

As we read the speeches, and still more when we go on to read the two conversations of Socrates in the condemned cell, we find it very hard to refrain from calling him a martyr. To this very day I can scarcely read the last pages of the *Phaedo,* describing his farewell and his death, without tears in my eyes. Thinking over his noble refusal to accept a chance of escape from prison (because that would mean violation of the laws of the democracy), and listening to the serenity and purity of his conversation, we are almost forced to call his trial a gross miscarriage of justice. And yet . . . and yet . . . can we be absolutely sure that it was? Socrates himself would not wish any thinking man to accept any impression without discussing it and trying to discover whether it was true or false; so it is our duty to keep our minds open and to examine the case fairly. We can do this best by rereading Socrates' speeches on his defense, and analyzing his treatment of the charges against him.

· The first charge was religious: Socrates did not believe in the gods of Athens. Now, how does he face this accusation? In his first speech, he meets it in a very curious way: he cross-examines one of the prosecutors and asks the man whether the complaint is (1) that Socrates is a complete atheist, believing in no gods whatever, or (2) that he is heterodox, believing in some deities, but not in the regular deities worshipped in Athens. The man (Meletus is his name) is represented as replying that Socrates is a complete atheist. Socrates then convicts him of inconsistency by showing that he does in fact believe in *some* divine powers, and therefore must believe in *some* gods. It is hard to take this very seriously. The prosecutor appears to have been exceptionally stupid — at least as Plato describes him — for he must have known that Socrates kept talking about a 'divine sign' which warned him against indiscretions, and that Socrates had also professed reverence for the god Apollo: so that he was not a 100 per cent atheist. On the other hand, Socrates does not produce any convincing evidence in his own defense, and treats the whole thing with levity, almost with derision. (For a dramatic contrast, compare the trial of Joan of Arc, with its long and intricate theological arguments.)

The second charge was that Socrates corrupted the young men. He scarcely defends himself against this charge, either. He brings no evidence, or very little. He merely cross-examines the prosecutor, and entices him into a logical quibble: if anyone corrupts the young, he will be harmed by them; no one wishes to be harmed; therefore Socrates cannot corrupt the young men intentionally; and with that he dismisses the second charge. It is noble, but it is naïve.

In *The Defense of Socrates* there appears to be no evidence, nothing but scandal and prejudice, to support the charges against the old man. But in fact there was some basis for both charges: there was some solid evidence, which could have been carefully stated and carefully examined. The Athenians who distrusted Socrates could point to young men who were devoted to him, and whom he appeared to have corrupted because he was the strongest single influence in their lives. These men were the rich and well-born opponents of the democratic republic. Although Socrates himself obeyed the laws and had fought for his country, he is always represented as criticizing the ideals of democracy as being wasteful and stupid, and many of his pupils were the young oligarchs. One of his devoted pupils and friends was the brilliant and unprincipled young nobleman Alcibiades, who betrayed his own country to its enemies in the middle of a terrible war against the militaristic power Sparta and her allies. Another was the brilliant and bloodthirsty young nobleman Critias, who, after the Spartans won, became one of the leaders of a reactionary government called 'the Thirty Tyrants,' and who impoverished, exiled, or killed many of the leading democratic statesmen. And there were others. (Plato himself was invited to join the group, or, as its democratic opponents called it, the gang. He did not. It was overthrown in blood and suffering. Yet to the end of his life Plato never believed that democracy was anything but a diseased form of government, a political insanity.) There were several men among the pupils of Socrates who did their own country as much harm as Benedict Arnold. Socrates resisted them when they came to power, and indeed risked his life by doing so. But by then (said his prosecutors) the harm had already been done; it was irreparable: simply by talking for thirty or forty years he had created a spiritual organization which was not a 'loyal opposition' but a treasonable conspiracy ready to help his country's foes, and regarding most Athenian citizens (including Socrates himself) as either subjects or enemies. This was the corruption of the young men to which the charge referred. This too (we may be reasonably sure) lay at the bottom of the charge of atheism. Before Socrates' pupil and friend Alcibiades deserted to the Spartans, he had been accused of two terrible acts of blasphemy — parodying one of the most sacred of religious rites at a drunken party, and then mutilating numerous holy statues all over the city of Athens. At this distance, nobody knows whether these charges were true, or false, or partly true and partly false; but Alcibiades' cynical career seemed to make them true, and once again his teacher Socrates got the blame.

These are the topics which are scarcely even touched upon in *The Defense of Socrates*. They had to be excluded, legally: for, after the oligarchic revolution in which Socrates' pupils played such a terrible part, there was a restoration of the democracy — followed by an amnesty (another splendid Greek invention, the first amnesty in political history). All the evidence which could either support or rebut the charges against Socrates was bound to come from the period covered by the amnesty, the thirty or forty years of his life as a teacher. That is why his defense seems so vague and sometimes so frivolous. That is why the charges against him seem so offensive and artificial, in fact so misconceived. Socrates was condemned, not for being an atheist, nor for being a dispassionate critic of democracy, but for being the teacher of traitors and tyrants who had betrayed and murdered hundreds of their fellow countrymen, and who might at the very moment be plotting against them in some hostile foreign country. His trial was a drastic illustration of the responsibility of the teacher — who may very well instil in others ideas which for him are manageable, or perhaps purely theoretical, but for them are dangerously exciting, sometimes explosive and destructive of both themselves and their surroundings. Even so, the trial and the condemnation of Socrates were wrong, for the Athenians had covered all the past, with its blood and its suffering, by the amnesty. As soon as the amnesty was passed, the case should have been ruled out of court; and it is a shame that Socrates was ever indicted. On the other hand, it is a pity that he and his pupils apparently failed to recognize how completely they had destroyed the morale and the social structure — yes, even the artistic impulses — of the society which they had so ruthlessly and so wittily criticized. Plato himself founded a college in Athens some years later, and in all his works there is hardly any conscious evidence that he realized how much Athens had given to the world.

It is strange that the three most famous trials in history have been so poorly reported. In the trial of Jesus, we can scarcely see what were the charges, still less the evidence and the defense. In the trial of Joan of Arc, we have only a distorted defense. In the trial of Socrates, we are given one side, but not the other. This is the only instance in which Socrates' pupil Plato fails to give both sides of a disputed question. It reminds us of the remark of the anxious Roman governor who had to examine Jesus. Jesus said, 'I am come to bear witness to the truth.' Pontius Pilate replied, 'What is truth?'

The immortal journalist

WE can all dispute what is the finest play or the most moving novel in our language; but there is not a shadow of doubt what is the best diary. It is the journal of the English civil servant, Samuel Pepys. (He used the old-fashioned spelling of his name, 'Pepys,' but pronounced it 'Peeps.') It is truly a delightful book — not to read straight through, but to keep at hand, to dip into again and again. Sometimes I take it up at random — say, on the 22nd of September, and then look up all the entries for the 22nd of September, year after year; and mighty strange it is to see how a man's life and fortunes alter from one year to another.

Of course the oddest thing about the diary of Samuel Pepys is that it is a secret. It was never meant to be read, far less published: heaven forfend.

Its author was perfectly well known, but not as its author. He has a modest but secure place in the history books as one of the men who created the British Navy, or rather reformed and improved it during one of its many periodical slumps. Born in 1633, he went (helped by scholarships) to Cambridge University, entered government service in 1660 as a complete novice, and learned the ins and outs of administration by hard and constant industry. He must have been a little like the First Lord in *H.M.S. Pinafore,* for he did not even know the multiplication table when he first took office. But since his time Cambridge has gone in more keenly for the exact sciences. Certainly Pepys became the very model of a permanent official, working energetically and continuing to learn all through his long life. By the age of forty he was a member of Parliament and secretary of the Admiralty; he earned more and more honors; he rose to be president of the Royal Society, and retired in 1689 after an adventurous and successful career. When he died he had a splendid library, for he had been collecting rare and interesting books throughout his life. He left it, together with his personal papers, to his own college, Magdalene. I have seen his documents preserved there, and I have felt his presence almost as vividly as though he were still alive.

Among his papers there were six volumes in his own handwriting. They look as though they were in a complicated and unintelligible cryptographic script, and they took three years to decipher at first; but in fact they are written in a standard type of seventeenth-century shorthand, with a few additional obscurities which Pepys himself introduced when he was writing anything particularly outrageous. They contain his journal for a period of nearly ten years, his twenty-sixth to his thirty-sixth year; and they stop only because his eyes began to give out, and

he feared he was going blind. They were first published
— at least in part — after Pepys had been dead for over a
century; they will never be completely printed, because
sometimes they are too disgraceful; but we may now read
nearly all of them.

One can enjoy Pepys's diary for quite a long time before
beginning to understand what is so good about it; indeed,
it has several different merits which rarely come together
in a single book. The most obvious one is usually over-
looked: it is that Pepys was a good writer. He had style.
He had variety. He had zest. He enjoyed words and sentences for their own sake. He did not write down vague
woolly phrases. As soon as we see this, we discover one of
the reasons why such a terribly busy man should bother
to keep a secret diary: it was the same motive which has
led many novelists to start writing novels — the wish to
create something more attractive than the general run of
books. If you can find nothing to read which really delights
you, then write a book yourself.

Then again, Pepys was an interesting man and he felt
he was leading an interesting life. To record it was, for
him, a way of understanding it.

He had a position very close to the center of public affairs. If we can imagine a modern Pepys, he would be a
civilian working in the Pentagon — say, during the Second
World War: on the policy-making level, closely associated
with Admiral King, sending reports to Admiral Leahy, and
reading the operational telegrams from Pacific Fleet HQ;
someone who was well enough known to the President to
be greeted by name and thanked for his services; someone who actually moulded history. (Much of Pepys's diary
is concerned with the naval war between the British and
the Dutch, which contained one episode almost as momentous as Pearl Harbor.) But a modern Pepys would also

have to experience two other crises: a terrible epidemic which chased the entire government out of the capital (Pepys sent his family out of town, but stayed himself, working like a dog), and a disastrous fire that destroyed four-fifths of the central part of the city in four days. All these adventures and many more, Pepys saw and appreciated and recorded day by day. No one can write a history of the seventeenth century in western Europe without reading Pepys.

His book is full of interesting people. One of his close associates was Admiral Sir William Penn. Pepys hated Penn (who returned his hatred), and was puzzled, even shocked, by Penn's son's book on the doctrine of the Trinity. The son was the founder of Pennsylvania. A little later we meet an alumnus of Harvard College, called Sir George Downing. (Downing Street is named after him.) Downing was high in the British intelligence service, whose principal target was then Holland. 'He told me,' says Pepys, 'that he had so good spies, that he hath had the keys taken out of [the Dutch statesman] De Witt's pocket when he was abed, and his closet opened, and papers brought to him, and left in his hands for an hour, and carried back and laid in the place again, and keys put into De Witt's pocket again.' Even three hundred years ago, people were breaking security rules.

In spite of all this interest, as we read Pepys's journal, we are apt to overlook his real talents. He was far more versatile than most modern officials seem to be. He makes very little of it, so that we are surprised to find that he was an able musician, who loved having concerts in his own house and actually composed several songs. He spent lavishly on books, and he read them, too. For the theater he had a passion. Some of it was due to the pretty actresses (Pepys had a wandering eye, which constantly vexed his wife) but much of it came from a truly intelligent interest in the drama. Far more new plays were produced in London in 1660 or so than today, and he went to almost every one, recording his impressions while they were still hot. Also, he liked travel: he kept gathering impressions of foreign countries from his acquaintances and his books, putting them all into his diary.

But more important than his versatility is his humanity. He was very real. He was very like most of us, both in his best and in his worst. Some people are shocked by the obscene parts of his diary; but it is far milder than the records of that filthy little monster Boswell, and the average modern novel shows far worse things not only being done but being boasted of. Also, he was a young man, living in London, with some position and some money, during one of the most licentious reigns in history: the reign of King Charles II, who himself had a long succession of beautiful mistresses. Wherever Pepys looked, he saw gallant young cavaliers and willing ladies, courtiers and courtesans.

Mr. Pepys and the Ladies would make a superb comedy. Even when he did not know them, he loved them.

> I went . . . to the Theatre; . . . and here I sitting behind in a dark place, a lady spit backward upon me by a mistake, not seeing me; but after seeing her to be a very pretty lady, I was not troubled at it at all.

His interest in handsome actresses caused some terrible rows with his wife. One of them started when she put on a new blond wig.

> My wife being dressed this day in fair hair did make me so mad, that I spoke not one word to her, though I was ready to burst with anger. After that, Creed and I into the Park, and walked, a most pleasant eve-

ning, and so took coach, and took up my wife, and in my way home discovered my trouble to my wife for her white locks, swearing several times, which I pray God forgive me for, and bending my fist, that I would not endure it. She, poor wretch, was surprized with it, and made me no answer all the way home; but there we parted, and I to the office late, and then home, and without supper to bed, vexed.

Next morning (which was Sunday), his wife came downstairs in her dressing-gown to have the matter out.

We begun calmly, that, upon having money to lace her gown for second mourning, she would promise to wear white locks no more in my sight, which I, like a severe fool, thinking not enough, begun to except against, and made her fly out to very high terms and cry, and in her heat, told me of keeping company with Mrs. Knipp, saying, that if I would promise never to see her more . . . she would never wear white locks more. This vexed me, but I restrained myself from saying any thing, but do think never to see this woman—at least, to have her here more; and so all very good friends as ever.

After that he took his wife out to dine at a French restaurant, downtown, as many a husband has done since then in a similar situation; and then they came home and Mrs. Pepys discharged the maid.

In those days there were just as many 5-per-centers as there are now. Pepys got his share of percentages. Since he was in the Admiralty, he had a particularly close connection with rich shipbuilders; and this is how he accepted a bribe (or, as he might call it, a compliment) from one of them:

Sir W. Warren . . . did give me a pair of gloves for my wife wrapt up in a paper, which I would not open, feeling it hard; but did tell him that my wife should thank him, and so went on in discourse. When I come home, Lord! in what pain I was to get my wife out of the room without bidding her go, that I might see what these gloves were; and, by and by, she being gone, it proves a pair of white gloves for her, and forty pieces in good gold, which did so cheer my heart, that I could eat no victuals almost for dinner.

Then he adds, reflectively,

I was at a great loss what to do, whether to tell my wife of it or no, for fear of making her think me to be in a better condition, or in a better way of getting money, than yet I am.

As his income went on increasing, he did exactly what people would do today: he bought a Cadillac. In his time it was even grander and rather more rare: it was a coach of his own, with a pair of matched black horses and a liveried coachman. It meant a great deal to Pepys as a symbol of success. He bought it in midwinter, so anxious was he, and he could hardly wait until spring. As soon as the weather improved, he took it out —

— to Hyde Park, the first time we were there this year, or ever, in our own coach, where with mighty pride rode up and down, and many coaches there; and I thought our horses and coach as pretty as any there, and observed so to be by others. Here staid till night, and so home.

Reading the diary, and smiling at all the little follies of Samuel Pepys, we can scarcely help liking him. Men like him rather better than women do, for some reason. He seems to tell us everything. What he sees in other people is usually sensible; what he records of himself is often silly.

Just as you and I have been, so Pepys was short-changed when buying seats at the theater:

> I was prettily served this day at the play-house door, where, giving six shillings into the fellow's hand for three of us, the fellow by legerdemain did convey one away, and with so much grace faced me down that I did give him but five, that, though I knew the contrary, yet I was overpowered by his so grave and serious demanding the other shilling, that I could not deny him, but was forced by myself to give it him.

(The last time that was done to me, the conjurer was an elderly woman in the change booth at one of the largest motion picture theaters in midtown New York, who looked like a contralto in the church choir. Whenever you hand over a ten-dollar bill, say, 'Ten,' or you *may* get change for a five.)

Again, one night Mr. Pepys lay sweating and trembling in bed because he thought he heard burglars in the house. He rang for the maids. After half an hour one of them got up. She found it was only the dog trying to get in. A few years later both he and his wife were terrified because they heard people in the next room, moving things, and concluded that their servants had already been stunned or killed. Finally Pepys braced himself, and went out 'with a firebrand in his hand,' and found that it was the people next door sweeping the chimneys. And so on, through incident after incident, until we begin to think Mr. Pepys must be a milktoast or a fool. And sometimes readers will say that this is what they enjoy most about his diary, that he tries to tell the whole truth, even if it is degrading to himself.

But this is not true. Mr. Pepys was an Englishman, and the English tend to underestimate themselves — personally, if not socially. So he leaves out many things. He puts in his follies, almost all, and leaves out some of his best virtues. He will say how frightened he was at the sound of possible burglars, but not praise himself for staying in London and doing his duty during the plague. He hardly ever gives himself any credit for his own energy and industry: now and then he notes (without a word of complaint) that he spent all Christmas Eve working in the office, alone, and got home late. And in particular, he does not record the steady growth of his own intellectual competence. He will mention the problems that confronted him, but he will not analyze them. He will say that he and a few other officials have worked out a set of formal instructions for commanders of British ships, but he will not explain his own contribution to this very important measure. All that he left in the office when he came home to enjoy himself and to write his journal. His famous diary is the mirror of only half a man.

Vanity, vanity, is what all readers exclaim on first looking into Pepys's journal; and it usually takes quite a long acquaintance with the man and his book to learn that he was in fact a sober, hard-working, intelligent, and unselfish official; and that the vanity was as inessential to the real man as the periwigs, the laced waistcoats, the velvet cloaks, and the pretty coach and horses of which he was so proud. No man can tell the whole truth, even to himself. No man knows the whole truth, even about himself. But even for half a truth we can be grateful, if it is set down with wit and charm and vitality. All art is a skilful way of telling half a truth.

The letters of Jefferson

IT is usually interesting to read the lives of important
politicians. It is usually very boring to read their letters,
for two reasons, because they are concerned only with the
manipulation of power, and because they cannot write
down the things that are really important.

But if a politician is something more than a power-seeker
and a power-holder, if he thinks of himself as a man with
many different interests (of which politics is only one), if
he can see and think of problems beyond the power of
legislatures to solve, and of activities which cannot properly be debated in senate or parliament, then his letters
will be not only fascinating but inspiring. Such a man was
the third President of the United States of America,
Thomas Jefferson. He was a tremendous letter writer. No

less than 18,000 of his letters survive. Many of them were written not because he wanted to put pen to paper, but because he felt he ought to. His enormous experience and his well-earned reputation for wisdom made people from all over America and Europe write to him constantly. He seems to have had no private secretary; he used to reply in his own hand, with singular courtesy and elaboration; yet we have one letter in which he says that, in a single year, when he was seventy-eight, he had written 1267 letters; and he called the relentless flood of mail a *corvée*, which means 'the forced labor of a serf.' No one except specialists would wish to read all this vast correspondence; but there is a good representative selection, called *A Jefferson Profile as Revealed in his Letters,* edited by Saul Padover and published by the John Day Company. In this it is easy, and indeed delightful, to study the remarkable range of Jefferson's interests.

Naturally his chief concern was politics. He was the author, and one of the signers, of the Declaration of Independence; governor of Virginia; chairman of Congress; ambassador to France; Secretary of State; Vice President of the United States; and twice President of the republic he had helped to found and to form. But it is notable that his letters on political subjects mainly concern matters of principle. Jefferson did not regard politics as a game or a dog-eat-dog contest, but as a perpetual examination of rival principles, the test of competing ways of life. For example, there are many things to be said against the institution of monarchy, but it has seldom been more clearly or more pungently denounced than in Jefferson's letter to Langdon (1810):

> Take any race of animals, confine them in idleness
> and inaction, whether in a stye, a stable or a state-
> room, pamper them with high diet, gratify all their

sexual appetites, immerse them in sensualities, nourish their passions, let everything bend before them, and banish whatever might lead them to think, and in a few generations they become all body and no mind; and this, too, by a law of nature, by that very law by which we are in the constant practice of changing the characters and propensities of the animals we raise for our own purposes. Such is the regimen in raising kings, and in this way they have gone on for centuries. While in Europe, I often amused myself with contemplating the characters of the then reigning sovereigns of Europe. Louis the XVI was a fool, of my knowledge, and in despite of the answers made for him at his trial. The King of Spain was a fool, and of Naples the same. They passed their lives in hunting, and dispatched two couriers a week, one thousand miles, to let each other know what game they had killed the preceding days. The King of Sardinia was a fool. All these were Bourbons. . . . These animals had become without mind and powerless; and so will every hereditary monarch be after a few generations.

Although we think of him as an optimist, Jefferson has a profound distrust of legislation, and political institutions, and group organizations. It is quite obvious from his letters that he would have loathed and despised the idea of 'social engineering'; he would have seen the worship of the state — any state, monarchical, republican, or dictatorial — as the reverse of liberalism; and he himself hoped for the *least* possible amount of government, with the *fewest* possible officials. About individuals he was optimistic; about political groups he was pessimistic. There is a remarkably far-sighted utterance in a letter he wrote to Madison in 1789: 'The executive, in our governments, is not the sole, it is scarcely the principal object of my jealousy. The tyranny of the legislatures is the most formidable dread at present, and will be for many years.' And then, in terms which forecast some of the struggles of the present century: '[The tyranny] of the executive will come in its turn; but it will be at a remote period.' And a similar pessimism was implicit in much of Jefferson's wary and even suspicious attitude to committees and legislative bodies in general.

Anyone who has visited that handsome house Monticello will know that Jefferson had two other chief interests, quite apart from politics. One of these was science and technology; the other was music and the fine arts. It is strange, by the way, that visitors to Monticello are always told about Jefferson's gadgets — the wind vane, the dumbwaiter, the clock wound by the movement of the door — but seldom about his artistic taste. It is a most beautiful house; with its situation, its grounds, and its furniture, it could have been created only by a true artist. Even its interior decorations, exquisitely tasteful, were planned by Mr. Jefferson. So, among his letters we find many which would strike us as extremely strange if coming from other politicians, but which show us Jefferson's fine taste. As early as 1778 he wrote to an Italian friend asking him to look for five musicians who might come to America to join his household — not professionals ('The bounds of an American fortune will not admit the indulgence of a domestic band of musicians'), but skilled workmen who could also play musical instruments — a gardener, a stonemason, a weaver, a cabinetmaker, and a vinedresser. As far as we know, that project came to nothing, but Jefferson had other artistic notions which were more deeply rooted and produced more lasting fruit. In 1787, when he was forty-three, he wrote to a Parisian friend to say that he was in love — in love with a little building in the southern French town of Nîmes. He called it, as no doubt its neighbors called it, 'the square house,' *la Maison quarrée;* we know it as the temple of the young Caesars. It is a fine creation of the best period of Roman architecture; and Jefferson not only admired it, he had it copied in the Capitol of Virginia, and used its inspiration for other buildings which set the tone for fine classical architecture on this half-continent.

Of course every visitor to Monticello sees the evidence of Jefferson's passionate interest in technology. His letters make this equally clear. We see him, in 1799, writing to Robert Livingston on the steam engine; in 1807, congratulating Fulton on his new submarine torpedo; and constantly searching out every invention that might help the progress of his country.

Jefferson knew that progress is impossible without firm roots. He was a devoted advocate of a solidly based system of education, including history, modern languages, mathematics and science, and Greek and Latin literature. As for the classics, his opinion was not perhaps 'progressive,' but none the less admirable. In 1800 (at the age of fifty-seven, writing to the British scientist Priestley), he said:

> To read the Latin and Greek authors in the original, is a sublime luxury. . . . I thank on my knees him who directed my early education for having put into my possession this rich source of delight; and I would not exchange it for anything which I could then have acquired, and have not since acquired.

He says the same to young men whom he is advising about their education; he repeats it when he is outlining the curriculum of the University of Virginia; and long after his retirement, he observes with satisfaction, to a friend who knows how he hates newspapers: 'I have given up newspapers in exchange for Tacitus and Thucydides, for Newton and Euclid, and I find myself much the happier.' His library, which was bought by Congress for $25,000, contained nearly 10,000 volumes, and became the nucleus of the Library of Congress.

Jefferson had one interest which, at first sight, seems rather surprising. Certainly it has been shared by few other Presidents. He admired the American Indians; he studied their customs and their languages. In 1801 he wrote to a Mississippi planter to thank him for sending him diction-aries of three Indian dialects, adding that he already pos-sessed vocabularies of about thirty different tribes. Fifteen years later he corresponded on the same subject with a Scottish-born scholar named Peter Wilson, who became Professor of Greek and Latin at Columbia College, New York. He told Wilson that he had intended to make a synoptic survey of many Indian languages, and had col-lected 'between thirty and forty vocabularies' of Indian tongues; but that, after his retirement from the Presi-dency, when his goods were being shipped from Washing-ton to Monticello, the package containing these valuable papers was stolen and destroyed. Even after that disaster, and at that distance of time, Mr. Jefferson's perception was correct — for he saw that more than half of the Indian languages differed as radically from one another as Latin from Icelandic. His wisdom appeared equally well when he rejected the theories of amateur ethnologists who tried to tell him that the Indians were descended from the Jews (a belief which is still maintained by the Mormons), and when he warned Meriwether Lewis, in dealing with the Sacs and the Foxes, to avoid military action, with the words: 'Commerce is the great engine by which we are to coerce [the Indians], and not war.'

As we read these letters, we become aware of two or three odd quirks in Jefferson's outlook. One is that, although he had been a successful lawyer, he seldom speaks of the law. Another is that, although he was devoted to the ideal of freedom of speech, and in particular to the freedom of the press, he despised and detested the contemporary newspapers, their editors, their writers, and even those who read them. Writing in 1807, he said:

> It is a melancholy truth, that a suppression of the press could not more completely deprive the nation of its benefits, than is done by its abandoned prostitution to falsehood. Nothing can now be believed which is seen in a newspaper. Truth itself becomes suspicious by being put into that polluted vehicle. The real extent of this state of misinformation is known only to those who are in situations to confront facts within their knowledge with the lies of the day.

Jefferson wrote these bitter words when he was President of the United States; and no doubt one of the most difficult conflicts he ever had to endure was the struggle between his belief in the fundamental decency of most men and his horror at the meanness and mendacity of some journalists. After all, he did face the conflict, and he wrote:

> Were it left to me to decide whether we should have a government without newspapers, or newspapers without a government, I should not hesitate a moment to prefer the latter.

On the whole, Americans are an optimistic people. We expect everything, or nearly everything, to turn out for the best. We believe that all excesses will correct themselves, and that all abuses can be corrected before they go too deep. It is good for us to read the speeches and writings of the Founding Fathers, who were, on the whole, pessimists.

They had a deep faith in men, but a deep distrust in any kind of state, as a machine for producing and exercising power. In fact, they were devoted to one ideal — the individual man. There was the end at which they aimed, and the state was merely the means to make that end attainable; and all its mechanism and pomp, all its power and proliferation, were, they believed, an endemic disease which might become fatal and was always dangerous. Men who are helpless before their own government must be either slaves or animals. So thought Thomas Jefferson.

The first deadly sin

THERE is something fascinating about watching a man or a woman going to the bad. If it is someone close to you, it is unutterably painful, an experience not to be discussed. But it is endurable to watch someone who has talent, promise of distinction, much energy, many potentialities; to see him choosing the wrong road, not once, but again and again, pushing downward until he ruins his own life; to conclude, as we observe, that he is wrecking himself not by accident, or by mistake, but deliberately; and to be deeply, passionately interested. I imagine that detectives must feel this very often; they will look at a really 'bad actor' whom they have watched growing up all the way from juvenile delinquency to major crime, and — not admire him, but contemplate him with the same interest as a fish fancier keeps for a weirdly inbred goldfish with six-teen tails, or a pathologist for a truly enormous tumor.

There are several wasted lives like this in art, in literature, in philosophy; there are many in politics. If the psychologist Jung is right, one of those who purposefully destroyed himself was Nietzsche; we can see some around us today; we shall see more. One of the most perplexing things about such men and women is that often they seem to derive extra energy from going wrong. It is as though they said, 'Evil, be thou my good!' and then found themselves inspired with a new force which, even though it was a destructive force, was still immensely powerful. In a side chapel of the cathedral of Orvieto there is a powerful painting by Luca Signorelli which shows the preaching of the Antichrist, as it is described in Scripture. Raised on a dais, among admiring listeners and thoughtful commentators, stands a dignified man in long robes, with flowing hair and beard and the hieratic gesture of an inspired, almost a holy preacher. All those near him are convinced by his energy and his authority, except for a few heretics who are being tortured or executed. His face is thoughtful and filled with deep controlled emotion; but his eyes, his eyes twist horribly to one side and are set in haggard pits. Just behind him stands a grinning naked demon, whispering in his ear. Such are the men who choose to waste their talents and their lives.

One of them was an extraordinary Englishman whose very name is still something of a puzzle (because he endeavored to make it so): a puzzle, or a mask. He was born in 1860, and died in 1913. The world now knows him — if it knows him at all — as Baron Corvo, which means 'Baron Crow.' He often signed himself Fr. Rolfe, which he meant to be read and interpreted as 'Fra' or 'Brother' Rolfe, but in fact his name was Frederick Rolfe, and both his attempt to make himself an Italian nobleman and his claim to be a priest were false. Not many men have put so much energy into pretense. Few have lived a life of such pervasive disguise that it penetrated beneath the surface, and altered their very manner of speech, their physical shape. Few have had such an odd assortment of talents and tastes, and misused them so grossly; few have wanted power and wealth so much, and, while possessing the dynamism to seize them, have failed so egregiously even to approach them. Poor miserable Rolfe: he wanted to be the greatest author in the English language; he wanted to be an artist worthy of the Renaissance; he wanted to be an opulent nobleman without attachments, practicing every possible kind of apolaustic accomplishment; he wanted to be Pope. He never had more than five hundred dollars in his possession at one time, and he died in a pitiful mixture of extravagant debt and nagging poverty at the age of fifty-three.

Baron Corvo would be forgotten by now, except by a few specialists in odd areas of literary history, if it were not for two distinctions which he earned. The first is that he wrote one unforgettable book. The second is that one remarkable book was written about him.

He wrote one unforgettable book, I said; of course he wrote more, much more; but of all that he produced, nothing is worth reading today except his extraordinary romantic novel, *Hadrian the Seventh*. This is a story set in modern times. It tells the story of a humble English Catholic layman who wishes to become a priest but is rejected. For twenty years he starves, living as a hack writer, while still preserving his conviction that he is intended to become a priest. After that long interval, his case is reconsidered by the Church. A cardinal and a bishop visit him, examine him, and are persuaded that he has been sorely wronged. They hear his confession, and admit him to the priesthood. He is taken to Rome. And then — during an insoluble deadlock in an election to the Papacy — he is (simply because he has suffered for so long and endured so much without tarnishing or wavering, because he has always been certain of his vocation with a certainty which was surely divinely confirmed) elected Pope. He takes the title of Hadrian the Seventh, because the last (and only) Englishman to occupy the Pope's throne was styled Hadrian the Fourth; he reforms the Papacy and the Church from inside — for instance, by selling the treasures of the Vatican and giving the money to the poor; and he is finally murdered by an envious Socialist agitator. It is a brilliant, though crazy, idea; it is brilliantly carried out. Understand, it is not a satire on religion; far from it: it is based on a highly idealistic view of religion, and is intended to be a reverent re-examination of the powers and duties of the Roman Catholic Church; and it is written in a style as eccentric, as individual, and as haughtily aristocratic as its hero.

Of course that book is not an autobiography, but an autolatry, or self-glorification, a piece of wish-fulfillment as impudent and yet as pathetic as any author has ever attempted. The real life of Baron Corvo was almost as romantic. Like the career of his fictional Pope, it began with twenty years of poverty and misery. But, instead of ending in nobility, and virtue, and almost superhuman power, it ended in folly, and poverty, and diabolical vice. He himself never told that story; but it has been told in a brilliant piece of biography called *The Quest for Corvo,* by A. J. A. Symons, written in 1934.* Brilliant it must be called, for

---

* *Published by the Michigan State University Press in 1955.*

it is a biography written on a new plan, exactly appropriate to such a fantastic character as Baron Corvo. Instead of telling the tale of Corvo's life from his birth through his youth past his maturity to his death, Symons begins by saying that he had never heard of Corvo (as most of us have never heard of him) until one of his friends lent him Corvo's book, *Hadrian the Seventh*. He read the novel and was deeply impressed by it. He went back to his friend, and proclaimed that this fellow Corvo must have been a genius. What had happened to him? And then his friend produced a long series of personal letters all in the highly individual handwriting and the unmistakable style of Baron Corvo, and all exploring with rapturous detail and unflinching sincerity the lowest conceivable depths of vice. Symons was appalled. Appalled, but fascinated. How was it possible that a man who had written a wish-fulfillment novel imagining himself as head of the Catholic Church should also have written such truly devilish letters, not only glorying in his own sins but enticing others to join him?

The rest of Symons' book, *The Quest for Corvo*, is a step-by-step description of his long-drawn-out effort to discover all the facts about that extraordinary man. He determined to find out what were the real talents of Baron Corvo; what were his central weaknesses, and (if possible) what was their source; and how he had lived for his fifty-three fantastically troubled years. He resolved also to search for the articles and stories which Baron Corvo had published and which had since been forgotten, and for the manuscripts of certain books which he was known to have written, but which had never appeared. In fact, he set out to build up the first factual biography of this extraordinary man and to compile a list of his writings: to make him, in some sort, a permanent figure in the history of literature.

But, instead of writing the straight biography of Corvo,

he wrote the story of how he himself had found out — with incessant labor, with many disagreeable diversions and disappointing false trails, and sometimes with ventures into bitter personal feuds and absurd personal vanities — most of the truth about that phenomenal character who had hoped to be a divine, and who had turned into a scoundrel. This story is filled with brilliantly drawn character sketches: there is an eccentric professor of Greek (modern Greek) at Oxford; there is a horrified British consul, who had the unsavory job of going over Baron Corvo's effects after he died in Venice, and who found enough there to have sent the man to prison for life in most countries throughout the Western world; there are several eminent publishers, several shy Anglican clergymen, and some ambiguous and complicated characters who might themselves have come out of the fantasies of Baron Corvo. It is a remarkable book.

Baron Corvo was a highly unusual man, simply because in most ways he was a monumental fake, and, like some monumental fakes, had nevertheless contrived to acquire an almost impenetrable air of mystery and authority which for a time imposed on the world. It is still imposing on the world, for there are people now who write of him as though he had possessed vast knowledge. They admire his facility in quoting Greek and Latin and his passion for using uncommon words derived from those languages. But they are sometimes deceived. For instance, an article on him written some years ago praises him for introducing into English the word *turpiludicrous* — which looks like a blend of ludicrous and turpitude. But what Corvo actually wrote was *turpilucricupidous,* which means 'having a shameful lust for money'; it is a word which occurs only once in the whole Latin language, in a poet whom Corvo had probably not read; he got it out of a dictionary and used it, as he used many others, to impress the less ingenious public. He was, in fact, a half-educated man with an enormous ego; and his so-called classical scholarship was always a superficial collection of words and phrases and vivid details, never a real attempt to penetrate into the past of Greece and Rome.

Still, he had distinction of manner, if not of substance. He had a handsome script, which has caused some of his letters to be preserved, however vile their content; he had a real sense of the history of the Renaissance; and he had worked out a very individual style. This is sometimes annoying. For instance, in writing a history of the Borgia family, he refuses to use the word 'poison,' he chooses to use the word 'venom' and would speak of a possibly poisoned glove as being a 'gauntlet envenomed.' Yet in such an odd little masterpiece as *Hadrian the Seventh* even this affected style is appropriate; and that is because once only, when his dream of his own life and his visionarily aristocratic style came together, he was enabled to make a book which would tell itself in terms fitting for his subject, which was his own dream of omnipotence.

Of course Rolfe was abnormal, painfully and disastrously abnormal. His sexual life varied between extremes of asceticism and extremes of debauchery — as his social life varied between extremes of loneliness and extremes of affectionate all-or-nothing friendship, as his financial life varied between abject poverty and ridiculous extravagance. In his last year or two, living in Venice on money sent him by a dupe with whom he had agreed to collaborate on a book, he used to have himself rowed through the canals in his own gondola with four gondoliers. (Ordinary people have one gondolier, occasionally; the rich and magnificent have two; only princes and kings have four.) Rolfe's bedroom at this time was said to be draped and curtained with the material of the robes of cardinals. A little later he was hopelessly impoverished, eating on credit, sleeping in his gondola on the lagoon and trying to keep awake to fight off the rats. After a few weeks, he was dead.

It is possible to go a little deeper, and to say that Rolfe ruined his own life by one central weakness: the sin of pride. In order to be great, one must be humble. In order to rise, one must stoop down. In order to learn, one must admit one's ignorance. In order to be a notable artist, one must accept discipline, and work, and erase, and revise, and throw away, so that eventually one may create something that will last. Rolfe was unwilling to do any of these things, except in his style and his handwriting. That is why he was a proud amateur in scholarship, in art, in religion, and in his entire life. His pride was a concealment for fear, for a bitter, terrifying knowledge that he himself was inadequate, and for a stubborn and stupid determination that he would never work and study humbly in order to make up his inadequacies. It was the first sin, the sin which they say the archangel committed when he cried *'Non seruiam!'* (I will not be a servant!) and so became Satan. It was pride, pride, which caused Rolfe, though he could write a magnificent dream-novel in which he became a servant of God and a saint, to end his life as a fraud, false to himself and to all who had trusted him, and in fact a miserable fiend, Mephistopheles without the confident smile.

The house high on the hill

IT is very difficult to understand anybody without visiting his home. Houses reveal character. Someone who appears to be a hard, tense, ambitious careerist when you see him at a meeting may live in a small, comfortable country place, with a garden full of flowers and birds, out of sight of the road. Talk to him there — or even look round the house and garden in silence, breathing the calm air — and you will understand that he is really a gentle soul, who is rather afraid of life and is struggling almost too hard to conquer it and to ensure his own safety.

It is this fact that makes it so interesting, indeed so necessary, to visit the homes of people whom we know only through their books. A. E. Housman's grim and graceless rooms in Trinity College, Cambridge; Ellen Glasgow's house in Richmond, Virginia, proud, gracious, but rather conventional and chilly; the dour, pathetic little cottage of Robert Burns in Scotland — these all tell us something new about the writers who lived there, and confirm much that we had only divined before. The danger, of course, is obvious. Too many people visit such a house merely because it is a sight to be seen and not because they have any real interest in the author, any considered appreciation of his work. The house soon comes to feel this. It becomes something as impersonal as a museum. The spirit of the author looks at the gaping crowds, and shudders, and departs.

This is happening to one of the most famous houses in the world. It was created by one man with a surprising and original character, almost incomprehensible even to himself. Millions of people got to know something of it through his book. Thousands of men and women visited it during his lifetime; many thousands more have been visiting it since his death. It is true of him, as of other authors, that he cannot be understood by those who have not seen his home. He was a doctor, born in Sweden: his name, Axel Munthe. The house is the villa which he built largely with his own hands, on a lofty promontory in Anacapri, the highest part of the island of Capri; he named it for the patron saint of the little parish where it stands, St. Michael, or San Michele. His book, *The Story of San Michele,* was published just over twenty-five years ago. Partly autobiography, partly social criticism, partly aesthetic appreciation, and partly spiritual meditation, it might have been expected to interest a small select public, sell four thousand copies, and go out of print. Instead, it has sold something like a million copies in the English language alone, it has been translated into over twenty foreign languages, it was a steady best-seller (though then quite an expensive book) during the depths of the depression, and it is still popular, still well worth reading.

Just as old Munthe was one of the queerest people in the world, so his book is one of the oddest collections of memoirs in the world. He was a tremendous raconteur, he was an acute psychologist, and so he could tell stories that illuminated an obscure epoch of social history, or made a bandit, a prostitute, a peasant, or a rich hypochondriac come vividly to life, speak in their own voices. But apart from the oddity of Munthe's anecdotes and the enormous range of his experience, the book has a permanent quality which not only accounts for its success in the depression but guarantees its continued value in our own troubled times. It is kind; it is consoling; it contains tenderness. On the whole, it is optimistic — not with the shallow optimism of certain creeds and teachers who deny or ignore the reality of suffering; no; Munthe was a doctor, he had worked in slums and fought epidemics, he had watched many people die in pain, he himself was ill and suffering when he wrote the book, and in its last chapter he recorded a strange conversation with his old opponent Death. But rather, *The Story of San Michele* is optimistic because it expresses Munthe's belief that even the worst sufferings can be lightened, even the vilest and most selfish people can be cured of their vices, and for a time at least purified, if we and they will learn to put trust more in emotion than in the cold intellect, more in instinct than in convention, more in gentleness than in strength. He himself was a Protestant, but he greatly admired one of the noblest of the Roman Catholic saints: Francis of Assisi, chiefly because — in an age of strong and violent men, the age of armored knights, proud noblemen, ambitious and masterful prelates — Francis quarreled with no one, gave kindness out as freely as the sun spreads its rays, and in his last illness blessed the fire of the red-hot iron which was about to cauterize his face.

Axel Munthe's book is not difficult to understand and to love. His character was not quite so lovable, and is not nearly so easy to understand. He did not show all aspects of it in his memoirs; some he deliberately concealed; some he neglected, or forgot; at some, he merely hinted so that we might reconstruct them. A book which attempts to Tell All is often less interesting than one which leaves our imagination still at work.

A man's character is shown in many different ways; but it is surely well revealed by the pattern of his career. Some men swing wildly from side to side like a car on a slippery road; some push steadily on like a liner crossing the ocean; some drift. Axel Munthe was a doctor — which usually means steady application and the acceptance of routine; but his life was as erratic as a comet. He was born and educated in Sweden; he qualified as a doctor in France; he practiced in Paris and in Rome; he married a British wife, wrote chiefly in English, served in the British Red Cross in the First World War, and was proud to have sons in the British army during the Second; his home was in a once lonely part of Italy; and he died in the Royal Palace at Stockholm. He had no home, in the sense in which most of us understand home — a place where we live among people like ourselves. Although he loved the house he built in Anacapri, and although he knew nearly all the people on the island of Capri very well, he was a stranger even there. They were peasants, many of them unable to read and write, or even to speak correct Italian; he was a scholar, a cosmopolitan, an aesthete, a polyglot. They were devout and indeed superstitious Roman Catholics; he was a lonely heretic — he tells an amusing story of the village priest who used to thunder out terrible denunciations of the abominable Lutherans, enemies of God, condemned to eternal torment . . . all except il Signor Dottore, all except Doctor Munthe! He cherished ancient things, relics of the Greek and Roman past; his house was full of exquisite fragments of sculpture, and coins, and pieces of mosaic, which he had dug up or rescued from oblivion. But the people among whom he lived, they had little understanding or love of the past. He tells how one of them found an old clay pipe in the garden — probably left by the British garrison that held the island for a time during the Napoleonic wars; the finder decided at once that it must have belonged to the Roman emperor Tiberius. He records the complaint of old Vincenzo who was digging the hillside to make a new terrace for his vines, and came across a lot of decorated stonework: it had pictures of people on it, *tutti spogliati, ballando come dei pazzi,* all undressed, dancing like lunatics; it took Vincenzo a good deal of hard work to scrape off the paintings, or break all that ancient rubbish into pieces and cart it away and throw it over the cliff into the sea.

It was the same everywhere. Axel Munthe was always something of a stranger to the people among whom he lived. He treated princes and millionaires in Rome, and spent their fees on feeding and curing outcasts in the slums. He enjoyed mixing with the great; reigning monarchs visited his home in Anacapri, famous people like Oscar Wilde and Eleonora Duse came to see him. But he dressed shabbily, lost his medals and decorations, let his money lie about in crumpled bundles of notes here and there, invested little or nothing, hated the machinery of social distinction and of accumulated wealth. (Therefore, he was a magnificent example of the truth that in order to write a real best-seller one must not think of sales or of money for a single moment.)

His character, then, was an enigma both to his friends and to his readers. He appeared modest in his manner and in his writings; and yet, if you reread his book, you will see that indirectly he contrives to praise himself more enthusiastically than any admirer could do. He will say that he was not a good doctor, only a successful one (as though that were not medicine but some cheap trick), and then he will allude to his own cures, and recall the days and nights he spent surrounded by frightful danger, working among the very poor after the earthquake at Messina and during the cholera in Naples. It is not vanity; but it is not self-effacing humility either.

For a long time, I thought he was a rebel. He speaks of his father with something like hatred: tells how the father flogged him, locked him up in a dark room on bread and water for several days and nights; explains that he bit his father's hand. He might have been one of those men whose entire lives are moulded by the wish to oppose their fathers and to be as unlike their fathers' ideal as they possibly can manage to be. Hatred sometimes produces those eccentric lives. But, no. I understood better after I saw his house high up in Anacapri. It is not a house of hatred and negation. It is positive. Still, it is very odd, almost mad. It is filled with works of art: so many that there was hardly room for a human personality; the walls are thick with fragments of Roman inscriptions, one entire room is a Roman Catholic chapel with ancient ecclesiastical furnishings, everywhere you look, you see something old, or rare, or beautiful. Yet it is the house of a single, lonely man. The garden paths are so laid out that two people cannot walk on them side by side. And the view! the view is something close to insanity.

Perched on the edge of a precipice about a thousand feet above the sea, the Villa di San Michele is so built that nothing appears to be above it, or even near it; it looks down on the Bay of Naples, down on the rest of Capri, with only a distant glimpse of the other peaks of that mountainous island. To look out even on a calm day makes one dizzy with height and godlike detachment; above is the sky, far beneath is the sea, all around is blue air and bodiless distance. Standing in San Michele, we begin to understand Axel Munthe a little better. He spent much of his life in Capri trying to stop the inhabitants from maltreating their animals and from trapping songbirds to be eaten in the restaurants of the mainland; he had a fantastic collection of tame animals whom he befriended, right down to miniature tortoises the size of walnuts, who lined up for lettuce leaves from his luncheon; the only people he really disliked strongly were the domineering Germans; his whole life as a doctor was spent in helping both the poor (who are prisoners of their poverty and ignorance) and the rich (who are prisoners of their own rank and wealth and stupidity); he himself was never quite well in body and, it may be, in spirit. Axel Munthe wanted one thing above all else for himself, and tried to procure one thing for other people. Since he saw illness and weakness and helplessness and even a regular routine of life as something like imprisonment, he tried to set others and himself free. His strange house on the edge of a precipice was not, like other villas on Capri, the home of a tyrant or an exhibitionist or a maniac. It was, as it were, the doctor's waiting room: on the other side of the wall, between the sea and the sky, there was liberty.

WE think of the English author Somerset Maugham as being an uncompromising realist. Even when they are set in strange distant places, his stories are scarcely ever fanciful or romantic. The chief power of his work is that it seems like a transcript of actual life.

However, there is one of his novels which is unlike all the others. It is called *The Magician*. Its plot and several of its characters are quite different from the usual hard photographic Maugham tale and easily recognizable personages.

The principal character is a modern wizard, called Oliver Haddo. He is a rich young Englishman, well-born, and very tall and strong, with a remarkable reputation for courage. When we meet him first he is living in Paris, studying occult books in Hebrew and Arabic, but we learn that he has already distinguished himself as a big-game hunter, and is the only man alive who has killed three lions with three successive shots. Once handsome, he is now bald and immensely fat, although he has lost none of his colossal strength; he looks like a very bad Roman emperor.

Oliver Haddo is not the hero, although the book is named after him. The hero is an English surgeon called Arthur Burdon. He is in love with an English girl who is studying art in Paris; her name, significantly, is Margaret. Oliver Haddo crosses their path once or twice, and then again. He performs several feats which, even to the realistic surgeon, appear to be magical: for instance, he allows himself to be bitten by a poisonous viper, and heals the wound by saying some words over it and spitting on it. Eventually he hypnotizes Margaret, makes her see terrible visions of evil, dominates her, and marries her. Some time passes. Margaret and Oliver Haddo are apparently happy, living the life of wealthy expatriates in Rome and Monte Carlo, but the girl's character degenerates rapidly. Eventually Haddo takes her to his huge old house in the north of England, and there her death from heart disease is announced.

Arthur, who has continued to love her, does not believe that her death was natural. He follows Haddo to his home to investigate; and there, in a dark room of the local inn, he is attacked by Haddo; he breaks his arm, and at last strangles him. But when he manages to find matches and light the lamp and turns to examine the body, he finds to his horror that the dead Haddo has completely disappeared. At this he knows what he must do. He goes up to Haddo's house and breaks in. It is richly furnished, but has no human inhabitants; yet he hears an extraordinary sound coming down from the top story — not a human voice, nor the cry of an animal, but an odious gibber, hoarse and rapid and wordless. On the top story he finds an enormous series of laboratories, fitted with the most modern equipment and heated to an overpowering temperature by a set of furnaces. And there, in a row of glass jars, he at last discovers the secret of Oliver Haddo, the secret for which he had dominated and at last sacrificed Margaret by using first her spirit and then her blood.

The jars contain Haddo's attempts to create life. In the first there is a mass of flesh about the size of a head, pulsating slowly and rhythmically; in another there is a thing like a large embryo, with its legs and arms not yet separated from the body; another contains an almost human trunk, with two heads which open their eyes slowly and separately as the light strikes them. In the last of all there dances and raves a furiously alive creature about four feet high, with a human shape, and an enormous human head; it is from this monster that the senseless gibbering comes. And then beside it, Arthur sees the body of the magician lying on the floor; its eyes are injected with blood, its throat dark with the marks of strangulation, and when Arthur feels the right arm, he finds that it is fractured. He turns away in horror and leaves the vast building which contains nothing but death and the caricatures of life. But before he goes, he uses the furnace to set fire to it, so that in a single holocaust all that iniquity will be blotted from the face of the earth.

An extraordinary story, is it not? Quite unlike the rest of Somerset Maugham's work. Yet he published it in 1908, when he was thirty-four years old, and therefore in the prime of his life. It is not the product of an aberrant imagination, nor of a decadent struggling with omnipresent sin. Maugham himself says that all his work blends fact and fiction so inextricably that not even he himself can distinguish them. The fact that his hero is a doctor leads us to interpret the story as somehow connected with Maugham's own life and experiences, or at least as based on someone whom he had known.

It is true. Or at least its basis is true. There was such a magician. He was a year younger than Maugham, he was well known in Europe for many years, and he died as recently as 1947. Not only Somerset Maugham, but W. B. Yeats and Arnold Bennett knew him quite well. He was called Aleister Crowley.

The real magician's story is nearly as extraordinary as Somerset Maugham's romantic novel about him. Some of the facts are almost the same. Crowley was not a hunter, but he was a daring mountaineer who made expeditions to the dangerous peaks K2 and Kanchenjunga in the Himalayas. He had strong hypnotic powers; and he had an extraordinary capacity for dominating women, using them in magical rites, and driving them at last to drink, insanity, and death. On the other hand, his chief interest was not the artificial creation of something resembling human life, but the establishment of a new world religion of which he would be both the apostle and the deity — a religion based on the controlled use of emotion raised to its greatest intensities, and on the abandonment of reason and the evocation of unconscious powers by every possible mystical release, including sex and drug-taking. And throughout his life, instead of studying (as Oliver Haddo did), he poured forth an interminable torrent of bad poetry, meaningless prose, and amateurish drawings and paintings. If he had not had such a deliberately destructive effect on so many men and women (even though they were weaklings), he would have been an essentially comic figure, like the adherents of those small absurd sects who have private gospels written by one of their own number — they usually talk much about the Egyptian pyramids, wear sandals, and weave their own clothes.

The facts in Aleister Crowley's life (the external facts) are these. He was born in the English midlands in 1875, from a rich, prosaic, middle-class family. His father had made a decent fortune out of brewing beer. Both his parents belonged to the tiny new sect called Plymouth Brethren. His father died young, leaving him lots of money; his mother tried to dominate him, and then gave up, saying that he was the Beast 666 of the Book of Revelation — a description which apparently moulded his career for the rest of his life. He tried for the first years of his adult life to become a poet and mystic like Yeats, but was not taken seriously. He spent the First World War in America, writing anti-British propaganda for the German agent George Sylvester Viereck — not from any admiration for the Germans, but, like many such propagandists, from a profound and irrepressible mother-hatred.

After the war, he returned to Europe and started to publish again; but once again he failed to make his mark, because his writing was so poor and his doctrines were so incoherent. In 1920 he founded what he called an abbey in northern Sicily, where he gathered a group of disciples with whom he engaged in fantastic rites of asceticism and debauchery, alternating in the way that only a very strong man or woman can endure. One of his pupils died. He was expelled from Italy in 1923 and from France in 1929. During the 'thirties he enjoyed an odd reputation, partly because he had published a book, *The Diary of a Drug Fiend*, which had a scandalous success, and partly because he had a certain personal impressiveness through which he dominated many groups and many goofy individuals. Also, although he was obviously a very evil man, blasphemous and perverted and fundamentally cruel, a hater of the world, many mixed-up intellectuals felt it their duty to defend him — not because they liked him and his doctrines, but because he was attacked by the cheap newspapers and magazines and the old-fashioned English officials who had just been condemning the paintings of D. H. Lawrence. This helped to give him a reputation which his own thought and work had done nothing to deserve. Gradually, in the face of a more real diabolism, it faded away. Aleister Crowley survived the Second World War, constantly repeating his slogan, 'Do what thou wilt shall be the whole of the Law,' and taking as much as eleven grains of heroin a day, which is sufficient to kill a roomful of people. He died in 1947, lamented only by a few loonies, and at his funeral service his own pseudo-Swinburnian *Hymn to Pan* was read. It gave serious offense to the authorities of the Brighton Crematorium.

He was not a fake, Aleister Crowley. He was a failure. As a magician, he was far less successful than many wizards — for instance, Saint-Germain. As a mystical writer, he was miserably inferior even to his contemporaries; if you want proof, see Yeats' *Vision*. As a teacher, he was not to be compared with Gurdjieff. He remained a boy all his life. He never lacked courage, but he lacked taste, and he lacked knowledge, qualities which come with maturity. He would not study, but preferred to evoke visions and oracles from his own subconscious, which anyone can do.

To the ordinary spectator Aleister Crowley must seem a wicked and foolish man. True; but he has some importance beyond his individual character. He was a symptom. He was a channel of the forces which appear in the later music of Scriabin, and the poetry of Lautréamont and Rimbaud and the novels of Huysmans, and in much Dadaist and Surrealist art — the forces which first found voice in the writings of Nietzsche, the forces which contributed to making the mind, and the power, of Adolf Hitler and others of the modern barbarians. The new gospel announced in Nietzsche's *Thus Spake Zarathustra* belongs to the same family as its weaker and more derivative successor, Aleister Crowley's 'Do what thou wilt shall be the whole of the Law.' These are the gospels of the chthonic gods, the gods of the lowest and most dangerous parts of the human soul. We all know the strength which these powers can exercise; those who can evoke them are truly magicians and witches; and, as in the old fables, such emanations always threaten and often destroy those who call them into the upper world of light and reason.

The animal kingdom

WHEN we talk of the animal kingdom, we imply that the beasts (wild and tame), the birds, and perhaps the fish and reptiles, belong to a single organized group. But it is not really so. The different kinds of walking and crawling and flying and swimming things all inhabit the same world; many orders of them live together in the same region, sometimes depending on one another for food and even shelter; but on the whole they exist for themselves alone. Like a dog and a cat in the same house, they pay very little attention to each other except at mealtimes. They have no common language. They share no emotions outside their groups. They make no attempt at mutual understanding. There is only one creature which does try to understand many different kinds of living beings, which has learned to interpret their ways by cross-reference, which often knows more about them than they know about themselves, and which has even inspired love in their hearts — a love which he himself has sometimes returned. This creature is Man. In some of the early accounts of the Creation we are told that Adam, first of men, was master of all the animals, gave them the names which were right for them, understood them, and — at least until the Fall — was loved by them, every one. These days are gone now. Many, far too many, human beings are indifferent or cruel to animals; most animals are indifferent or hostile to us; and yet it is still possible, with care and thought and love, to regain something of that old friendliness which appears in Milton's delightful description of the animals in Eden playing with all their wonderful subtlety and grace, to charm the young man and woman who were their masters.

> About them frisking played
> All beasts of the earth, since wild, and of all chase
> In wood or wilderness, forest or den;
> Sporting the lion ramped, and in his paw
> Dandled the kid; bears, tigers, ounces, pards
> Gambolled before them, the unwieldy elephant
> To make them mirth used all his might, and wreathed
> His lithe proboscis.   (*Paradise Lost*, IV, 340–47)

Two remarkable books by a man who really understands animals have come out within the past few years. He is Konrad Lorenz. His first, *King Solomon's Ring*, was issued by Crowell in 1952; his second, *Man Meets Dog*, by Houghton Mifflin in the spring of 1955. They are simply delightful — and made more delightful by very skilful and amusing pictures drawn by the author himself. He is an Austrian, now in his fifties. By profession he is a naturalist — but not the kind of naturalist who collects different species in order to describe their physical structure. He is not an anatomist or a physiologist, but something more like a psychologist. His interest is in the behavior of animals, we might almost say in their minds, rather than in their bodies. That mysterious subject *instinct* is one of the problems which he is no doubt trying to solve; and he has thought a great deal about that equally mysterious subject *intelligence,* with all its ramifications — *learning, teaching, remembering* — and with its intimate but still hardly understood links to the emotions. He told an interviewer for *The New Yorker* that his wife was a medical doctor and earned the money they lived on, while he did his research. Evidently he is very Austrian, with something of the Austrian imprecision, humor, and disregard of sordid things like money and property, and with the Austrian delight in life for its own sake. In one of his books there is a description of how he attended the funeral of an old professor whom he had deeply loved, and whom he sincerely mourned . . . but in his briefcase he had a new puppy, an Australian wild-dog puppy, which he was taking home to see whether it could be reared with tame dogs. As the mourners stood by the grave, the little dingo broke out into the high, shrill, irresistible wail of the homeless, motherless pup shut up in the dark; Lorenz had to push his way out of the funeral service. One of his friends told him, I think with perfect truth, 'Everyone there was angry at you — except the old professor whose funeral we were attending.'

The danger for us men and women of paying more attention to animals than to human beings is that sometimes we begin to humanize the animals. We see them as filled with human emotions — such as fidelity, honesty, courtesy, even charity; we credit them with human intelligence, and we think their transient fancies are more meaningful than they really are. ('I think he understands every word we say;

I am sure he knows more than we do — you saw he was un-happy all last night, even before father was taken ill.')
However, Konrad Lorenz does not make this mistake. In-stead of humanizing the animals, he has gone far toward animalizing himself, a human being. He has become the parent of an orphaned jackdaw; he has been the playfellow of a savage wolf; he has been the foster mother of a large group of ducklings, to the extent of crawling round his garden for hours at a time, quacking, so that they would learn to follow him. He is really something like Mowgli, the jungle boy — except that he has moved the jungle into his own home, with geese waddling through the drawing room, jackdaws sailing through the windows, monkeys climbing up the curtains, hamsters sauntering about on the table, several types of fish going about their compli-cated business in aquariums near the window, and a large number of dogs wandering about everywhere — dogs which we might call mongrels, but Lorenz calls real indi-viduals, without the 'typical exaggerations' created by pro-fessional breeders.

Konrad Lorenz has learned about the animal kingdom in a number of different ways, some of which would seem to most of us eccentric, and several quite impossible. For instance, he knows a lot about the family life of animals and birds. The young thing, when just hatched or born, looks at once for a protector. If it does not find its own mother, it will adopt any living being which pays any at-tention to it and feeds it and talks to it, and treat that being as its parent: *any* living being, whether it is of the same size and shape or not. Lorenz once bought a young jackdaw from a pet shop, and fed it personally. The jackdaw there-fore elected Lorenz as its parent, flew after him from room to room, accompanied him as he cycled about the countryside, and finally settled down as the patriarch of a jackdaw tribe on Lorenz's rooftop. Another jackdaw actually fell in love with Lorenz. Like all lovers, it brought presents to its beloved, and fed poor Lorenz with worms. He says he did not much like the taste of finely minced worm, mixed with jackdaw saliva; but he *had* to accept the gift, for if he did not open his mouth, the jackdaw would fill up one of his ears with the same delicacy — which corresponds to the finest box of candy that any human lover could present to his beloved. And in case you think that is extraordinary, consider Lorenz's other story about a lovely white peacock in the Vienna zoo. It was the only survivor of a brood which died of cold. To save it, the keeper put it in the warmest place available. This was the reptile room, along with the giant tortoises. There the young peacock grew to maturity. And therefore, for the rest of his life, the poor peacock loved only tortoises. For them alone he would display his handsome crest and his magnificent tail, and he remained insensible to the charm of even the prettiest peahen. Sheridan has told us that even an oyster may be crossed in love; but it is more of a comedy when one of the loveliest of all birds lavishes his affection on one of the most repulsive of all reptiles.

Besides the family life of animals, Lorenz knows about their play. They play a great deal, almost as much as human beings; and they also enjoy playing with human beings, if they can treat them as part of their own group. The difficulty is to gauge the fine distinction between play and fighting. The most exciting episode in *Man Meets Dog* is the chapter which tells how Lorenz mated a bitch with a wild Siberian male wolf in a cage at the zoo. He introduced them carefully, first; they wagged their tails, and soon they were romping together. Then Lorenz himself entered the group of cages, first taking the precaution of emptying them all, so that the wolf should feel he was in his own territory, rather than in a single barred enclosure where he was at the mercy of the man. The wolf bristled, and retreated. Slowly, he returned, now not bristling, but watchful. He was trying to decide whether Lorenz was a friend or an enemy. But at this point the girl-friend recognized Lorenz and welcomed him. At once the huge wolf galloped up to him, with a clumsily playful canter which was an invitation to play, like wolves tussling together. Lorenz was flung crashing against the wall, and again and again dropped to the floor under the impact of the powerful animal, which did not want to kill him, or even hurt him, but merely wanted to cut up touches with a strong male comrade. No doubt Stasi was watching her two friends playing together, with wagging tail and broad smile.

Furthermore, Lorenz understands that animals have rudimentary languages. They can talk to each other, within their own species: he has learned many of these languages, and can make communications, transmit warnings, give commands. He tells some terribly funny stories about his use of such languages. For instance, he bought a beautiful white cockatoo which had become psycho from long imprisonment. He set it free in his home, and trained it to wander about his house and garden, but not to fly away. But once he went away on a short trip. When he returned, he got off the train in the middle of a week-end crowd of tourists from Vienna. Walking home, he saw a strange bird high in the air: it was heavy and slow: not a buzzard, not a stork; by heavens, it was a cockatoo; it was *his* cockatoo, in full flight; in five minutes it would be gone forever. Lorenz could do only one thing. He stopped in the middle of the crowd and gave the shrill, piercing, horrifying screech which is the flight call of the crested cockatoo. The crowd was paralyzed with terror; but the cockatoo hesitated, looked down, dived, and landed on Lorenz's arm. Only then did the Viennese decide that he was not a dangerous lunatic.

Behind language lie other processes, which for want of a better word we have to call thought. Of course many things that animals do, like many things that human beings do, are purely automatic. But when there is a problem to solve, when there is a decision to make, when there is a choice between equally powerful alternatives, then even quite small animals, usually guided by instinct, do something like thinking. Lorenz has several amazing stories about thought in animals. Once, for instance, he had a pair of tiny jewel-fish in an aquarium. They built a careful nest, where they laid their eggs. After the eggs hatched out the young fish were taken out into the pool and taught to swim by their father and mother. In the evening — I know this is hard to believe, but I trust Lorenz — in the evening the mother fish waved her fin to signal for the children to come home and enter the nest. Meanwhile, the father searched the pool, and when he found a straggler, took it in his mouth, carried it to the nest, and blew it in. Once Lorenz came home late and remembered that he had to feed his jewel-fish. He dropped some chopped worms into their tank. The father fish at once gobbled up a juicy piece of earthworm; but as soon as he had taken a bite of it he saw one of his children swimming all alone. He started, rushed after the baby, and took it into his mouth too. Lorenz says, 'It was a thrilling moment. The fish had in its mouth two different things, of which one must go into the stomach and the other into the nest. What would he do? I must confess that at that moment I would not have given five cents for the life of the baby.' But the father fish remained absolutely still for many seconds. Although he was hungry, he was not eating, but obviously *thinking*. Finally, he solved the problem. He spat out the whole contents of his mouth. Both the worm and the baby fell to the bottom of the tank. The father then turned resolutely to the worm and ate it up, keeping an eye on his child meanwhile. When he had finished, he ingested his offspring once more, and carried it safely back to the nest. This is a problem which I hope will never confront us, but if it did, I trust we should think it out as clearly and satisfactorily as the little jewelfish.

Behind language, even further, lies the wonderful problem of the relationship of two beings — male and female, parent and child, master and servant, friend and friend. Lorenz is very good on this, particularly in his discussion of the friendship between men and dogs. He believes there are two kinds of dogs, with different ancestry and emotional make-up: one, largely descended from the jackals, is almost universally friendly, and regards all men and women as potential providers and allies; the other, in which there is a strong strain of wolf blood, pays little attention to most human beings, is hostile to a few, and is devoted at most to one alone. The first type of dog thinks all people are substitute parents; the second thinks of one man as the leader of his pack, and treats him as a superior comrade. My wife and I once had a noble elkhound like that, bless his strong heart. He met my wife first, after leaving the kennel where he had been born and bred: so he became utterly devoted to her, and ignored my son and me almost completely. In time, perhaps, he might have included us in his friendship. He was really a cave dog, and he would have liked to be back at home in the Ice Age, with the glaciers thundering outside the cave and the carcass of a hairy mammoth steaming placidly inside, to be dissected at leisure, with occasional squabbles between men and children and dogs but with absolutely unflinching loyalty. When we admired him, we were not humanizing him. We were all animals, or were like animals, for many thousands of years before we became fully human, and some of our best virtues as well as some of our worst vices come to us from our animal friends.

Ruler of the world

———————————

THERE are many beautiful towns in central Italy. Some of them have been alive for nearly three thousand years, and seem to have acquired a new kind of loveliness at every stage of their history — at least until the immediate present. One of the most beautiful is a little place about twenty miles from Rome, called Tivoli. It is cool when Rome is hot; it is surrounded by pleasant woods and vineyards; it is romantically placed, on a steep craggy hill through which there flows a rushing river.

A few miles outside Tivoli there is a curious spectacle which many travelers miss. Their feet get tired; they have not realized what to look for; they gaze, and pass on. Yet in some ways it is one of the most fascinating places in Italy. It is the ruin of a gigantic palace. Not one single building, no, far from it, something more vast and varied: many different buildings united only by the personality of the man who conceived and created them — libraries, swimming pools, banquet halls, galleries for pictures and sculpture, together with fountains and forests and lakes, hills and quiet valleys: a private world. The first time I saw it, I could think of no adequate way of describing it except in the words of Coleridge's most famous poem:

> In Xanadu did Kubla Khan
> A stately pleasure-dome decree . . .
> So twice five miles of fertile ground
> With walls and towers were girdled round:
> And there were gardens bright with sinuous rills,
> Where blossomed many an incense-bearing tree;
> And here were forests ancient as the hills,
> Enfolding sunny spots of greenery.

That at least conveys the amplitude and splendor of the grounds, but it says nothing of the curious diversity of the buildings in this place. It was the country palace of the Roman emperor Hadrian, who ruled the whole of the civilized Western world for over twenty years, from 117 to 138 A.D. It was ruined in the Dark Ages, silted over and forgotten. In modern times people have dug into it here and there, finding many beautiful statues and clearing out some fine buildings. But it still has not been thoroughly excavated. Unknown treasures may lie beneath that innocent hillock, and the roots of those peaceful trees may twine themselves around some unimagined masterpiece from the past.

Hadrian spent most of his life traveling all over the enormous empire, solving difficult and important administrative problems. When he returned to Italy, he wanted a palace, near Rome but quiet, which should contain memories and curiosities from many different parts of the world.

This is the palace: almost a small city. One part of the grounds resembles a famous valley in Greece, a canal with buildings and a temple at its end reproduces the strange Egyptian sanctuary of Canopus, and so on. The whole palace ran and rippled with water, in fountains, pools, cascades, and marble-bordered brooks. It is an eccentric notion. If Hadrian had not been such a brilliantly original man, so wise and so far-sighted, we might dismiss it as a mere vulgarity, like William Randolph Hearst's palace of San Simeon, but what we know of the emperor makes us sure that his palace must have had an imaginative quality far above that: something magical.

The Roman emperors are a fascinating group of men. Not one of them is dull, not even the good emperors. Some of them are wildly funny; some are admirable in their self-control; some of them are tyrants, terrifying bureaucrats; a few are profoundly puzzling. Of them all, the two most difficult to understand are Augustus and Hadrian. Of course we know the facts of their lives: when they came to the throne, what wars they had to fight, what laws they passed, the aims of their policy, and the chief opposition they encountered, but we do not know the inmost springs of their character; we do not know their souls. They did not intend anyone to know their souls. The seal ring of the emperor Augustus showed a sphinx.

And yet it is tempting to speculate about them. Anyone interested in history must endeavour to catch a whisper from the sphinx's smiling lips. Frankly, I should have thought it was almost impossible to write anything nearly complete and nearly convincing about either of them, and harder to write about Hadrian than about Augustus, because we have fewer facts about him. And yet one book has done much to re-create his character. It does not explain him fully, but it is extremely subtle, and it creates something like an intellectual and emotional sympathy for the man; also it is written with a grace fully worthy of its subject. This book is *Hadrian's Memoirs,* by Marguerite Yourcenar, translated from the French by Grace Frick and published by Farrar, Straus & Young.

The first thing that is hard to understand about Hadrian is his greatness. He was one of the wisest statesmen who ever lived. His genius touched every problem of the civilization of his time, and did something to solve every one. He created and enforced humane rules to diminish the horrors of slavery. He was a tireless town planner, constructing huge public buildings and irrigation works. Finding the empire terribly overextended by his predecessor's policy of military conquest, he re-established stable peace and a proper system of defense: in Britain alone he showed his wisdom by abandoning Scotland to the northern barbarians, and building a huge wall across the north of England to keep them out. (The wall is still there, but Englishmen nowadays complain that it is not high enough.) He was a financial genius, and stamped out nearly every trace of bureaucratic extortion; he was one of the founders of systematic Roman law. Now, we do not want to explain greatness in the sense of explaining it away. But it is hard to see why Hadrian became so great when his antecedents were comparatively ordinary. He came of a family of Italians which had been settled in Spain for several centuries without producing anyone distinguished. He became a possible candidate for the imperial throne merely because his kinsman and guardian was a promising Roman officer, who himself became emperor. But the Roman empire was not hereditary; there were other candidates for the appointment, and many a young man of more distinguished birth turned out far less well, as a drunk, or a voluptuary, or a formalist, or a fool.

Mme. Yourcenar's book takes up this problem first, and gives the only explanation possible — which is the three-fold one, that Hadrian was born with exceptional talents, that he was well taught, and that, seeing his possible destiny ahead, he set out to make himself worthy of it. Two of these factors contributed to the greatness of Lincoln. Lincoln had no teacher who could help him, but Hadrian had:

> To my dying day I shall be grateful to [my teacher] for having put me early to the study of Greek. . . . I have loved the language for its flexibility, like that of a supple, perfect body, and for the richness of its vocabulary, in which every word bespeaks direct contact with reality; and because almost everything that men have said best has been said in Greek.

Marguerite Yourcenar goes on to describe a thoughtful, ambitious, self-centered, self-disciplined young man practicing the various techniques of thought, of decision, of organization, of personal intrigue: moulding a character fit to be that of a great ruler. Several paragraphs in this particular chapter of her book can be recommended to anyone who wishes to strengthen his, or her, will:

> I determined to make the best of whatever situation I was in. . . . Thus the most dreary tasks were accomplished with ease as long as I was willing to give myself to them. Whenever an object repelled me, I made it a subject of study, ingeniously compelling myself to extract from it a motive for enjoyment.

Such a man deserved to become a statesman.

And yet, this training ought to have made Hadrian into a stone figure: one of those marble emperors who stare impassively from above their marble robes in every museum. On the contrary. The second problem about him is his peculiar emotional life, which was strongly aesthetic in tone, and was sometimes marked by outbursts of passion. His very face is different from the traditional Roman face. His predecessors had firm, clean-shaven features; he has a light graceful beard, like an artist's or a philosopher's, and eyes which look both anxious and astute, like those of a surgeon performing a dangerous operation. And the great tragedy of Hadrian's life was the mysterious death of a handsome young man to whom he was devoted: Antinous. We do not know why he died or how, by murder or suicide; we know only that the emperor made him a god and founded a city named after him. This too is explained in Marguerite Yourcenar's book, with exquisite tact and remarkable penetration. The death of Antinous she interprets as a ritual suicide, by which the youth hoped to give the remainder of his unlived years to the aging Hadrian, in an act of utter self-sacrifice. And throughout *Hadrian's Memoirs* we see again and again how the statesman conceals the artist: the emperor enjoys a successfully completed set of military maneuvers not because it proves that the Roman army can fight, but because, beyond that, it is a work of art.

Statesmanlike, artistic: two qualities hard to combine. With them went another still stranger quality in the emperor Hadrian. He was frivolous. Without being a silly show-off like Nero, he took serious things — some serious things — lightly. He was a wit and an epigrammatist. His palace in Tivoli was not a monument like Versailles, but a delicate pastime, a fancy, almost a folly, a world to be visited in a day's walk. And, strangest of all, he wrote a cheerful poem about his own death. Here it is, in a meter and style like that of the original:

> Little soul, you pretty gipsy,
> guest and playmate of the body,
> tell me, where now must you travel,

poor and pale and stiff and naked?
Where are now your jokes, your gambols?*

This frivolity is the third problem in Hadrian's life. It is the only one which Mme. Yourcenar does not explain. She makes him a mystic, a solitary, determined to preserve his own individuality. Of course, she is partly right, but I should like to suggest a more complete explanation. Hadrian thought, and thought profoundly. If he did so, he must have had a philosophy. It is clear from his poems, from his attitude to the arts, and from his frivolity, that he must have been a follower of Epicurus. He was an Epicurean statesman. He believed in this world and its pleasures, and he knew that its pleasures could be achieved only by wisdom. Wisdom, for Hadrian, was the means; enjoyment and lightness of heart were the end. His successors were to be Stoics, working for duty alone and believing in the stern rule of inevitable law. But the principle of the Epicurean is λάθε βίωσας, 'live in hiding.' Was that the ultimate secret of the man who was monarch of the world?

----

* 'Where be your gibes now? your gambols?' (Hamlet to the skull of Yorick, *Hamlet*, 5.1. 207–8.)

Writing and Reading

An unknown world

THERE is, in one corner of the United States, a small society which is virtually unknown outside its own frontiers, although it has a tremendous effect on the other citizens of America, and indeed on the inhabitants of most of the civilized world. Hundreds of millions of people know the faces of its principal members. Thousands of millions of people have been either nourished or nauseated by its products. Yet comparatively few people have ever visited it on their own feet — although many millions have dreamed of going there. Only a few thousand, perhaps, have met its inhabitants face to face, and talked with them. It is an unknown world; and it has all the fascination of a realm which is filled with fabulous imaginings, and yet practically unattainable. Every now and then an explorer from the outer regions penetrates it, but the reports which he sends out are scanty, distorted, often unintelligible. The explorer himself scarcely ever returns. If he does, he is terribly changed — wearing fantastic native costume, sumptuous but semibarbarous native jewelry; talking in a strange patois; practicing unusual and sometimes repulsive rites apparently inculcated in him during his visit; and (what is worse of all because it makes communication so difficult) thoroughly brainwashed — brainwashed and transformed by the inhabitants of the mysterious world which he set out to investigate as a dispassionate explorer, and which ended by dominating and drastically reorienting his own personality. A few, a very few hard and intrepid pioneers have entered this peculiar world and emerged apparently uninjured: men like William Faulkner, John Marquand, and Ogden Nash; but they can seldom be brought to speak of their experiences. The unknown world remains a dark abyss surrounded by blazing light.

It is the small, new, volcanically active region called Hollywood, California. Its effect on the outer world is really astounding. In fact, you cannot understand how intensely it has influenced several generations of mankind unless you have traveled in Europe and the other continents, and there seen for yourselves how movies from Hollywood fill the theaters, styles from Hollywood are imitated by both men and women, and even by designers, and the characteristic gait and mannerisms of Hollywood players provide models for youngsters who want to be bright and up to date, over half of the inhabited planet.

If it is so well known and so influential as this, how can Hollywood possibly be described as an unknown world? Surely it is well, excessively well, documented. It has been pouring out motion pictures for half a lifetime. The faces of many of its leaders are better known than any other faces except those of powerful politicians. Reporters never stop manufacturing richly succulent stories about its principal inhabitants, illustrated by even more succulent photographs, so that everyone who can read may learn that the new starlet, Miss August Strawberry, measures no less than thirty-nine inches round the chest, and that Robert Taylor was originally christened Spangler Arlington Brugh.

True, there is plenty of documentation to help us in penetrating the mysterious world called Hollywood — almost too much. The trouble is that the documentation is incomplete, and often self-contradictory. There are the movie magazines, full of glitter and glamor and gunk. There are the gossip columns and the new 'confidential' magazines, which give a very different picture, often characterized by stupidity, vulgarity, and vice. There are some social and historical studies of the motion pictures, and a very few biographies of eminent players such as W. C. Fields and John Barrymore. But the histories are too few and too discreet, while the biographies apparently are left incomplete until their subjects are well and truly dead. Then there are some interesting novels dealing with life in Hollywood. And of course there are the motion pictures themselves — a truly awesome number of them, perhaps the biggest single output of drama since the theatrical achievement of Greece and Rome, although perhaps not the best. From all these sources, a diligent researcher could surely construct something like a true picture of Hollywood.

Perhaps; but it would be terribly chancy, terribly difficult. It seems that many of the secrets of that world have never been set down in writing. And the spirit of the place — several competent writers have tried to describe it, and none of them has completely succeeded. There is now a sizable shelf of novels about life in Hollywood, and although they are interesting (and frequently repulsive and occasionally appalling), they make a strangely incomplete and fragmentary picture. Scott Fitzgerald's *The Last Tycoon*, Ludwig Bemelmans' *Dirty Eddie*, Budd Schulberg's *What Makes Sammy Run?*, Nathanael West's *The Day of the Locust*, J. R. Kennedy's *Prince Bart*, and Maritta Wolff's *The Big Nickelodeon* — they make a picture full of dazzling lights and foul shadows, but a picture which is neither coherent nor complete.

It might be easier to understand Hollywood if we put together the realistic novels which are written about it and the romantic motion pictures which it turns out. Even then it is difficult to make these two types of evidence cohere.

For instance, the novels about Hollywood seldom show anyone in the place as having the slightest concern with artistic beauty. Yet one of the chief contributions made to our culture by the motion pictures is that they have helped to raise photography to something like a fine art. The photographers and directors who produce the good Westerns (like *Shane* and *Stage Coach*), those who are responsible for the magnificent 'spectaculars' such as *Gone with the Wind* and *War and Peace*, and those who have brought out the lovely features of Garbo and a few other inimitable women — such men are true artists. Further, there are some composers of incidental music (we all know the work of Dmitri Tiomkin) who write genuinely moving scores for dramatic motion pictures; and some of the men who design costumes and stage settings have real taste. Yet such people never seem to appear in the novels about Hollywood — just as they seldom appear in the gossip columns and get only rather limited credit on the screen itself. As for the aesthetic beauty of a motion picture regarded from the point of view of drama, that is practically never discussed in the novels about the screen capital; and, to judge by the majority of the movies, it is rarely considered by writers or producers in real life.

The chief characteristic of life in Hollywood — if we are to judge by the novels about it — is that the place is swept by tornadoes: tornadoes of emotion, conflicts of will-power, punctuated by outbursts of physical and spiritual violence, abrupt and horrifying outbreaks of hatred, furious grudge fights between both men and women duelists, melodramatic denunciations and massacres, plots, ambushes, and assassinations. The climax of *Prince Bart* is that a dynamic male star who is just beginning to feel himself growing older is challenged to a duel by one of his enemies. A duel? Yes: a tennis match, singles, with some enormous sum, fifty thousand dollars or thereabouts, bet on the outcome. The aim of each of the duelists is to conquer, impoverish, and humiliate the other; and the end of the tennis match is nothing less than the death of Prince Bart himself.

Now, this particular characteristic of Hollywood does come out in many of the pictures it produces. We do not see them all — we couldn't possibly see them all, it would drive us mad; and most of us do not often see the average product, the run-of-the-mill B and C pictures. But the average films are shown abroad. And I assure you that it is apt to shock the American visitor to certain countries over seas, when he walks through the streets of a foreign town and sees that his United States is represented most prominently not by books, not by the fine arts, not by philosophy, but, first of all, by technical products such as refrigerators and Coca-Cola, and almost equally by the films playing in the movie houses. One of these films will be called *Bloody Frontier,* and the poster advertising it will show a cowboy shooting down another cowboy at point-blank range in a barroom. The other will be called *Blood in the Gutter,* and its posters will show a carload of criminals firing a machine gun at a policeman, while ordinary citizens scurry for cover or lie bleeding on the ground. The American visitor will be still more shocked if he is told, by a European or Asian critic, that America must be a backward country, because most of the dramas it turns out on the picture screen deal with violent struggles between bestial criminals and an almost equally ruthless group of law-enforcement officers; and that, even if this is an incomplete view of American life, there must be something wrong with Americans, because they enjoy watching people hurting one another and killing one another. Perhaps these critics are right; perhaps they are not. But if we look for some time at the motion pictures through their shocked and revolted eyes, we shall see how terribly Hollywood distorts the American life that we know; and we may wonder whether Hollywood makes pictures filled with savage and bloodthirsty conflicts simply because life in Hollywood is filled with savage and bloodthirsty conflicts.

The novels about Hollywood have something else in common with the motion pictures. This is their almost entire neglect of the enjoyment of culture. You know how, in almost every single film that shows the interior of a family dwelling, there are never any books (real books, which someone has been reading), nor pictures (except something junky put in by the interior decorator), nor musical instruments (unless perhaps a silver-painted piano at a penthouse party), and none of the apparatus of civilized living: just furniture, more or less plushy. It is the same in the novels about Hollywood. The closest that anyone gets to leading a more or less civilized life in them is to buy enough phonograph records to have a 'collection.' No one ever seems to go to a concert, to have music at home, or even to read a book. You could scarcely imagine that anyone like Edward G. Robinson had inhabited Hollywood and had not only collected but understood some of the best of modern art. I suppose, nevertheless, that this must be true to life. One of the most profoundly depressing things about the motion pictures is that they often appear to be controlled by men who are imperfectly educated, do not read books, and know practically nothing about the drama as a major art. (Remember Thurber's exquisitely funny story, *The Man Who Hated Moonbaum?*)

Furthermore, the novels all agree in emphasizing the tremendous power of sex in Hollywood, or rather of both sex and drink. Maritta Wolff's *Big Nickelodeon* goes to depths hitherto untouched in describing this aspect of Hollywood life. The statistics are probably unobtainable; but if we are to judge by this and other novels, more time and energy are devoted to these two (often conflicting) interests in 'the film capital of the world' than in any other social group outside the African jungles. Careers are built up on sex, with talent almost excluded. Careers are broken down by drink, however talented the performer may have been. The furious extravagance of Hollywood's sexual life comes out into the cold light of day only now and then, when there is a particularly nasty trial or divorce case; but it is mirrored constantly in the weird and unnatural emphasis on sex which appears in three out of five motion pictures. As for Hollywood's drinking, that is scrupulously controlled in the films; but every now and then members of the ordinary public will notice that a prominent actress suddenly looks much older, or that a distinguished actor has changed into an eccentric clown; and if they have any perception, they will know why.

It is a weird place, Hollywood. It is really out of this world. The pitiful thing is that it continues to purvey, for the consumption and the credulous acceptance of hundreds of millions of people, a series of skilfully and often beautifully photographed dramas, directed with shrewd technique and staged with exorbitant expense, which pretend to describe the real lives of men and women both in history and in contemporary times, but which, because of the self-imposed limitations of the leaders of the motion-picture world and the extravagances of their followers, are glaring and repulsive distortions of humanity, and too often prove to be merely the reflections of Hollywood itself, at its stupidest and basest.

History on the silver screen

SUPPOSE we go to the movies.

We might see a new epic about the War of Independence, starring Audrey Hepburn as Martha Washington, Charlton Heston as George Washington, and William Holden as all the other Founding Fathers. (He is a very versatile actor, William Holden.) Among the most stirring scenes are the battles. There is a splendid re-enactment of the Battle of Trenton. On one side, the Hessians, with their red coats and their long muskets and bayonets; on the other side, the small forces of General Washington, in motley uniforms and ill armed; but they have the advantage of surprise, and they are fighting for their own country: they charge gallantly. The Hessians, with the power of long-established discipline, resist. For a moment the issue hangs undecided. Then Charlton Heston jumps forward carrying a heavy machine gun: *trrr, trrrrrrr*, he mows down the Hessians, the first rank, the second, and the third; the American forces move onward in triumph, shouting 'Victory!'; Washington waves his machine gun, and the camera pans from it to the Stars and Stripes.

Or else we might see an epic about the Civil War. The hero is the Southern general, George Edward Pickett (played by William Holden). The big scene is the Battle of Gettysburg. The forces of North and South struggle, locked in deadly conflict, swaying this way and that. The ground is dark with blood, the sky, with the smoke of guns. Pickett's division is held in reserve, until at last, on the fateful July 3rd, the attack on Cemetery Hill is launched, with Pickett and his men in the forefront. Up the deadly slope they charge, with rebel yells almost drowned by the thunder of Federal cannon. Just at the summit, as the lines are about to meet, up spring the defending Federal troops. They are led by a Sioux Indian in full war paint, who is followed by eight hundred whooping Indian tribesmen brandishing stone tomahawks. This decides the battle.

Exciting, isn't it? No? Incredible? Almost disgusting? Yes, it is. But neither of these fantastic scenes is any more incredible, any more disgusting to a man with a sense of history than the distortions of historical fact which are repeatedly perpetrated by the makers of motion pictures. The Civil War is usually quite well represented — because we have photographs of it and reminiscences of it; the very weapons and uniforms used by the combatants still exist; and somehow we understand their manners, their attitude toward life. By the time we go as far back as the War of Independence, a certain vagueness sets in — about manners if not about material objects (I still have in my mind's eye a delicious scene in which Meriwether Lewis, played by Fred MacMurray, said to President Jefferson with a genial grin, like a basketball coach talking to a difficult school principal, 'Oh, congratulations on the Louisiana Purchase!'); and any period beyond that seems to be dim and fabulous. By the time we reach the Greeks and the Romans everything is lost in a world of fantasy.

I must say that I am fascinated, in a horrible way, by motion pictures about ancient Greece and Rome. However silly they may be, they are usually photographed quite beautifully; the costumes are very becoming, particularly to the women; there is a certain thrill in seeing all the famous buildings, like the Acropolis at Athens, looking brand-new and so clean; and then the mistakes and the distortions are uproariously funny. They are just as funny as George Washington waving a machine gun, or Meade's troops headed by a detachment of Sioux Indians. And sometimes they are far funnier. The unconscious humor of the movies is one of their strongest assets.

In movies about ancient Greece and Rome, the static parts often look quite real and convincing — no doubt because they have been modeled on pictures and statues. It is the active parts which are usually so funny. Almost every motion picture about ancient Rome I have ever seen showed somebody driving through the streets of the city in a chariot, while the citizens cringed away from his mad career. This is as absurd as showing a cowboy on horseback galloping along the sidewalk of Fifth Avenue, New York. Chariots and such things were absolutely prohibited in the streets of Rome; they were kept for war, or else for hot-pole driving on the highways outside the cities. Everybody walked. The average Roman never rode in a chariot from the day of his birth to the day of his death.

The Greek and Roman armies are usually wrong too.

Most Hollywood producers know very little about military tactics, and still less about the more difficult science of strategy. Even in modern movies, they constantly make both the Good Ones and the Bad Ones commit elementary blunders in the art of war.

In *The Robe* we see a group of Roman legionaries rushing into a town and shooting at everyone visible with bows and arrows. In other pictures about Rome we see the legionaries throwing spears with great care and accuracy, as though those were their essential weapons. The reason for these mistakes is quite obvious. The people in Hollywood think that everyone fights by shooting; if not *bang bang*, then *fft fft;* if not smoking guns, then whizzing arrows and hissing spears. But this is nonsense. The Romans conquered the world with swords — short, strong, efficient swords which were used both for cutting and for thrusting. Spears were thrown at the opening of a battle, much as grenades are thrown now, without very careful aim, merely as a device to disrupt the enemy's line; what mattered was the body-to-body conflict. As for bows and arrows, these were left to Arabs and the like, who stayed out in the wings together with slingers. It is as ridiculous to show the Roman soldiers using bows and arrows as it would be to show the U.S. Marines using blowpipes and poisoned darts. The Romans, like the Marines, were realists; they knew that if you want to kill an enemy and defend yourself, the surest way is to face him, eye to eye, and put a sword into him.

In the same way, and probably for the same reason, Hollywood often gets the strategy of Roman warfare quite wrong. (I believe the people out on the Gold Coast think the Romans were stupid, primitive fellows with no power of long-term planning, no maps and no experience in warfare — early medieval minds; whereas in fact they were shrewd statesmen and hard pragmatic thinkers, with a long, long experience of both war and politics reaching over many countries and many centuries.) There was a good motion picture version of Shakespeare's *Julius Caesar*, in which most of the acting and the characterizations struck me as truly splendid; the conspirators might have been the actual men whose faces one sees on the sculptured portraits of the old Roman tombs. But when we came to one of the great crises of the play — a crisis which Shakespeare himself well understood, and did his best to explain within the limits of his small theater — the battle at which the forces of the Republic were beaten by the forces of dictatorship, then we saw that it was misunderstood, or vulgarized, or both. In actual fact, the battle was touch and go; it was one of those supremely difficult contests in which the two sides are approximately equal, and each has a chance of winning. One side was victorious on one wing, the other side on the other wing, the center remaining undecided. It was one of the Republican commanders, Cassius, who misinterpreted the situation, gave up too soon, committed suicide, and wrecked the chances of his army. This is a powerful and highly dramatic situation; Shakespeare grasped it. But as Hollywood presented it to us, the army of the Republic marched blindly into a long canyon, without sending out any reconnaissance units to guard their advance and their flanks. The hills above the canyon were occupied by the enemy; and, at a given moment, Mark Antony (played by Marlon Brando) raised his hand in the old gesture so familiar from Western movies, and the stupid Republican forces were destroyed like walking ducks, mowed down by Sitting Bull.

This kind of oversimplification is supposed to make history clearer, bolder, more dramatic. In fact, it destroys many of the best values in history, and therefore destroys many of the possibilities of drama which lie in history. For example, take the screen treatment of the Polish romance about the emperor Nero and the first persecution of the Christians, *Quo Vadis?* If I remember correctly, the screen play began with a Roman general (well played by Robert Taylor) leading a triumphal procession into the city of Rome — and, as he rode at the head of his victorious troops, saluting the indolent and selfish young emperor Nero. I wrote a piece for *Harper's Magazine* about this absurd scene, pointing out that, under the Roman empire, no Roman general except a member of the imperial family could ever lead a triumphal procession — for a very good reason: namely, that the triumphant general was, for the time being, supreme in the state, almost God, and could have seized power in fifteen minutes. I got a letter back from Hollywood saying that this was all very well for pedants and specialists, but that people who wrote motion picture scripts had to give the public big spectacular crowd scenes, and what could be better than a triumphal procession? Well, the answer is that truth is always better than falsehood, and that it nearly always makes better drama. The end of the movie version of *Quo Vadis?* was equally false to history; it had the emperor Nero overthrown by a mutiny of some of his troops mixed with a popular revolt stimulated by horror at the persecution of the Christians. The man who was supposed to lead the mutiny was Robert Taylor. Now, the writers could have made this final piece of nonsense more credible, or 'motivated' it in depth, by sticking to historical truth in the first scene. They could and should have made the Roman general lead his victorious troops up to the very gate of Rome, and then have them taken over by the young emperor, too weak to command but too vain to omit the opportunity of a triumphal procession; wearing a suit of specially made gold armor,

Nero would lead the army through cheering crowds, while the war-hardened officers rode grimly in the rear, smouldering with rancor and beginning to plan his final overthrow.

Sometimes, again, entirely imaginary or palpably false scenes are placed on the screen, for no reason whatever that any sane being can conceive, except sheer carelessness or ignorance. Quite early in the film version of *The Robe* we saw the aging emperor Tiberius — looking fairly convincing (although much less sinister than he was in reality), but complaining bitterly about his troubles with his wife, the empress Julia, who appeared for a moment with a magnificent costume and a proud manner. An amusing domestic scene. But at the time when the drama was supposed to take place, Julia had been dead for about twenty years, and Tiberius' inclinations had turned in far different directions. Think of the trouble, the expense, and the needless ingenuity expended on writing in a scene, working out dialogue, providing dress and make-up and hair-do, for a character who was not only unnecessary but impossible.

I wonder why they do this sort of thing. Partly it is because they know little or nothing about historical research. They do not believe it is possible to find out the truth about how the Roman army fought, or how a Roman emperor treated his wife. They do not know, apparently, that there are dozens and dozens of reference books filled with details. Often they seem to use cheap and more or less fictional accounts of the life which they are going to put on the screen. Usually, their banquets are as unlike a real Roman banquet as a party given by Al Capone would be unlike a normal American dinner party. This is because the most detailed description which we have of a Roman banquet is a bitterly satirical account of a vulgar millionaire's party in which everything is either exaggerated or in outrageously bad taste — and yet the simple-minded 'researcher' who cannot distinguish satire from truth is apt to accept it as normal. In the same way, I suppose, the Asian nations will accept the portrayal of American life given in such films as *Guys and Dolls* as being truly representative of our culture at its most characteristic.

But partly, also, the people who make such films about history are cynics. They live for the moment. They think that history does not matter; or in the immortal phrase attributed to Henry Ford, 'History is bunk.' And, what is worse, they think that everyone else believes the same. They believe that no one cares about the truth of anything that happened beyond fifty or a hundred years ago. Perhaps that is the worst thing that could be said about them with any pretense to truth: that they despise us, their fellow-citizens and their customers. They imagine that we cannot tell the difference between truth and lies, between sense and stupidity, provided the screen is made extra wide, and covered with beautiful colors, lovely women, expensive costumes, and competent actors (Robert Taylor, Charlton Heston, and William Holden). We are all supposed to be seventeen years old, but almost without the conflicts of seventeen-year-olds. The French had a phrase for this attitude: they said their theater managers sometimes spoke of 'les cochons de payants,' 'those swine who pay for admission,' or more bluntly, 'the stinking customers.' But that is too bitter for Hollywood. The people who make these epics do not think we are swine. They merely think we are children.

Scottish words

No two people speak the same language. Even a couple
who have been happily and harmoniously married for
thirty years will notice, whenever they pay attention to it,
that each of them has a small private set of words and
phrases, private even from his or her nearest and dearest.
Even in the closest family group, the individuals do not
use precisely the same words and phrases — partly because
each has a slightly different age and environment, partly
because everyone is an artist, and art is exercised in the
choice of words.

I thought of this the other evening when I heard my
wife use an unexpected and interesting word. She often
does. Sometimes I think she makes them up. But this one
struck me because it was neither imaginary, nor American,

nor English, but Scottish. It was Scottish, it was a fine vivid word, and I knew its meaning perfectly well. It was *glaikit,* which means something like 'goofy'; yet I had never used it in my life, although (like her) I was born and brought up in Scotland.

This set me to thinking about the use of dialect words. Every country is full of dialects. Even apart from the difference in accents, an experienced listener could tell the origins of five soldiers in the same outfit, from Missouri, Vermont, Oregon, New Jersey, and Louisiana, simply by their choice of words and phrases. Basically, they would all be speaking standard American, but each of them would instinctively avoid certain words and use certain others special to his own home. The correspondence between the patterns of their speech would be enough for them all to understand one another, but it would not be 100 per cent. In the choice of words it would never be nearly 100 per cent, and sometimes as little as 80 per cent. No two people speak the same language.

My wife and I were both born in Scotland, but we were brought up to speak 'standard English.' That is, our teachers expected that we would be easily understood by people born and brought up in Yorkshire, or Cornwall, or Canada, or the United States, or Australia, or any of the English-speaking areas of the world. We are so understood (I hope); and yet each of us as an individual has a little private language, and the two private languages do not quite coincide. And in conversation between ourselves we occasionally use words which we do not think about, but which (on reflection) we see are plainly dialectal words. They are not standard English, not even British English, but Scottish.

Still, they are interesting and expressive words. Neither of us thinks of giving them up. They are strong. They are vivid. Occasionally they are ugly, but they are usually unforgettable. We use them not to be quaint, still less to be nationalist, but because they describe something better and more graphically than any word or phrase used in standard English. That is the best thing about dialect words — not their beauty, but their strength. Shakespeare occasionally drops into dialect (for instance, 'blood-boltered' in *Macbeth*), and that mistress of French prose, Colette, spiced her lively stories with rich Burgundian words almost too strong for the Parisian palate.

As I thought over the Scottish dialect words which were known to both my wife and myself, I was rather surprised to see how many and how vivid they were. There must be three or four hundred, all told.

The first group, and in some ways the strangest, is a set of words which were originally French. They came into Scots four or five hundred years ago, or even more — either during the time when Scotland was allied with France in order to resist English domination, or at an earlier stage, when all the tongues that grew into English were being penetrated by words from France. The best known of this group is certainly the word *bonny,* which seems to come from *bon,* and is actually used by Shakespeare ('Blithe and bonny,' *Much Ado*). Most people also know the word *caddy,* which is simply *cadet,* a 'youngster'; and the word *poke,* which means 'bag' or 'pocket' (from *poche*) — we use it in the proverb about making a blind investment, 'to buy a pig in a poke.' Some of us also know the adjective *dour,* which means 'stubborn'; but I have heard it mispronounced to rhyme with 'sour.' (The people who mispronounced it had seen it written, but had never heard it spoken, and did not realize that it came from the French word for 'hard,' *dur.*) I know, but I never use, two more

Scottish dialect words which come from French: *bien* and *douce*, from *bien* and *doux*, meaning 'respectable' and 'gentle.' But almost every Scottish housewife, if asked to name the large plate on which the main dish is served, would call it an *ashet*, which comes from *assiette*. That is one of the advantages of dialect: it often makes it possible for us to describe a thing more precisely.

Then there is a second group of words which are now known throughout the English-speaking world, but which were originally pure Scots. For instance, *tartan, plaid, clan*, and probably *porridge*. (Yet only the Scots know that *porridge* is not singular, but plural; you say 'these are good porridge.') *Whisky* came into English from the Gaelic of Ireland. But *slogan*, meaning 'a war cry,' and now much debased, is Scottish. Everyone knows *canny* and *uncanny*, although the difference between them is not simply the difference between 'wise' and 'unwise'; *uncanny* seems to mean 'incomprehensible' and therefore 'unsafe.' Most of us know *daft*, which is old English, but survives only in the north. And surely everyone uses the affectionate little adjective *wee*; it is somehow more natural to say 'a wee baby' than 'a small infant,' and to wait 'a wee while' rather than 'a short time.'

Much less known outside Scotland are the words which describe places. Such is *loch*. It does not exactly coincide with 'lake'; there are lots of fresh-water lochs, but what the Norwegians call a fjord, a long arm of the sea, is also a *loch* in Scotland. (Never shall I forget the disgust with which once, traveling by train through northern Scotland, I looked out at the station of Lochawe, and heard two English school teachers cry out 'Oh, what a pretty name, *L*oshawee!') A *brae* is a hill, but somehow it does not seem so steep as a hill, nor so rugged as a mountain. A mountain is a *ben*, and of course a *burn* is a stream. It is wilder and rockier than a brook, and it is not so large as a river; it is just a wee stream. Then there is one word which goes back very far into history, and which most Scots use and pronounce correctly, more or less by instinct: this is the old Celtic word *dun,* which means 'a hill,' or 'a fort on a hill.' I think that is the *-don* in *London,* and I know it is the first syllable in names like *Dundee, Dunbar, Dumbarton.* (Because it means 'fort,' the accent is put on the following syllables, the definers. It shocks me to hear Dun*bar* pronounced as *Dun*bar, as it would shock any American to hear, instead of Fort *Worth* or Fort *Knox, Fort* Worth and *Fort* Knox.) Not so many people know the word for a heap of stones, a *cairn,* or the semiprecious stone named after the mountain where it is found, a *cairngorm.* But almost everyone knows the pretty word for a valley (usually with a stream flowing through it), a *glen.*

Then there are a few words which were brought into general English use by distinguished authors remembering them from their childhood. Thomas Carlyle, for instance, introduced *outcome,* in the sense of 'result'; and *feckless* for 'ineffectual'; and the beautiful word *lilt.* (Probably he recalled that from one of the finest Scottish poems, the lament for the men killed by the English at Flodden Field; it begins 'I've heard them lilting at the ewe-milking, lasses a' lilting, before dawn of day.')

Still, after all these words which are more or less known outside Scotland, there is a large residue of dialectal expressions which are known only to the Scots and yet continue to be used. Quite often a Scotsman will have two different modes of speech: one in which he talks to Englishmen and other less fortunate people, and the other which he uses with his intimates. John Buchan, for instance, spoke and wrote very correct and graceful English, but he

could also tell Scots dialect stories with inimitable vigor
and realism. Robert Louis Stevenson actually wrote stories
both in English and in dialect Scots.

Of all these special words, I think my favorite is *scunner,*
used both as a noun and as a verb. To *scunner* is 'to
shrink back and feel nauseated.' If you have once had a
dish which violently disagreed with you, whenever you see
that dish again, and perhaps whenever you hear it named,
you will have a *scunner.* If you must engage in some repulsive but unavoidable task which makes you bitterly depressed, you will, whenever it comes up, have the same
experience. Regularly, every year in the spring, I think
of compiling the figures demanded by the income-tax
authorities, and I *scunner* at them.

Similar is the word to *swither,* which means 'to hesitate'
— not only that, but also to move back and forward between several choices. If you hesitate, you simply pause
before taking action; if you *swither,* you undergo the rapid
change of opinions which Homer puts into poetry when he
says that a hero 'this way and that divided his swift mind.'
This is not the same as to *haver,* which is 'to talk meaning-
lessly,' to ramble on and on. And that in turn is not the
same as to *blether,* which is 'to talk too much.' The man
who *havers* really says nothing. The man who *blethers* may
say something, but the proportion of words to meaning is
about a hundred to one. (This particular word came into
American slang during the War of Independence, through
a Scottish song called 'Maggie Lauder'; we know it here as
blather and the man who does it as a *blatherskite.*)

You notice that many of these Scots dialect words have
a harsh and yet vivid sound, more like Dutch or Norwegian
than English. It is partly their harshness that makes very
correct speakers in Scotland exclude them from current
use; but I like it. So much language is flat and lifeless.

Swither; scunner; then there is *shoogle* — which is 'to shake violently and all over.' A table may shake, because it moves all in one piece, but a cup of jelly *shoogles.* To *shauchle* is 'to walk without lifting the feet and without straightening the legs.' Old, old waiters often *shauchle;* and when they do they are apt to *scliff* their feet. (On their feet they will wear those pathetic old shapeless shoes which are well described as *bachles.*) On the other hand, to *sprachle* is 'to rush forward with great effort and hurry,' like a commuter catching a train just as it moves out, dropping papers and missing the step and generally *sprachling.* But if you move violently but purposefully and effectively, for instance, if you charge into a revolving door without caring who else is going round in it, you are said to *breenge* in.

If you do that kind of thing, you are apt to be either a *sumph,* which means 'an essentially stupid and impercipient fellow,' or else a very *thrawn* man; *thrawn* means 'obstinate to the point of being twisted and distorted.' (The word *thraw* means 'twist,' and Stevenson has a remarkably fine story about witchcraft, with a horrible heroine called Thrawn Janet.) But you could also be *glaikit.* I constantly see *glaikit* people on the streets. Usually they are in a car; and either they are trying to turn right starting from the left-hand lane of traffic, or else they are getting slowly out of the driver's seat into the main stream of oncoming cars. They are not busy and preoccupied. Their minds are not on anything else. They are just *glaikit.* When I see them I usually *girn* at them. Not grin, *girn.* (It means 'to snarl and feel snarly,' with a *girning* noise, *rrrr.*) But then, even thinking of the traffic in city streets gives me a *scunner.*

A few words were used only in school, and have been all but forgotten since. For instance, a slap from an angry teacher — in Scotland the teachers were allowed to use force if they found their pupils *glaikit* or *thrawn* — is called a *skelp*. One pupil who tells tales about others is said to *clipe*. A boy with a squint is *skelly* — but I think that means only 'an inward-turning squint,' 'a convergent squint,' not what we call 'wall-eyed.' If you enter the classroom and leave the door slightly ajar, you may be asked to *sneck* it, which means 'to push it until the lock catches'; if the door had a push bolt, you could *snib* it. After school, if you climb a tree or a wall on the way home, and then, after hanging by your hands, let yourself fall, you are said to *dreap* the distance.

Last of all, I still remember and use a few deprecatory words, some of which are Middle English in origin but are preserved only in Scottish, perhaps because Scotland is exceptionally favorable for the experiences and characteristics they describe. One is *gyte*, which is 'crazy,' 'featherheaded,' just crazy enough not to be locked up. One is *shilpit*, which is 'frail' and 'meager' — the opposite of *sonsy*. A *shilpit* woman is a *skinnamalinky*. Then there is the beautiful word *dreich*, which means 'endlessly long and tedious'; a sermon lasting forty-five minutes spoken in one unchanging monotone is apt to be *dreich*. And a woman who goes on and on about the same subject is said to *deave* her husband, which is 'to deafen him and exhaust him.' But in case I *deave* my readers with Scottish words, I shall not *swither*, I shall stop *blethering*, and close the subject before it gives any of them even the slightest hint of a *scunner*.

English shibboleths

EVERYTHING you do reveals your personality. A good detective, a good psychologist, can judge, after watching you for an hour or two, whether you are aggressive or retiring, clever or stupid or confused, verbal or manual, social or antisocial, and so on into deeper qualities. Most of us practice the same art of discrimination in an amateurish way whenever we meet new people. But something else is revealed in everything you do and say: the social group you belong to. A man can usually type another man by watching him eat a single meal or by spending a single evening in company. A woman can usually type another woman in an even shorter time, with one of those long, all-embracing, all-penetrating glances.

This happens in every country. In the East it is more

marked than anywhere else; the different Indian castes have different ways of walking, and eating, and drinking, and even sneezing. In England also these distinctions have long been very marked; Bernard Shaw, about fifty years ago, said that no Englishman could open his mouth without making some other Englishman despise him. Indeed, one of the first things an Englishman learns while growing up is how to size up another man by his appearance and his accent, and then (if possible) to put him in his place.

This subject has recently been brought up again by an English expert on social distinctions. This is Miss Nancy Mitford, a witty and charming authoress, with a sharp and sophisticated pen. (She is the daughter of the second Baron Redesdale, and is married to the son of the second Baron Rennell; she has written several novels in which most of the characters are Honourables, which means they are the sons and daughters of viscounts, or at least of barons.) In the autumn of 1955 she produced an amusing and knowledgeable article which raised a good deal of interest in England. It appeared in the magazine *Encounter* and was called 'The English Aristocracy.' Now it has been reprinted, together with the essay which inspired it and several rejoinders and comments, in a pleasant little book called *Noblesse Oblige* (published in 1956 by Harper, with a witty preface by Russell Lynes).

The main body of the article does not interest us so much. It was pretty localized. In it, Miss Mitford stated once again the idea which she and Miss Thirkell have put much more forcibly in fiction: the idea that the British peerage is the salt of the country, and of the earth. She added the more surprising notion that it is still very rich; there is a report that, of the hundred finest diamonds in the world, sixty are in English hands.

What caused the sensation in Britain was the opening

of the article, together with some sentences toward its close. In these paragraphs Miss Mitford pointed out what many English readers apparently did not know — that, even if they spoke grammatically, and even if they spoke in an unchallengeably cultivated voice, they could still be typed at once by their choice of words.

Let us look at some of the examples she gives. (But let us remember that she is speaking only for the English.) When you write somebody a letter, what do you write it on? Letter paper, note-paper, or writing paper? When you send someone a message through Western Union, what do you call it? A wire, or a telegram? When you are brushing your hair, what do you look into? A mirror, or a looking-glass? If you are a woman, what do you put on in the evening to make you smell pleasantly? Scent, or perfume? If you are short-sighted, what do you have on your nose? Spectacles, or glasses?

You and I would not know, by the light of nature. (And, I gather, neither would most of the English, or else they would not have been so distressed by the article.) We might remember what we had heard people saying, and try, rather faintly, to conform with their usage; but we probably would not think it was important. I think I should say note-paper, telegram, mirror, perfume, and glasses. But Miss Mitford tells us that the upper-class words are writing paper, telegram, looking-glass (remember Alice?), scent, and spectacles.

She has known this distinction in speech for a long time, but her article is not an authoritative and complete description of it. She is merely commenting on a much more scientific account of upper-class and non-upper-class English. Anthropologists are always doing comparative studies of the social habits of tribes and nations — the Balinese, the Mundugumor, the Americans, and the Arapesh. Linguists do the same. And Miss Mitford's article is merely a comment on such an article, called 'Linguistic Class-Indicators in Present-Day English,' which appeared in the *Neuphilologische Mitteilungen,* Volume 55 (1954), pages 20–56, published in Helsinki, Finland. Its author is the Professor of Linguistics at Birmingham University, England, A. S. C. Ross, a competent scholar who has written several penetrating studies of Anglo-Saxon language and literature. Mr. Ross explains that there are still very clear distinctions in language between the English upper class and the others. It is not a matter of money, or manners (he says), or education; it is simply a group distinction.

If you look at the Bible, you will find that a similar test was applied by the Hebrews during a civil war. In Judges 12 we are told that the men of Gilead fought against the men of Ephraim, and won. During the retreat of the beaten force, the Gileadite field security units seized the fords over the river Jordan. Whenever a fugitive arrived, they said to him, 'Do you belong to the forces of Ephraim?' If he said no, then they ordered him, 'Pronounce the word *shibboleth.*' No man of Ephraim could pronounce it, for he said *sibboleth.* 'Then they took him, and slew him at the passages of Jordan; and there fell at that time of the Ephraimites forty and two thousand.'

In the same way, Professor Ross divides the English into the U's and the non-U's: members of the upper class, and hoi polloi. This is an anthropological technique. People in every primitive tribe belong to the fox clan or the tortoise clan, and there are rules about foxes marrying tortoises, and who can hold the priesthood of the sacred groundhog, and who must kindle the fires on the second Thursday of each month, and so forth. The English, says Professor Ross, are divided almost as sharply. A member of the upper-class group, the U's, knows a long list of words and formulae and names which only his group will employ; and similarly a member of the non-U's can be recognized at once by his utterance of certain phrases or verbal gestures which no real U would ever speak.

To take a simple example, there are U names, and non-U names, for children and even for dogs. (Not doggies: that is non-U.) A girl called Marleen, a boy called Frank, are both non-U, for obvious reasons. I think the names of the kings and princes of the Hanoverian monarchy are non-U in England, simply because the upper classes never cared very much for those originally German monarchs; or perhaps it is because the non-upper classes seized on their names in an upsurge of loyalty and thus made them impossible for U children. When you hear a woman calling 'George, George,' or 'Here, Bert,' in England, you can place her and her family even without the accent. That subtle psychologist T. S. Eliot observed this thirty years ago, and put it into *The Waste Land*. There is a splendid sequence in a Cockney pub, in which a woman says

> Others can pick and choose if you can't.
> But if Albert makes off, it won't be for lack of telling.
> You ought to be ashamed, I said, to look so antique.
> (And her only thirty-one.)
> I can't help it, she said, pulling a long face,
> It's them pills I took, to bring it off, she said.
> (She's had five already, and nearly died of young George.) *

Notice that the Cockney husband was named after the Prince Consort, and his son after the Georges.

Professor Ross's article gives a long list of words and phrases which are specifically U and non-U. Some of these

---

* From *Collected Poems, 1909–1935*, copyright 1936 by Harcourt, Brace and Company. Reprinted by permission of Harcourt, Brace and Faber and Faber, Ltd.

are indicators. If you heard a man in the Middle East saying 'Bismillah,' you would know that he must be a Moslem. So no one who was not a middle-class or lower-class Englishman would ever say 'Well, really' or 'Ever so nice' or 'Thanks very much, I'm sure.' Such phrases are shibboleths. The simplest of all shibboleths is the very first greeting between English people. They are introduced. One says 'How do you do?' The other says 'Pleased to meet you' or 'Quite well, thank you, and how are you?' At once the second man is typed as non-U. He should simply have said 'How do you do?' in the same tone and if possible at the same moment as the other, depending on age and rank.

No one claims that U speech is any better or clearer than non-U speech. It is not the intellectual content of speech which matters in these things, but the emotional and social charge. So it would be possible for us, as outsiders — neither U nor non-U — to work out a few principles which govern the distinction.

U speech, upper-class speech, always prefers the simple to the complex. If you have a house in the country, it is better to call it something quiet rather than something noticeable and bold, something dull rather than something which sounds as though you had spent weeks thinking of it: *Smith Farm* rather than *The Village Smithy;* no name at all rather than *Dunroamin* or *El Nido*. Again, U speech prefers to be civil rather than gushing. If you do not know someone to whom you have to write a letter, you will address him as 'Dear Sir,' and put his name at the foot of the page; you will not begin the missive 'Dear John Smith.' U speech also prefers to be leisurely rather than hurried; so it looks down on abbreviations, such as 'wire' for 'telegram' and 'phone' for 'telephone.' And U speech and U speakers prefer to be cool and distant rather than cozy and gushing; not 'this is a lovely home,' but 'this is a pleasant house.' In England, or at least in U England, a house is not a home, except to those who live in it. If you have nothing to say you will not talk for the sake of bridging the gap of silence — unless you are the unfortunate hostess. And you will always cut formalities down to the essential. When you leave, you will not say 'Good-bye, it's been so nice meeting you, we must see each other again soon, do call me up,' but simply 'Good-bye.'

We must not think that these distinctions are felt *only* by Miss Mitford, as an Honourable, and Professor Ross, as a linguist. The English, both U and non-U, think a good deal about them. In a London musical show produced during the autumn of 1955, one of the most successful songs was a collection of very refined phrases which — although apparently graceful and even cultured — were terribly and nauseatingly non-U. It began with four awful blunders: 'Phone for the fish-knives, Norman.' This little song is reprinted at the end of *Noblesse Oblige,* and is a sort of self-marking examination paper by which U people can distinguish themselves from non-U boys and girls. And even in the early novels of Evelyn Waugh we see members of the upper class, perhaps just a little bit shaky, assuring themselves of their own place by deliberately using non-U phrases — to show that they know what is wrong, and therefore what is right.

All these anthropological groupings seem rather upsetting. We hate the idea that we can all be ticketed and put into cases, like fish or spearheads. Remember Marquand's anthropologist Malcolm Bryant, in *Point of No Return,* who infuriated Charley Gray by listening carefully to his talk and then saying 'Yes, you had to say that, it's just right for you.' Still, it is useless for us to pretend that these groupings do not exist, both in England and in the United States, and in every country. It is important to be aware of them, even if one tries to forget them after learning their subtleties. Authors in the United States recently have become more and more sensitive to such distinctions. They have been publishing novels and writing plays which often dealt with characteristics as simple as the shape of a man's shirt collar, or the sound of a woman's speech. Shibboleths, all these. Those who believe they are all-important would perhaps say that they distinguish the noble from the vulgar: the people you would like to meet, from the others. Some might say they were tests of good manners, like the ability to smoke without puffing filthy breath and stale nicotine vapor in other people's faces and putting smelly butts down in the middle of the table; or the ability to eat and drink without making loud noises. What shall we say? Shall we say that good manners are the expression of kindness and self-control, and that, if these qualities appear in speech and action, no shibboleth need matter very much? Even if we do not know the correct U speech or U action, if we have these qualities, we shall be neither U nor non-U, but real.

I'm going to write a book

THE young couple were newly married. One of them had been a pupil of mine some time before. I congratulated him, and wished them well. I said, 'For the first few years, it will be a bit of a struggle for you; but it nearly always is. You are young, and you have each other. Good luck.'

They smiled happily. The bride's eyes glistened with love and hope. She said, 'Oh, it will be wonderful. Joe is going to write a novel.'

Poor girl. And poor Joe. They think that, if he writes a novel and has it published, their troubles will be over. Well, in one blunt way, perhaps it may be a relief. Almost everyone who has gone through college feels that he or she could and should write a novel. When Joe gets his book published, the family will rest easier. But, apart from that, no.

What do they expect from Joe's novel?

To begin with, I believe they think it will bring them distinction; it will raise them out of the common; it will convert them into something more than two average individuals. They may become famous. I can understand why they hope for all this; but it is a slim and uncertain hope. To say, 'I am going to write a book' nowadays in the hope of becoming famous is not like saying, 'I am going to become a lawyer' or 'I am going to drive to California.' It is much more like saying, 'I am going to become a distinguished inventor.' Every Saturday *The New York Times* publishes a selection from the inventions which have been patented in Washington during the preceding week. Some of them are brilliant and highly practical; some are ingenious but unnecessary; and some are mad dreams, the outcome of years of meditation on an obsessive idea which seems vital to the originator but will appear utterly trivial to the rest of the world. So it is with novels — particularly first novels. Some of them express thoughts which are urgently important to the author but signally fail to interest the rest of the world. Some of them describe peculiar people and events in an unusual way, but are unimportant and easily forgotten. A few of them say something which mankind will think to be new and important. These are the really valuable novels; and they are few, very few in number. The odds against Joe's writing such a book are, I grieve to say, about 25,000 to 1.

Then think of the result of failure. Having an unsuccessful first novel is not like setting out to drive to California and turning back at Chicago. It is rather more like building your own house and forgetting to put in any drainpipes, or having the whole thing slip downhill because the foundations disintegrated. You are a bit ashamed of it. If one critic dislikes it, that might be ignored; but if twenty pan it and the rest cold-shoulder it, then it leaves a scar which never heals. Instead of being a symbol of distinction, your novel may prove to be a symbol of inadequacy; you never want to hear its name mentioned; you avoid passing bookstores of a certain type, in case you see it there, still in its gallant original paper dress, marked down to twenty-nine cents. The philosopher Jean-Jacques Rousseau had five children, and dropped them all, one by one, into the foundling hospital, so that he never (consciously) saw them again. But what if he had met them begging their bread on the streets, and wearing bright jackets marked BY J.-J. ROUSSEAU?

Yet perhaps Joe does not want the novel to bring him distinction? Perhaps he and his wife think of it chiefly as a money-making proposition? They have heard of the vast sums of money made by authors whose books become best sellers and remain on the best-seller lists for many months, are chosen by a book club for distribution to its members, are purchased by Hollywood for conversion into a motion picture, and so forth. Well, such books and such authors do exist. The world of contemporary literature contains unbelievable successes as well as miserable disappointments. But, in the quest for money as for distinction, the odds are enormously against the player. For every single success, there are hundreds, thousands, of relative failures. On the average, Joe's novel will sell 2000 copies.

Surely, you ask, surely he will make some money out of that? Yes, he will — a little, but very little. A few hundred dollars, perhaps. Not much; not enough to pay for a long effort such as he has made. And remember, the odds are that Joe's book will be average, not one of the few which hit the jackpot. Even the phrase 'hitting the jackpot' is wrong and degrading. It implies that a man writes a novel solely in order to gamble in a difficult and unreasonable game of chance; whereas in fact, if he is going to be a good author, he tries never to think of the gambling aspect of authorship at all.

However, suppose Joe's novel has both exceptional merit and exceptional good luck. No matter how much money he makes on it, he will have to pay a great quantity of it over to the Federal Government in taxes — a higher proportion than any ordinary citizen. Let us say he started writing his book in the spring of 1955, worked at it all that year and most of the next year, handed it to the publishers in the fall of 1956 after eighteen months of hard work, and had it published in the spring of 1957. Most of the money he makes out of it will come to him in 1957. He will be taxed on that money (over and above his regular income, if any) in 1957 — although he has been working on the book for eighteen months or so, and incurring expenses in typing, office space, and the like. Then, in 1958, he will scarcely have another novel ready; but he still has to live — on the remains of his 1957 takings. And he will find that the income-tax authorities are apt to question him very pointedly because his income appears to have undergone an inexplicable fluctuation. They are anxious to find out why he does not report so much income for 1958; perhaps he is concealing something; perhaps he is operating under a false name; hmmmm. Year after year that same attitude is apt to continue. Income-tax investigators apparently do not read books; they do not seem to believe that writing novels, irregular as it is, can be a legitimate way of making money. When they hear that someone makes a good deal of cash out of one book, they are liable to distrust him, and attach a special warning marker to his file so that they may investigate him next year and in all succeeding years until he writes another best-selling book (if he has any energy left after answering their questions). In the last few years, the laws have been amended, so that, if you can prove you have spent quite a long time on one book (I think it is three solid years), you may spread your income from that book over more than one year, for purposes of taxation. But that is still rather harsh; and it neglects the central problem, which is that very few people go on writing novels regularly until the age of retirement, in the same way as they go on doctoring, or selling stocks, or doing income-tax investigation.

Once upon a time, to be sure, it was possible to become rich by writing novels. It was possible to become rich even by writing short stories. It was possible to become opulent by writing both novels and short stories, unless you threw the cash out of the window with both hands, like Scott Fitzgerald. My elders and betters tell me that, before the present tax system was built up, a man might get five thousand dollars for a single short story from one of the big magazines; he might make fifty thousand dollars from a single novel. With virtually no income tax to pay, he could treat that not as income, but as capital; he could, and some did, try to save most of it, buy annuities, build a house, and provide against the possible drying up of his talent. Those were the days in which writers could become rich merely from writing stories. But now, all such windfalls are taxed as income, and disappear as rapidly as all income seems to do.

Very well, then. Joe is a dogged character. Suppose he says, 'I agree, times have changed, authors used to have it easy, now they have to face hard realities. It is a trade just like any other trade. I'll work at it. I'll be a novelist, just as my brother Bill is a dentist. I'll keep accounts, and work regular hours, and not expect too much. How about that?'

We must admire Joe's courage, but we must deplore his inexperience. Writing is not a profession like dentistry. People will always have toothache and pay for its removal; they will not always want to read novels, and they may never want to read Joe's novels. Or, even worse, they may begin by liking Joe's novels and then grow tired of them. Like painting, composing, and acting, writing is a hazardous and painfully irregular way of making a living. I remember a bitterly funny cartoon by Richard Decker in *The New Yorker* which showed a poor cold-water apartment, without comforts; there were a harried young wife, and two thin children playing on the floor; there were piles of typescript in one corner; and there was a table with a typewriter, at which sat a husband, rolling up his sleeves with an air of grim determination. The wife was saying to him 'Bernard, if you won't think of me, think of the children. Please don't start another trilogy.'

The income from authorship is usually so irregular that it depresses and even warps the author, unless he has some income from elsewhere. He can be a teacher; some have been doctors; many have been and are journalists; I know at least one who is a professional scientist. But he ought to have a regular income, just enough to keep him from worrying himself into extremities of rage or extravagance or despair.

And there is more in it than merely freedom from anxiety. If Joe sets out to be a novelist, he must be constantly broadening his experience. Many young writers start well, with their first and second novels based on their own memories and their immediate surroundings; but then — if they either remain in the small town where they wrote them, or, like Bernard, bury themselves in a cold-water flat to complete a trilogy — their horizon narrows, they meet hardly any new people, they have no new emotional revelations or intellectual stimuli, they lack standards of comparison, and usually they do not even buy and read interesting new books. Travel and movement are essential for growing novelists; in the last generation the most introspective of all were inveterate travelers and indefatigable party-goers: Proust, Joyce, and Gide. Now, in order to travel — not necessarily abroad, but within this wonderfully diverse country — Joe needs a little money and a sense of security. Frankly, I think he will do best if he treats his job as his regular source of nourishment, and then takes anything he makes out of his novels as a gift from heaven (subject to Federal and State income tax), and uses it to travel through the Far West or to spend four weeks in the Caribbean islands.

These are depressing thoughts. But they are realistic; and novelists must have a grasp of hard facts.

To offset them, there is one pleasure which Joe will have: the pleasure which all real novelists enjoy. It appears in the biographies of men like Balzac and Dickens, and several living novelists have spoken to their friends about it. It is this. Reading a novel is sometimes exciting, sometimes boring, and sometimes merely narcotic, like chewing aspirin-impregnated gum. But writing a novel (if you are not doing it for money) is really delightful. To see the characters who never existed except in your own imagination take shape and say words that you invent for them, to feel them taking on an independent life (like children as they grow older), to watch the story spreading into new episodes almost spontaneously, to feel unexpected grace and vigor running into the sentences out of an imaginative source unknown even to yourself — that is a pure and almost unparalleled delight. If Joe is writing a book in order to capture that experience, then good luck to him. He will have nearly all the happiness he needs in the work of creation. Compared with that, both money and fame are infinitely insignificant.

The first few words

———————

IF you have ever tried to write a book, you will know that it is an exciting experience. It is full of passionate moments. The greatest, no doubt, is the wonderful instant when you open the parcel from the publishers, and, for the first time, see your own offspring: your own long-nourished thoughts, and your own carefully arranged words, at last objectively real, independent, alive. But there is another moment, almost as exciting: the moment when, after thinking about your book for many months or years, you take up a pad of paper and write down the first words.

The first words of a book — they are intensely important. They will kindle the reader's interest; or they will puzzle him; they may repel him or challenge him. Both for him, the reader, and for you, the author, they are the opening of a new experience.

Whether he is conscious of it or not, the first words of a book are likely to remain in the reader's mind. And, if the book proves to be a good one, whenever he thinks of it later or picks it up to reread, he will find that his enthusiasm is rekindled simply by those first sentences. To put it another way, it seems to be a reliable rule that great books very rarely open badly, and very often open with a few impressive sentences. The first words need not be dramatic; they need not even be clear; but they must grip the mind of the reader and begin to mold his mood.

Here is the most famous beginning in American literature, three words only:

Call me Ishmael.

This is the opening of *Moby Dick*. In those three words, Melville has shown us the character of his hero, or his narrator; an exile, a wanderer, with a taste for the Bible, and a rough, lonely, combative character. In its abrupt power, its violence, and its sense of doom, that is the right beginning for a book which is to end with a lonely ship sinking deep in the desert sea.

But here is another opening, far less clear, and very undramatic:

It was the best of times, it was the worst of times, it was the age of wisdom, it was the age of foolishness, it was the epoch of belief, it was the epoch of incredulity, it was the season of Light, it was the season of Darkness, it was the spring of hope, it was the winter of despair, we had everything before us, we had nothing before us, we were all going direct to Heaven, we were all going direct the other way—in short, the period was so far like the present period, that some of its noisiest authorities insisted on its being received, for good or for evil, in the superlative degree of comparison only.

That is the overture to Dickens's *Tale of Two Cities*. It describes the years just before the French Revolution, in the same satirical tones as Dickens used about his own period; it warns us that that was a period of confusion, it makes us feel much of its unrest, it prepares for the extremes of the French Revolution, and at the same time it shows, without announcing the fact directly, that Dickens will take no sides: he will neither oppose the French Revolution as a frightful crime, nor praise it as though it were heaven on earth. He was a skilful writer.

Now take a contemporary. Here are the first words of one of his best novels:

> Through the fence, between the curling flower spaces, I could see them hitting. They were coming toward where the flag was and I went along the fence. Luster was hunting in the grass by the flower tree. They took the flag out, and they were hitting. Then they put the flag back and they went to the table, and he hit and the other hit.

Is this unintelligible? No. It makes sense. It describes something we have all seen; but it describes it as seen by a special mind. It is simply an account of two golfers approaching the green, holing out, and moving on to the next tee. But the description is given in the words of a man who is mentally defective: he can recognize people and simple events, but he cannot follow the structure of anything so complicated as a game of golf, he can merely describe it as a disconnected series of actions. These sentences are the opening of William Faulkner's *The Sound and the Fury* — a tale told partly by an idiot. They take you at once inside the mind of poor imbecile Benjy; they hint at one of his obsessions (golf balls); and they prepare you for the effort of understanding his story, not in the terms he uses, but in our own more rational and complete context. And also, in a pathetic simple way, they are beautiful. 'Through the fence, between the curling flower spaces, I could see them hitting.'

The chief mistake made by many authors in their opening sentences is to try to put in too much. Turn to the best known of all modern American books, and read the first sentence:

> Scarlett O'Hara was not beautiful, but men seldom realized it when caught by her charm as the Tarleton twins were.

It is a good novel, *Gone with the Wind,* full of spanking incident and vigorous character drawing, but it is not sensitively written. It is clear, but it is clumsy. This opening shows that Margaret Mitchell was an amateurish stylist. She wanted to describe her heroine on the very first page, to show that she was unusual, not the regular classical Southern beauty. That she did, and did quite well; her description of Scarlett goes on for two paragraphs. But she also wanted to get the story going, and so she dragged in the Tarleton twins, who do not even speak for two or three pages, and the result is a sentence with a stumble. She ought to have been more courageous, and written:

> Scarlett O'Hara was not beautiful, but men seldom realized it when caught by her charm.

Or even, if I might venture to suggest it:

> Scarlett O'Hara was not beautiful, but men seldom realized it.

The same mistake appears in the opening sentence of a world-famous novel, Dostoevski's *The Brothers Karamazov.* It begins with a long and absorbing character sketch of the man whose murder is the central theme of the book, old Karamazov: he occupies the reader's attention for the first ten or twelve pages; therefore he should have been introduced first. But Dostoevski also had in his mind the son, Alexey, who was to become the most important and most positive character in the novel: so, foolishly, he dragged him into the first sentence and then dropped him, thus:

> Alexey Fyodorovitch Karamazov was the third son of Fyodor Pavlovitch Karamazov, a land owner well known in our district in his own day, and still remembered among us owing to his gloomy and tragic death, which happened 13 years ago, and which I shall describe in its proper place.

No, it is better to be simple. One of the most remarkable of all modern novels begins with a sentence which is brief, undramatic, almost naïve:

> For a long time I went to bed early.

Silly, isn't it? And yet it is the opening of Marcel Proust's *Remembrance of Things Past,* one of the *least* naïve books of our epoch, and composed in a most exquisite style. Gently, imperceptibly, after that sentence, the reader is drawn into a meditation on sleep and dreams so subtle that — although sleep and dreaming is a universal experience — almost every thought in it seems quite new to him. Proust goes on:

> Sometimes, almost before my candle was out, my eyes closed, so quickly that I had no time to say to myself 'I am falling asleep.' And, half an hour afterwards, the thought that it was time to try to sleep would awake me: I attempted to put down the book which I thought I was still holding, and to blow out the light; as I slept, I had gone on thinking about what I had just read, but my reflections had taken an unusual turn: it seemed to me that I myself was the

subject of the work: a church, a quartet, the rivalry
of Francis I and Charles V. . . .

And this prepares the reader for the long voyage through
the world described by Proust — a world which, even
while the author describes it, changes as curiously and ir-
rationally as the phenomena of a dream, and from which,
at the end, as though life were itself a long slumber, we
awake to find ourselves facing one of the few permanent
realities: Death.

Equally clear, but less apparently naïve, is this introduction:

> It is a truth universally acknowledged, that a single
> man in possession of a good fortune must be in want
> of a wife.

In that epigram there is a dry and almost bitter tone; we
know from it that we are to read a comedy; we are prepared for irony; there is something both of amusement
and of derision in the author's trick of elevating the vulgar
wish to catch a rich husband into a general principle,
half way between economics and psychology. That is the
exquisitely appropriate overture, almost Mozartian in its
simplicity, to Jane Austen's *Pride and Prejudice*.

Many of the bad novels in the world are bad because,
throughout, their author has no clear conception of the
emotional tone he wants to create. This also often appears
in the opening paragraph. I have a particular blind spot
for Henry James; I can never read his books with any
interest — apart from *The Turn of the Screw* and *The
Aspern Papers*. The first sentence of *Daisy Miller* will explain why:

> At the little town of Vevey, in Switzerland, there is a
> particularly comfortable hotel. There are, indeed,
> many hotels; for the entertainment of tourists is the

business of the place, which, as many travellers will remember, is seated upon the edge of a remarkably blue
lake — a lake that it behooves every tourist to visit.

Well, are you interested? Do you find that perceptive, or
amusing? Does the description make you long to read on
and on? Is there not something a little snobbish about
'as many travellers will remember,' something a little
patronizing about the crack at the touristy charm of the
Lake of Geneva, something bored, something boring about
the whole sentence?

But consider this opening, somber, romantic, and mystical:

It was late in the evening when K. arrived. The village
was deep in snow. The Castle hill was hidden, veiled
in mist and darkness, nor was there even a glimmer
of light to show that a castle was there. On the wooden
bridge leading from the main road to the village K.
stood for a long time gazing into the illusory emptiness above him.

That comes from Franz Kafka's weird unfinished book,
The Castle, in which the hero K. constantly tries, in vain,
to get into communication with a mysterious castle which
dominates his life, yet which he can never visit, and sometimes not even see.

A mystical aphorism and a mystical question stand together at the entrance to a novel which may or may not
be a masterpiece: the reconstruction of the story of Joseph
by Thomas Mann. Its Prelude begins:

Very deep is the well of the past. Should we not call it
bottomless?

So says Mann, because his entire book is devoted to taking
us back, far back, into the remote past, where figures almost mythical become real individuals; and to showing

us that they thought of themselves as modern, and felt behind them a long, long reach of tradition and history: so that, when we read of their acts and lives, we feel ourselves not creatures of a single generation, but inheritors of the ages.

While Mann was working on his Joseph stories, another author even more deeply fascinated by the process of history was exploring the past. His novel, issued in 1939, is not much read; yet it haunts those who know something of it. This was James Joyce's *Finnegans Wake*. While Mann saw history as a movement in one main direction, Joyce thought of it as following a pattern of constant recurrence, the rains to the river, the river to the sea, the sea to the rain clouds, and so forever on and on. Therefore *Finnegans Wake* begins in the middle of a sentence and ends in the middle of a sentence, the two joining to give the effect of a continuous cycle. Here is the opening, without even a capital letter to break its continuity:

> riverrun, past Eve and Adam's, from swerve of shore
> to bend of bay, brings us by a commodius vicus of
> recirculation back to Howth Castle and Environs.

That half-sentence contains the theory on which the book is based, the initials of its hero, the name of the philosopher Vico who helped to inspire it, its setting, Dublin and the River Liffey, and half a dozen other themes of great interest and charm. Joyce expected his readers to devote their entire lives to reading his works; he is not a great enough man to justify that demand, but as a hobby, to be taken up from time to time, he is fascinating.

The first words of a book are not simply those which happen to stand at the top of the first page. They are the beginning of a new experience for both the author and the reader, and they point toward the end of that experience.

Once we have read the blunt ominous opening of Melville's *Moby Dick,* we can never forget it. That short hammering sentence prepares for the terrible last scene, in which the doomed whale crashes into the whale-ship, and the ship sinks, carrying down all its men, a sea hawk enfolded in its flag.

> Now small fowls flew screaming over the yet yawning gulf; a sullen white surf beat against its steep sides; then all collapsed, and the great shroud of the sea rolled on as it rolled five thousand years ago.

What's in a name?

O NE of the finest scenes in the theater is that which
opens the tragedy of *Hamlet, Prince of Denmark*. It is midnight. Two anxious sentries meet on the ramparts of the
castle. They are joined by a third, together with a foreign
visitor. The first sentry leaves, with obvious eagerness.
Those who remain talk with a strange urgency in the darkness, and almost before they can say what they mean, they
are confronted by a majestic and terrifying ghost. The
anxiety and the urgency tower into magnificent drama.

Nevertheless, when we begin reading *Hamlet,* we experience one disappointment. It is a minor one; yet if we
are sensitive, we must feel it. The play is laid in Denmark.
The soldiers are Danish soldiers. The visitor apparently
comes from no further away than Germany. But the sol-

diers are called Francisco, Bernardo, and Marcellus; the visitor is called Horatio. These are neither Danish nor German names. Three of them are Italian, one is Latin. Still, there is no hint that the soldiers or their companion are mercenaries, or southerners. They are meant to be three Danes and a German. If they were all outlanders — mercenaries or the like — the scene would lose much of its importance. There are many fine resounding Danish and German names which Shakespeare could have used: Harald, Eric, Sven, Otto, and Sigurd. He did not, because he was careless in making up names for his characters. He was — as his enemies and friends said — careless in many things, but he was exceptionally careless about the names of his people. Evidently, he saw the characters and cared little about the labels. (In *Hamlet* itself, one of the main characters, Polonius, was originally called something quite different — Corambis.)

Contrast this with another popular writer: Dickens. Charles Dickens took a great deal of trouble about selecting names for the characters whom he created, and he was splendidly successful. Some of his names are lovable: Pickwick and Micawber. Some are comical — Winkle and Jingle. Some are repellent and yet absurd, like Stiggins and Podsnap. Some are sinister, like Squeers and Krook. Some are horribly sentimental, like Little Nell. But they all correspond very closely to the people whom they identify — so closely that they become part of the people. When you hear the name Podsnap, it is impossible for you to think of a slender neat man with a black moustache and a pleasant smile, like David Niven, or a rough craggy individual with pessimistic eyes and a kindly modesty, like Spencer Tracy. If you are sensitive to syllables, you must think of a middle-aged man who is rather tall, certainly overweight, slow-spoken, pompous, self-satisfied, and inwardly a weakling — a grown-up baby, if you could ever puncture his armor of fat.

This is one of the many problems which face everyone who tries to write a play or a story. He has to create characters. He has to describe them, directly or indirectly, showing whether they are young or old, strong or weak, handsome, nondescript, or ugly, stupid, clever, enigmatic or inarticulate. He must make them real. But one of the essential facts about every person is his or her name — which has surprisingly often a peculiar and penetrating connection with his or her character. It is a part of the mask, and so it should be created and described.

Authors differ very greatly in the skill with which they solve this problem. Shakespeare took most of his names from history; he was casual or crude about most of the others. But Dickens actually collected strange and interesting real names, just as he collected strange and interesting real people. He would copy down names from shop-fronts and advertisements and directories, in the hope of using them later. The result is a splendid collection, each of them a picture: Sairey Gamp, Betsey Prig, Mr. Sowerberry, Bill Sikes, Wackford Squeers.

Very few other novelists have managed to build up such a variety of expressive names. Walter Scott, in his time, was a famous name-giver: there is still a romantic charm about such names as Ivanhoe, Kenilworth, Waverley, Quentin Durward, and Brian du Bois-Guilbert. Thackeray coined a few good names, especially the name of his adventuress, Becky Sharp, and the name of her corruptor, the Marquis of Steyne; but we can seldom recall more than those few.

It is true that some writers do not want to create outstanding names. They wish their people to be average, to merge into the crowd. So their hero is called Mr. Roberts, or (as in Marquand's *Point of No Return*) Charley Gray, or (as in Jane Austen's *Pride and Prejudice*) Elizabeth Bennet. Almost all the characters in Roman comedy and in the comedies of Molière are given perfectly commonplace names which scarcely characterize them at all — as in our own soap operas, where the lovers are called David and Linda, or John and Marsha.

Still, authors lose a great deal of effect if they do not give their characters memorable names, just as they do if they fail to describe the physical appearance of their men and women, so that we can see them and hear their voices. Names are important, for several different reasons.

First, their sound. In every language, sounds convey emotional impressions, partly because of their intrinsic quality, partly because of their suggestions and alliances. Take the hypocritical villain in Dickens: Uriah Heep. Quite apart from its Biblical background, Uriah seems to writhe, and Heep seems to creep and to peer and to sneak meanly. Another of Dickens's novels is named after an important commercial firm: *Dombey and Son*. Dombey sounds pompous and rather dumb, and it has a weak ending: DOMbey. The helpless, optimistic bankrupt in *David Copperfield* is named Micawber: his name begins weakly, swells out into a bubble of empty sound, and then disintegrates again: MiCAWber. Elsewhere in Dickens there is a splendidly empty-headed society lady whose name sounds like empty-headed society conversation: Julia Wititterly. On the other hand, his mean financier, whose money all turns out to be trash and worse than trash, is called MERDle, because *merde* means 'excrement,' and the cruel stepfather who nearly kills David Copperfield is Mr. MURDSTONE, because he is murderous and stony-hearted. In the novels of William Faulkner the most aristocratic family is called Sartoris — which, apart from its implied meaning (sartorial perfection), has a lofty sound depending on perfectly pure articulation. But the low family of peckernecks is called Snopes — a name which begins with the horrible sound of sneering and snarling and snitching and underhand sniping, and goes on into a syllable which closes up like two mean lips. In Balzac, one of the most ruthless villains is Rastignac.

Secondly, names have their own meanings. Becky *was* Sharp. The Marquis *was* a Stain on the nobility of his country. In *David Copperfield* there is a young man who is brave and reckless and selfish, rather like Byron. At the end he is drowned in a ship, wrecked by a fearful storm. His name is Steerforth — because he does not guide his life, but drives it straight forward without precautions. A character in *Bleak House* who is a strange combination of bitter violence and youthful charm, now threatening lawsuits and prosecutions and now chirping to his pet bird, is called Boythorn. (He was modeled on a real English eccentric, whose name also shows his double nature: *Walter Savage* LANDOR.) As for Mr. Podsnap—he is fat and empty; one day he will burst like a seedpod. The noblest and most superficial parvenu in Dickens is called by the name of a Byzantine princess and the name of a cheap furniture finish: Anastasia Veneering. So the hero of a famous American novel of the disorderly 'twenties is called Gatsby. He is a criminal masquerading as a gentleman (like Stevenson's Mr. Hyde), so his name ends with a rather noble syllable, as in Disraeli's Coningsby and Kipling's Gadsbys; but it begins with the word *gat,* which is crooks' slang for 'gun.'

Then, thirdly, names have their social suggestions. Every name has its background, its milieu. We may not all know them, but they exist. There are two favorite American characters called Tom Sawyer and Huck Finn. Samuel

Clemens chose their names well. Sawyer is a trade name, like Cooper or Carter or Carpenter or Miller. It implies that the man who bears it is a sound, reliable workman, and also that he is of English descent but has no claims to being aristocratic. Finn is an old Celtic name. It has nothing to do with work or reliability; it is allied to the name of the great and slightly crazy hero Fingal, Finn Mac-Coul. Thus, Sawyer is the steady fellow descended from the English immigrants, but Finn is one of the wild ones who sprang from the Irish (and the wilder they were, the farther they sprang). Sawyer's first name is Tom, the name of one of the disciples of Jesus: a good religious name. Finn's first name, Huck, is bold and blunt and means nothing unless it is expanded into Huckleberry, a strong sweet wild berry. Tom is human, and expected to be saintly; Huck is a thing of wild nature, who does not even like wearing clothes.

This is one of the chief difficulties which everyone has in understanding a foreign book, even if it is well translated. We cannot catch the shades of meaning — we cannot catch even the main significances — of foreign names. One of the chief characters in Proust is called the Baron de Charlus; it may be an aristocratic name in French, but to us it sounds cheap and poor. The main figure in Dostoevski's *Crime and Punishment* is Raskolnikov. We may like the name because it sounds bitter and distorted, but we have to know Russian to understand it: it means 'dissenter,' 'nonconformist.'

'What's in a name?' asked Juliet; but she knew too well how dreadfully important her lover's name was. There is a great deal in a name, real or fictitious. Are you a man? How would your nature have been changed if you had been named Caesar? Or Percy? Or Huckleberry? Are you a woman? Would you not have been miserable if you had been called Salome — and miserable in another way if you had been called Charleen? The two old Irishwomen were right. When they asked what the new baby was called, the proud mother said, 'Hazel.' They waited till she had gone, and then one of them said, 'With all the saints there are in the calendar, she has to go and name the baby after a nut.'

The birth of a book

SEVERAL correspondents have written me personal
letters filled with curiosity, yes, and even with anxiety.
They are anxious to learn more about the actual process
of authorship. One such letter is from a gentleman in Connecticut, who writes:

> Dear Mr. Highet,
>
> Several times I have heard you speak of friends of
> yours who have written and published books, and are
> now happy, mature beings. I understand that your
> wife has gone through this experience, and so have
> you in your time. Tell me, Mr. Highet, how does one
> have a book? Is it terribly painful? Is it true that some-
> times one may suffer so much that one loses one's
> mind? And what happens if one cannot afford the

proper care? Is there anything in these new theories about prenatal exercises and psychical conditioning, which are said to prepare for natural book-production? I am terribly worried, for I should dearly love to have a little book myself, and my wife has often urged me to give way to my natural instincts and go ahead; but the whole process is wrapped in such mystery that I am almost afraid to embark on it . . . in case. . . . Please tell me the truth, won't you?

That is very sympathetic. I fully understand what my friend in Connecticut thinks and fears. Although it is now many years ago since I had my first book, I still remember what a shattering experience it was. I sometimes thought neither I nor the book would ever live through it. I could feel myself drifting away on waves of agonizing pain, drifting away into the unknown, and could scarcely hope that I should ever be able, even for a moment, to look on the face of my little first-born volume. For two days and two nights before the deadline I did not sleep; and then, when I first saw the frail red morsel, so feeble, so infinitely pitiful, only eight inches by five (small octavo) and weighing only about six ounces, I scarcely knew whether to be glad for myself or sorry for it. Yet very soon, within a few months, I learned to love it. I got to know every line in its dear little form, every tiny hyphen and accent; and years later, when a ruthless publisher starved it to death (he let it go out of print) something . . . died within me. Yes, it is a unique, a marvelously rewarding experience, even with all its heartbreaks and dangers, to produce a book.

But quite seriously, several correspondents have written to me asking how a book is produced, from start to finish. To people who are engaged in what is laughingly called 'the book industry' the whole process appears pretty natural and simple; but from the outside it is what printing used to be called, a Mystery. For instance, a lady in Philadelphia wrote to me asking whether the pages of a book were printed in consecutive order — 1, 2, 3, 4 and so on; a gentleman in Rhode Island wanted to know what was the difference between a printer and a publisher; and so on. I should like, therefore, to describe the adventure of producing a book, from beginning to end.

A book is a public utterance. It is a means of communication. The author of a book is telling other people something which he wants them to know, and which he thinks they will be better for knowing; or he wants to entertain them; or he wants to impel them to some kind of action. Therefore every book is an enterprise in which there are two partners: the author and the publisher. The publisher is not the public, but he is the only way that the author has of reaching the public. He has been sending communications of various kinds to the public for many years, and he ought to know what kinds of messages will be received, and by whom. A really good publisher can read a new book by a new author in manuscript, and say with something like certainty, 'This will go to 20,000 people in the first year, and to about 2000 people every year after that for a good long time.' An ineffective or conceited author does not always realize that he is trying to communicate with other people; he is apt to write so as to please himself alone, and then to be very glum when no one will listen to him; and he will usually shriek to high heaven if a publisher explains to him that he is talking into a dead wire.

Therefore the first stage in producing a book is to write it for a definite purpose, and to aim it at a definite public. It is obviously possible to write a book aimed at an indefinite posterity, but it has much less chance of being printed and published, and unless you are a very great genius it is unwise to work in this way. It is also possible to write a book aimed at a public which does not yet exist, but which you yourself wish to create; this is a risk, but it is a good risk; and it is the risk taken by many competent writers.

Suppose the book is written. What is the next stage? The next stage is to have it clearly (which usually means professionally) typed: at least three copies, double spaced, on uniform paper. (This is so that, if and when it is printed, the printers will not have to waste time while transferring the text from your typescript into their lines of print.)

Next it should be sent to the publisher. Suppose you have no publisher? Suppose it is your first book, and you know nothing about publishers? If you have aimed it at a definite public, you have probably read other books which were following a similar line, and were more or less addressing the same public. If so, you should send your book to the publisher who has produced those others. If not, if you are vague about whom you are addressing and what publisher ought to produce it, then you have two options. One is to consult a book called *The Literary Market Place* (the publisher is Bowker), which gives almost every kind of author vast amounts of information about publishers of all sorts. Use that book, and make a thoughtful choice. Send your typed manuscript to the right publisher, with a letter giving your name and address, and enclosing an envelope with postage paid, to enable him to send it back if he does not want it. Or else — and this is my own preference — choose a reliable literary agent (also from the *Market Place*), and send the book to him. (Remember to enclose a stamped envelope for its possible return.) He will read it without charge, if he is reliable; and if he thinks it can be published, he will send it out to the right publishers without expense to you. If the book is accepted, and printed and published, he will take 10 per cent of all your profits, and in return he will save you all the trouble of drawing up contracts and reading the small print (some publishers have awfully small print) and watching your own interests thenceforward. If he sends the book back to you, it means that he thinks it has little chance of being published in its present state. Some literary agents will offer advice about how a book should be changed to improve its chances of publication; sometimes this advice is valuable. Not always.

The book is accepted, either directly by a publisher, or indirectly through the work of a literary agent. Good. You must have a contract, signed by both parties, author and publisher, and witnessed by the agent if there is one; it must state the whole future of the book, in particular its financial future. Some publishers will for some kinds of books offer you a lump sum down — quite a good lump sum, it looks, too, and the proviso in the small print that the publisher gets all the profits on your book for ever and ever is almost invisible. It looks wonderful, especially when the publisher gives a cocktail party for you and pats you on the back and offers you a large cigar (deductible). You feel like the flower in Omar Khayyam:

> Look to the Rose that blows about us — 'Lo,
> Laughing,' she says, 'into the World I blow:
>   At once the silken Tassel of my Purse
>   Tear, and its Treasure on the Garden throw.'

However, it is unwise to sign any such contract, even if you are new and naïve and need money. Keep the income from your work. Keep the royalties, however small they are. This applies even to what might seem like hack work. I once knew a young couple who worked awfully hard to do a translation of a book written in a difficult foreign language. They needed some money to pay for the baby; and they translated the book by working late at night and getting up early in the morning to do another half chapter after the first feeding. They got the lump sum. It looked fine and lumpish at the time, and it paid for most of the baby. The book was published; it went on and on and on into more and more printings, perhaps more than it had ever had in the original language; it is still selling today, nearly thirty years after they translated it, and the publishers must have done comfortably well out of it; but all that the young couple have ever had from it is six complimentary copies and the original lump sum of five hundred dollars.

Now, suppose the book is accepted by a reliable publisher, and a fair contract is signed. Then the interesting part begins. The publisher decides *when* the book will be produced. He knows, from his experience, that certain books do very well if they come out just before Christmas, others in the spring, others in midsummer. That is his job. Do not argue with him. If the book does well, it will continue selling for months and years. If it does badly to begin with, it is likely to disappear after a few weeks. Let the publisher decide the strategic time of publication. He is almost as deeply concerned as you are.

Next, he gives your typed copies to three experts. One is the man who will design the book — the book as a physical object. This man can read, of course, but he is chiefly interested in shapes and colors. He is to your book what the stage designer and light expert are to a new play. His job is to put it into the most attractive, most durable, and most appropriate dress, so that it will look well in the bookseller's window, on a table in a private house, and on the shelf in a library. There are very few top men in this particular profession, and they are underestimated geniuses. They know how to choose type styles, how to select paper and ink, how to plan the shape of a book (short, thick, and imposing, or long, thin, and distinguished?), and how to lay out the title page and the outside paper jacket which (whether the average reader knows it or not) often helps to make him buy a new book he has scarcely heard of until that day. Do not interfere with this man. If he offers you a choice, make a choice. If not, shut up. He will usually do what is best, anyway.

The second expert is the man or woman who reads the book to discover and eliminate your mistakes. He or she is called the copy editor (there are some very shrewd and knowledgeable women copy editors), and he or she is necessary. As education has been more and more widely spread in every Western country, more and more people have been writing books, however imperfect their grasp of language. It is quite common now to find a long novel, filled with intricate psychological analyses of motives and delicate descriptions of foreign lands and peoples, written by a man or a woman who does not clearly know the difference between 'lay' and 'lie.' You will find elaborate paragraphs like this:

> Subtly, as Joe gazed round the deserted atoll, a new consciousness of meaning emanated into* his spirit. Even the miniscule* shells laying on the beach seemed to be instinctive* with a fresh spirituous* life.

It is the job of the copy editor to remove these blunders, and to look for all the inconsistencies which you have

---

* Yes, this is wrong, too.

missed. And you have always missed some. He will write little notes to you, telling you: 'On page 128 Carla had black hair. On page 313 you say that Carla combed out her blond curls. When did she go to the hairdresser?' Or he will say, 'On page 8 Hegel is called a follower of Kant, and on page 88 a supplanter of Kant: which shall we print?' It is very painful to have one's own book gone over by these sharp, critical eyes. If the copy editor (as sometimes happens) is imperfectly educated or pedantically inclined, your book will have a bad time. But if he is efficient, as he usually is, then you will find his questions exhausting but healthful, like a Turkish bath.

The third expert is the editor. He has a very difficult job indeed. He has to advise you to how to improve your own work, not only in matters of spelling and grammar, but essentially and formally in its shape and in its content. Of course, if your work has been decently planned and written, and if you yourself have gone over it again and again with a really critical eye, then the editor may never appear. (Several authors whom I know, both in fiction and in nonfiction, see their 'editors' only at the party which celebrates the publication of their newest book; and they prefer that distant relationship. As one of them said to me, 'Why should a happily married man need a marriage counselor?') But if you are inexperienced — and particularly if you have written a long autobiographical novel — you will probably need an editor.

I read many scores of books every year, and I find something good and genuine in nearly every one of them. But again and again I am disappointed by shapelessness and carelessness and repetitiousness in a book, far more than by weakness and lack of vitality. This means that the author had energy and experience and was trying to make his book into something durable; but that the book was poorly planned and poorly edited. A good editor can make a book. Even a poor editor can scarcely ruin a good book; but he may delay its success.

However, you may be lucky: you may strike a good editor, conscientious and wise. What is the next stage? How is your book transferred to print and converted into a bound volume?

Up to this point your book is still in typescript. By now it is beginning to look rather terrible, for the pages, once clean and white and smooth, are covered with smudges and pencil notations and ink marks, some intelligible to you and some not. Don't worry. This is the professional look, like the darned stockings of the prima ballerina, the broken nails of the virtuoso pianist. At last, you say good-by to it, and it goes off to the printer.

The printer is usually (though not always) a specialist who operates quite apart from the publisher. Often he has his premises hundreds of miles away from the publisher's office, in a different state. He is like the man who makes textiles and sells them by the roll; the publisher is like the man who creates curtains or dresses or neckties out of the textile fabrics. Every publisher has his favorite printer. All the time that you were having your book edited and corrected, the designer of your particular publisher was looking over the different styles of type, makes of paper, and shades of ink which were available and which would best combine into an artistic whole. Some publishers pay a great deal of attention to these matters, others do not care. Some produce books which look as though they had been made out of last year's newspapers. If a book is cheap and vulgar, perhaps its appearance ought to be cheap and its type ought to be coarse; yet it is still an insult to the reader to tell him that he is an insensitive oaf to buy a volume so miserably printed and produced.

Your book is transferred to print by three or four expert printers working with big intricate machines, each the size of a normal bedroom and costing many thousands of dollars. They sit at a keyboard like a large complex typewriter, and type out your book. As they type, the letters which will make the printed page form themselves into lines and drop into place and are marshaled mechanically into long columns called 'galleys.' One of the pleasantest things about having a book published is to see the names of the separate experts who have been helping to produce it. My wife once picked them out. When she got the proofs of one of her novels, she saw, from the notations at the top of the galleys, that it has been transferred to print by two experts, Mr. Brevig and Mr. De Feo. Because they had done such a splendid job, she wrote them individual letters and sent them copies of her book; they were surprised but delighted.

The next stage is that your book returns to you again. Now you see it in print for the first time. Usually it is not in pages, but in long strips of paper two to three feet long. Each of them is a galley proof; it contains imprints of all the type that could be fitted into one tray. Your job is to read the book in this form, line for line, word for word, letter for letter, and to correct any mistakes made by the printer, or — although in theory there should be none — by yourself. If you make big changes, which mean that the printer will have to do a great deal of work in pulling out discarded sections of type and setting new type, then you will have to pay the cost yourself. Some authors prefer to do this, because they cannot see their work clearly until they get it in printed form. For instance, Sir Winston Churchill always has his books set up in print, and then starts slashing and jabbing at them, slicing out big sections and squeezing in new material until some chapters are almost rewritten. One of his publishers (Mr. Edward Dodd, of Dodd, Mead) remarked that this must be expensive. He replied, 'Everything I do is expensive!'

Correcting proofs is never much fun. To read your own book over in print for the first time is of course delightful, even on those long strips that look like Tibetan prayer flags; but to read it over several times, finding trivial misspellings and annoying repetitions at every reading, can be pretty painful. Yet it is only by doing this that you will improve your book, and remove blunders which otherwise will be perpetuated.

The chief difficulty in doing this is very simple. It is that as soon as you start getting really interested in the chapter you are correcting, you read on and on more and more smoothly, and follow the story or the argument, and so miss a dozen little slips and omissions. To avoid this, you must *slow up*. You must — however hard it may seem — treat your book as though it had been written by someone else and turned over to you for revision. And even then. . . . The most painstaking jobs of proof correcting I have ever seen were done by two distinguished scholars: Mr. David Magie of Princeton and Mr. Werner Jaeger of Harvard. Mr. Magie showed me the proofs of his great book on the Roman dominion in Asia Minor. Of course all the text had been carefully read and reread, but — since figures are more subject to error than words — every single digit in every single number had been ticked once in red pencil, when it was verified, and once in blue pencil, when it was cross checked. When I saw Mr. Jaeger last, he was correcting the proofs of his edition of the Greek divine St. Gregory of Nyssa. Greek is a fairly difficult language, with many apostrophes and accents which must be got right. Mr. Jaeger was reading every line *backwards,* so that he could check each letter individually.

After this job is finished you send your book back to the publisher again, and he forwards it to the printer.

The printer begins by making the corrections you have indicated. Then he takes the long trays of type and breaks them up into smaller blocks, each the size of a page. He makes sure that the balance of each page is right — for instance, the page must not begin with half a line overlapping from the end of a paragraph, because that looks silly. He adds the page headings and the page numbers and inserts the footnotes in the right places, and so on. Then, on a huge, perfectly smooth, perfectly flat steel table, he arranges the pages into groups of sixteen, or thirty-two, or even sixty-four pages, inside a huge frame called a form. He packs them in tightly, with strips and wedges of metal and wood, so as to hold them absolutely firm; he looks the whole thing over to see that the blank spaces — which will be the margins of each page — are even; then he fastens the frame so tightly that (in theory) not a single letter, or comma, or dot, can possibly fall out or even shift its position. This big pattern of, say, sixty-four pages can all be printed at once on a single big sheet of paper. The printer's job is to arrange the pages so that, after the big sheet is printed, it can be folded and refolded down to the size of an ordinary book, and still have consecutive pages come out next to each other. (On one system pages 1, 16, 17, and 32 are horizontally next to one another, and vertically opposite to pages 8, 9, 24, and 25.)

Now your work is in pages, and it comes back to you looking like a rather shabby book, smudgy and unbound, but still shaped like a book.

Next you correct the proofs *once again,* making sure that all the corrections you put in last time were made, and that no new errors have crept in. If you have to make any large changes at this point, you will infuriate the printer and cost yourself a good deal of money. It is easy to see why. Your book is now set up in pages. Suppose you cut out a sentence from one page, because it seems repetitious. The sentence is three lines long. Unless you write in another sentence exactly three lines long, the printer is going to have to break up and readjust the page which you have now mutilated, and he is also going to have to rearrange the three, or even seven, other pages which come next to it in the big framework called the form. This takes time. This costs cash. A skilled printer is paid a minimum of $2.70 an hour, which is rather more than all but the most highly skilled authors get for their work. Therefore, unless you see any absolutely monumental boner sticking out of your book at this point, you will try to avoid changing more than a few letters, or removing any word unless you replace it by a word of the same length.

At this point you have still another unpleasant task to perform, if you are not a writer of fiction. Every book of nonfiction needs an index. Only the author can make a really good index, because only the author knows all the things in his book which he considers important. That means you. Therefore, with a heavy sigh, you obtain several hundred 3″ x 5″ cards, and start working through your book, page by page, writing down each important name or subject on a separate card, keeping the cards in alphabetical order, and adding entries for every page on which each name or subject is mentioned. This takes weeks. By the time the job is completed, you are heartily sick of your book and wish never to see it again. You have read every single word of it so often that you are apt to think it was a ridiculous idea to write the book in the first place; and now, when it is too late to do anything about it, you see all the horrifying omissions which are irrevocable. And yet, indexes are so valuable to the reader, they are such an es-

sential part of every nonfiction book, that they are inescapable Musts. You simply go on and on and on, reading every page and filling up the little cards. When you
reach the end, all you have to do is to transfer all the
figures from the cards to a set of typed pages, and send
these to the printer together with his page proofs. Your
work is over. You vow never to write another book as long
as you live.

Now there is a pause.

If your book has finally left your hands in March, it
will probably not be published until September. This will
surprise you, but it is natural enough. Every author would
like to have copies of his work in the bookstores on the
first day when it can be bound up and jacketed; but that
would not be wise. The United States is an enormous
country. Books must be sold in every one of the forty-eight
states (although some buy much fewer books than others);
and in order to make the maximum impact a new book
must be published all over the country on the same day.
Therefore the publisher must have nearly two months in
hand, in order to let his shipments cross the country and
reach distant states. And furthermore, all the book reviewers must get a chance to review the book on the day
of publication. Some of them work as much as six weeks
ahead — for instance, on monthly magazines such as
Harper's Magazine. Therefore they must get copies of
every new book about two months before the book is due
to appear. And obviously there are good and bad seasons
for publishing books. The publishers know these seasons
— or are supposed to know them. It would not be terribly
judicious to bring out a large book of reproductions of
Botticelli's paintings priced at forty-five dollars, on the
black fifteenth, income-tax day. Light novels go well in

summer. Cookery books go well in the fall, and so on. Therefore the publisher has to arrange to publish your book at a time when it will give full opportunity to the critics to consider it, the bookstores to stock it, and the public to think of buying it.

At some time during the waiting period, you actually get some copies of your book from the publisher. Usually he sends you six copies, free. These are your perquisites; you keep two of them for yourself, and give the other four to your nearest and dearest.

Yes, but thereafter you find that you have a long list of friends and acquaintances who ought to get gift copies. There are a dozen of them, thirty of them, fifty of them, scores and scores of them, an address book full of them, worse than sending Christmas cards; you go over the list and, like Macbeth in the witches' cavern, cry, 'What! will the line stretch out to the crack of doom?' However, at last you reduce it to a reasonable number. You send the names and addresses of your friends who expect to receive copies to the publisher. You ask him to send out a copy of your new book to each of them, 'with your compliments,' and to charge you with the cost of the book and the postage, to be deducted from your royalties, if any. He agrees. He doesn't mind; he likes distributing his books; but it costs you good money, which is somehow seldom recognized. Out of every fifty people to whom you send your book, three write to thank you.

And now it is all over. There is nothing to do but wait. Weeks pass, during which you feel like the parent separated from the new baby by a set of hospital regulations, permitted to see it now and then through a glass partition, but not to touch it or get on friendly terms with it. No doubt it will emerge from confinement one of these days, with its birth certificate tied around its neck and its personality firmly developed, but then it will be something different — not the you, or the projection of you, which you had tried to create.

One day in September your book is released; or rather, it is published. Strange that you feel so numb. The hue of the daylight ought to have changed, but it has not. Traffic runs and smells in the streets, just as before. People walk along, missing one another by hairbreadths, and concerned about their own affairs. If you are lucky and if your book is good, it may be reviewed on the day of publication. If not, a few days or weeks later. . . . In any case, you will bleed slowly and painfully as you read the reviews: how could they have misunderstood you so blatantly, how could they have picked out the one paragraph which you had intended to change in proof, is there any justice, any fairness, perhaps all critics really hate creative writers, anyhow they are all old, poor, and jealous — and with that you tear up the reviews and grind them down into the waste basket.

A week or two later, other reviews will come in. A month or two later, letters from your readers will come in. If they are not bitterly hostile, if they are even moderately friendly, you will begin to relax and to look at your book with something approaching kindness. Poor little monster, you say. It gave me a terrible time; how I suffered, it will never know; and yet now it is almost worth it; there are others who admire it; this is not merely the fondness of a parent; bless every page, every paragraph, every line of it; and if you are sentimental, you pick up the book, and heap kisses on it, all warm and damp and wriggling as it is. Then, for the first time, it opens its pages to you with genuine trust and affection. You handle it with the confidence of a true parent. And, just before you put it away on the shelf definitely and forever, you can say, 'There, I have given birth to a book.'

But then, just as you feel calm, relaxed, rewarded, fulfilled, a little voice whispers in your inner ear, 'Now, how about the next one?'

The face in the mirror

———————————

THEY say that every man and every woman has one
book inside him or her. Some have more, but everybody
has at least one. This is a volume of autobiography. We
have all been talked almost to death by bores who attached
themselves to us in a club car or a ship's smoking room,
and insisted on giving us a play-by-play account of their
marital troubles, or their complete medical history. I once
met one who carried a set of his own x-rays. Yet even these
people might be interesting if they could tell the whole
truth. They are boring not because they talk about themselves, but because they talk about only one aspect of themselves, that phase of their lives which fascinates and worries
them personally. If they were really to tell us everything,
we should listen with amazement.

Most of us cannot tell the whole truth, or even the important parts of the truth. This is one reason why there are not many good autobiographies. People cannot, or will not, put down the facts. The wife of the philosopher Carlyle said that the story of her life, written down without falsification or disguise, would have been a priceless record for other women to read, but that 'decency forbade her to do any such thing.' Think how many millions of people have told secrets to their wives or husbands, to their psychiatrists, to their doctors, their lawyers, or their priests — secrets which they would rather die than see printed in a book and published under their own names. And the other reason for the dearth of readable autobiographies is simply that most people cannot write. Writing an interesting story, a fictional story, is difficult enough. Writing eloquently about oneself is still more difficult; it needs a style even more subtle and a finer sense of balance.

Apparently there are three kinds of autobiography: three different ways of telling the story of one's life. (We can leave out journals like Pepys's *Diary,* which was not meant to be published, and collections of letters, and disguised autobiographies, which so many modern novels are.)

The first group could all be issued under the same title. They could all be called 'What I Did.' They are essentially success stories. In them, a man who has achieved something of wide importance explains how he did it, what were the obstacles in his way, how they were overcome, and what was the effect on the world. Self-made men often write such books — or have such books written for them. There is a splendid one by Ben Franklin, and an equally good one by his English opposite number, William Cobbett: these are optimistic works, a good tonic for anyone who despairs of solving his own problems.

Sir Winston Churchill's six-volume work *The Second*

World War (published by Houghton Mifflin) is really an autobiographical record. He himself says it is 'the story as I knew and experienced it as Prime Minister and Minister of Defence of Great Britain.' Therefore it cannot be called anything like a complete history of the war. For example, Churchill tells the story of one of the crucial events of the war, one of the crucial events of this century — the reduction of Japan to impotence and surrender by intensive bombardment culminating in what he calls the 'casting' of two atomic bombs — in only eight pages, while a greater amount of wordage is devoted to a reprint of the broadcast which he made to British listeners on VE day.

A similar personalized history of the last twenty years is *The Secret Diary of Harold L. Ickes* (issued by Simon & Schuster). This is a view of the New Deal and of the war years, as experienced and interpreted by a single, rather lonely politician. It is not a traditional success story. Ickes was so fantastically vain and ambitious that he saw the world as a conspiracy designed to deprive him of his rights; he would scarcely have been content with anything less than the perpetual presidency of the entire solar system. Therefore he accepted, and recorded in his diary, every piece of flattery which was offered to him — however blatant or insincere — and, while freely and gladly delivering cruelly effective attacks on his rivals and enemies, he bitterly resented any personal slight to himself. There is one very funny chapter in the latest volume, in which Ickes explains why he stopped going to the Gridiron Club dinners in Washington. At the last one he attended, a reporter dressed up as Donald Duck caricatured Secretary Ickes: 'crowing like a rooster, he strutted and patted himself on the chest, and indicated by sound and action that evidently he thought that Secretary Ickes was the greatest man in the world.' Ickes goes on to comment, 'I have completely fooled myself if I give the impression to anyone that I am conceited and possess a feeling of superiority over other men.' Obviously he did give just that impression, and every entry in his diary confirms it; but he refuses to face the fact. On the very same page he describes Governor Thomas Dewey as 'a political streetwalker,' and similar delicacies occur throughout the book. Still, there is no doubt that Ickes conceived of himself as a champion fighting alone against tremendous odds, and for that reason his diary is a success story.

One instructive contrast between the autobiographies of Churchill and Ickes is in the matter of discretion. Churchill has often been charged with talking out of turn, and dropping rash remarks to provoke the opposition, but anyone who reads his book carefully will be surprised to see how much is tactfully omitted. For example, he spends a page on describing his meeting with King Ibn-Sa'ud just after Yalta. His account is full of vivid and interesting details — such as the fact that the king's cupbearer gave Churchill a glass of water from the sacred well at Mecca, 'the most delicious' (he says) 'that I had ever tasted' — and probably the first such drink he had had for a very long time. It is only when we reread the episode that we realize how discreet the old statesman has been: he has not said a single word about the purpose of the meeting, and not a single word about its results, although his book purports to be a history of the war. On the other hand, Ickes seems to have attended confidential meetings of the Cabinet and of other bodies, at which data of great importance and secrecy were given out, and then to have come straight home and dictated a verbatim report to his secretaries, who then typed it up and kept it in a folder. No doubt it was a relief for him to do so, and certainly it makes interesting reading now, but surely it was a shocking piece of indiscretion for a man in a position of confidence to betray everything to his employees, particularly secrets which were not his to keep or to disclose.

So much for the first type of autobiography: 'What I Did.' The second type might be called 'What I Saw.' Here the emphasis is not on the achievements of the narrator, but rather on the strange sights he saw and the strange experiences through which he lived. Most good books of exploration are like this. Both the book *Kon-Tiki* and the film were absorbingly interesting, not because the author was an unusual man, but because he could describe to us some unique adventures. We shall never cross New Guinea on foot, or spend a whole year alone with two companions on the Arctic ice, or climb Mount Everest; therefore we are delighted when a man who has done such a thing can tell us about it clearly — and modestly. The greatest of all such books in the English language is probably Doughty's *Travels in Arabia Deserta*. Some good adventure autobiographies have been written by ordinary soldiers and sailors. Many of our finest descriptions of the Napoleonic wars come from such books as the *Recollections of Rifleman Harris,* and there are similar documents from the American Civil War. Such also are the pathetic and marvelous books of reminiscence written by men and women who have survived long terms in prison. It would be virtually impossible for us to tell how the German and Russian prison camps worked, if we did not possess such books as Christopher Burney's *Dungeon Democracy,* Tadeusz Wittlin's *A Reluctant Traveller in Russia,* Seweryna Szmaglewska's *Smoke Over Birkenau,* and Odd Nansen's *From Day to Day.* Finally, a great deal of social history is best conveyed through autobiography. At or near the top of the ladder there is a rather snobbish but delightfully written work by Sir Osbert Sitwell, in five volumes, which came out at intervals during the last decade, and which he himself describes as 'a portrait of an age and person.' At the bottom of the ladder, there is a painful but unforgettable description of the life of tramps and outcasts by George Orwell, called *Down and Out in Paris and London*. What Orwell tells us about the filth and calculated vileness of the kitchens in smart Parisian restaurants (where he himself worked as a dishwasher) is enough to sicken the strongest stomach, and I know that I personally have never enjoyed a meal in Paris since I read his book. One paragraph about the handling of food in the smart hotel kitchens ends, 'Roughly speaking, the more one pays for food [in Paris], the more sweat and spittle one is obliged to eat with it.' A good book of this kind has a perfectly unequaled impact: if its author can write at all, it is very hard to forget what he says.

Then there is a third kind of autobiography. It does not describe 'What I Did,' or 'What I Saw,' but 'What I Felt,' 'What I Endured.' These are the books of inner adventure. In them there is achievement, yes, but it is a struggle and a victory within the spirit. In them there are dangerous explorations, and the discovery of unknown worlds, but the explorer is making his way through the jungles of the soul. Such are the books of failure, disaster, and regeneration which are now so popular: for example, Lillian Roth's *I'll Cry Tomorrow*, which tells how a woman wrecked her life with drink and then rebuilt it. Such also are the books which describe one of the most dangerous of all adventures: the process of growing up. My own favorite among them is Edward Gibbon's autobiography, partly because it is unconsciously funny. More famous perhaps are the self-studies of John Stuart Mill,

Herbert Spencer, and Henry Adams — all of which seem to me excruciatingly pompous and dull. There is also an exquisite little book, now out of print and very hard to procure, which tells how a little boy brought up in a sternly intellectual and narrowly religious family fought his way out and remade his character. This is *Father and Son,* by Edmund Gosse. I wish it could be reprinted. It is both very sad and very amusing. The famous records of religious suffering and conversion could all be subtitled 'What I Felt': the *Confessions* of St. Augustine, the journals of John Bunyan and of the first Quaker, George Fox. And many of the most famous autobiographers have concentrated on reporting the events which happened during their lifetime, not as objective facts, but simply as occurrences which impinged upon their own personalities: in books like the reminiscences of Benvenuto Cellini, of Rousseau, of Boswell, Yeats, and André Gide, we see the world as in an elaborate distorting mirror.

'What I Did,' 'What I Saw,' 'What I Felt.' . . . Really, it is difficult to make a sharp division between the three types of autobiographical writing. The emphasis in one book is more toward reporting of external happenings, in another toward self-analysis, but a man can scarcely describe what he did without also letting us know what he felt and saw. Even the most egoistic of men, like St. Augustine and James Boswell, do from time to time give us valuable information about their outer as well as their inner worlds. The most interesting of these books give us something of all three kinds of experience. For a time, while we read them, it is possible to enjoy one of the rarest artistic pleasures — complete escape: escape into another sphere of action and perception. From that escape we return — with what relief! — to the real center of the universe, which is our own self.

I married an author

———————————

I HAVE the honor, and the pleasure, of being married
to an author. My wife has written no less than nine novels,
which have all been published, have sold hundreds of
thousands of copies, and are still in demand. It would be
wrong for me to try to appraise them, so I shall say nothing about their style, their characterization, and their plots
— except that I personally enjoy them very much and
frequently reread them. What I can describe without offense is the unusual experience of having a professional
author in one's home. It is very pleasant, most of the time,
but it *is* peculiar.

In fact, the whole thing came, and still comes, as a colossal surprise to both of us. When we got married, my
wife had done some writing, but she had never had any-

thing published. I was the purveyor of fiction, having published quite a lot of poetry and several short stories; and we rather expected that I would continue with what they call 'creative writing.' Instead, I got more and more absorbed in scholarship and in teaching (research and teaching are not one profession, but two; they often conflict; and it is pretty hard to learn them both at the same time) until I virtually gave up imaginative writing altogether. My wife collaborated with me on producing two long translations from German into English; indeed, she taught me what Mr. Sherlock Holmes calls that unmusical but expressive language, German. But for a time we were so busy with bringing up our son and moving to the United States and establishing new routines of work and housekeeping, and so forth, that neither of us had much time to think about original writing. And then — much to my surprise, much to the surprise of most of our friends, and (I think) rather to her own surprise — my wife suddenly produced a highly imaginative novel. This was in the winter of 1940–41. I had been working rather hard at Columbia; we had been out at summer school in one of the western state universities, where I made the ridiculous mistake of offering a brand-new course on a subject I had never tackled before and writing the lectures as I went along, day by day: so that, sitting at the desk every evening and plowing away, I had — I confess it — paid the minimum of attention to my poor wife. Meanwhile, she was sitting on the couch nearly every evening with a growing pile of pencil-written manuscript beside her. After some months, she stopped twisting her back hair round her index finger, drew a firm line on the paper, and said with a sigh of relief, 'There. That's done. Would you like to read it?' In a rather vague way, I said, 'Yes, of course.' I started to read several hundred pages in her fine clear handwriting — and was unable to stop until half past two in the morning, when I had come to the final page.

That was a surprise I still remember. It was less of a surprise that, when my wife sent the book to a literary agent, the agent was able to place it at once with a reputable publisher; but it was a surprise again some months later, when it appeared in print and immediately jumped onto the best-seller list. Meanwhile, I had been given leave by Columbia and was engaged in war service; so, partly to relieve the monotony and partly to divert herself from worrying about the possible fate of her first novel, my wife started a second — which was to surprise us all even more by being bigger, more original, and more solidly successful than the first.

If I have used the word 'surprise' rather often, you can see why. It is awfully odd to think you know someone — after all, I had been engaged and married to the woman for fifteen years before she suddenly up and presented me with a novel — to think you know someone well, and then to discover in her or in him entirely new and unsuspected abilities. What would you feel if your husband came home one day and told you that Knoedler was giving a one-man show of portraits he had painted during his lunch hour; or if your wife invited you, without warning, to hear the first performance of her Passacaglia for Strings in F minor, played by the Little Orchestra Society?

And then imagine if that kind of thing continued. This is another aspect of the general feeling of astonishment which still possesses me. Of my wife's nine books, all are different. Not one is repetitive. All have different settings, ranging all the way from Poland to Wyoming, from Edinburgh to San Francisco. All are different in tone: two are so sad that they leave me always with a heavy heart, others are full of suspense, and one is unashamedly comical. It is really very curious indeed for me to see my own wife sitting meditating peacefully, and twisting her hair, and gradually beginning to write, and filling page after page until a big pile of handwritten manuscript has grown up beside her — and yet not to know anything, scarcely even to be able to guess anything about the new book; to wonder where it will be set, what kind of a story it will be (perhaps a historical novel this time? perhaps an exploration of the future? a social comedy, or a tale of suspense?); and to go on wondering, until she looks up and says — still, even now, rather diffidently — 'It's finished. Would you like to read it?' The few hours after that always provide the biggest surprise of all. As I read, I look up at her from time to time, and think (or even say), 'How on earth did you ever dream this up?'

Another fascinating thing about being married to an author is to watch how she works. (That is one of the most interesting things about all creative people, not only artists, but scientific discoverers, scholars, statesmen; and it is one of the things usually treated with inexcusable inadequacy in their biographies. No biography of any intellectual worker is complete unless it contains a careful study of his hours of work, his absences, his methods of concentration, his peculiar techniques, even down to his habits of keeping notes for future work and answering correspondence.) One experience I shall always remember is this. After my wife started her third novel, I attempted to explain to her that she was using the wrong method. Quite patiently and kindly, I showed her that it would be far easier and more logical if she first made a skeleton outline of her plot, wrote out 3" x 5" cards for the main characters, then broke the whole thing down into individual chapters and planned them out as separate units, so that she could, if she liked, write ten pages regularly every day and count on finishing the novel in six weeks. She listened. She smiled very charmingly. She said something like this: 'That sounds wonderful, but it would be a little difficult for me. I think just at present I'll go on as I've been doing, telling myself a story and writing it down as I tell it.'

After a year or two, I began to realize she was right. Most nonfiction must be planned out ahead, in the same detail as that with which an architect designs a building. Fiction and poetry, and probably music, can scarcely ever be planned. As the creation is being carried on, or after it has been virtually completed, the material must fit itself into a plan; and of course there must be an original concept: no one starts out to compose music without knowing whether he is going to write a five-minute nocturne or a fifty-minute symphony; but the difficulty and the fascination of imaginative creation lie in the fact that the material, as it emerges from the subconscious, does very largely dictate its own form. Ever since I realized this, I have appreciated creative work much better, and I realized it first while watching my wife writing her novels.

People often ask my wife and myself if we help each other. The answer is that of course we do — simply by being there. I sit and write at the desk, and she sits and writes on the couch; we put on the records, or we turn on the musical programs, which we like best (Haydn quartets are excellent, and so are Ravel's piano works); now and again we look up and exchange glances; and if that isn't helping each other, what is? But I can never offer any more concrete help than that, until she has completed a book. I don't even know her subject or her setting, so it would be quite impossible; it would be like saying to a composer, 'Put in a little allegretto passage in D flat minor,' when you didn't even know his theme. My wife occasionally suggests subjects for these essays — although, needless to say, not for this one. She never suggests subjects for my books, such as they are; nor I for hers. That is the only possible way to ensure independence.

But after a book has been finished by either of us, then we each can and do help the other. We do not, we cannot suggest major changes, such as altering a plot, adding a chapter, enlarging an area of criticism; still, we do read each other's work very carefully for style, for accuracy, and for congruity of detail. Helen will say to me, 'You have never explained this about the life of Catullus, and I can't understand it; you need another paragraph at this point.' I sometimes say to her, 'The action here is very quick, almost bewildering; could you put in a sentence saying how long the whole operation lasted, ten minutes or half an hour?' Yet most of our mutual aid program is confined to what the publishers call copyreading — in particular, to watching for repetitions. Every author repeats himself. He repeats his own thoughts because he thinks they are important. He repeats certain words because they fascinate him, often unconsciously. (You know how Hemingway puts in phrases like 'He felt good' again and again.) Usually the copy editor, a quiet little man with a pipe and a dictionary and a copy of Fowler, sitting in the back of the publisher's office, eradicates the repetitions before the manuscript reaches the printer. My wife and I help each other principally by eradicating them before the manuscript goes to the publisher.

The next stage is the worst of all. This is the stage when the printer sends back the proofs of the book: long strips of paper, each containing the equivalent of three or four normal pages. These have to be read and corrected, not only line by line, but word by word, and in fact letter by letter. My wife does this tedious job dutifully and accurately, but without enthusiasm — rather in the same way as if she were darning a sock, or, no, mending a prized old tablecloth. She usually says to me that the only time a book is really finished is when she remembers every sentence of it so intimately that, if the entire novel were destroyed, she could restore it, word for word.

After the proofreading, some weeks pass. The author whom I had the good fortune to marry sometimes looks at me a little disconsolately, as though she had sent off a message to outer space, and were beginning to despair of getting a reply. Nothing is heard from the publisher, except faint hoots and toots from the advertising department. Nothing is heard from the printer, except a continuous muffled rumble, which may be either human or mechanical or both. And then, one enchanted morning, a large parcel arrives, with my wife's name on it. She tears it open, upsetting a cup of coffee. It contains six copies of her latest book. With a charming smile, she presents one to me. I open it, and begin to read — and once again I realize the fact that, of all the avocations open to intelligent people, one of the most delightful is writing; and the next most delightful is reading a book.

Compulsory reading

EVERY now and then, at a party, you meet someone who tells you about a book she has just read. She describes its tremendous reception and the growing fame of its author. Finally, in a tone of friendly authority, she says 'You *must* read it. Do remember its title, now, and don't forget. You *must* read it.'

At once your stomach — assisted by the canapés — turns. You thank her civilly. You fix the name of the book in your memory. You resolve never, never on any account, to read it.

Yet it might have been quite a good book. She explained how important it was. What made you feel it must be revolting? Was the evidence in its favor inadequate? No. The evidence was fairly sound. But you were biased against the book simply because someone told you that you must *must* MUST read it.

We have all felt this. It goes back to the days when we were in school, when we were told that we were obliged to read some book about which we usually knew nothing, nothing whatever, except that it was a Must. Now, there are some people who naturally hate reading because of some psycho-physical quirk in their make-up: they live through their hands, they can hit a ball anywhere or fix anything, but they are made dizzy by looking at print on paper. Still, such people are few. Most people can read, most people like to read; yet many of them are discouraged from reading, in school. Surely that is worse than a blunder: it is a crime. Reading, for most people, is a natural pleasure. They would enjoy it without any suspicion or reluctance — in fact, it would be difficult to keep them away from it. But compulsion does so: for some, completely; for all, partially.

Surely, if we wanted to make boys disgusted with baseball, one very good way would be to institute baseball classes in every school, to make baseball efficiency compulsory for graduation, to set up baseball curricula and baseball quizzes and baseball Regents' Examinations, to distribute lists of baseball facts which had to be learned off by heart and interpretations of baseball trends which had to be discussed, to work out long courses in pitching, catching, fielding, and strategy, to treat the entire game as something deadly systematic and deadly serious, and to build it up as a painful dedicated occupation leading to a Ph.D. degree. Of course, a few noble souls would take it all in, and stay with it; the others would be sickened of baseball, and never think of it again for the rest of their lives.

However, it is not only the repellent force of compulsion that makes the young disgusted with the books they are forced to read. Partly it is the quality of the books. They are often bad.

The other day, one of my friends showed me a book of modern Spanish short stories which he was expected to use in teaching Spanish. I read some of them. It would be a compliment to call them mediocre. Any sensitive boy or girl who read them would be forced to conclude that Spain had no modern literature worth a *caramba,* that Spanish was not worth learning for its own sake, and that his or her teachers were tasteless idiots. It is often the same in English literature. A month of my life at the age of fifteen or sixteen was blighted by one of the books of that distinguished bore, George Eliot. *The Mill on the Floss,* I think it was: a decent enough little work for its time, but now utterly without relevance or distinction. They tell me that some schools are still plagued by another work of that obsolete author (or authoress), called *Silas Marner.* It is the same in other tongues. My wife still speaks with horror of the endless tedium of Balzac's social-documentary novels, which she was compelled to read when studying French in school. I myself like Latin; but all the time my classmates were reading the works of Caesar in Latin, I (having read them the night before) was working through Victor Hugo in French, under the desk. A dashed good book, too, *The Toilers of the Sea.* But I was detected. The schoolmaster saw that something must be wrong. Instead of looking as consumedly bored as the other members of the class, I was actually showing signs of interest. No wonder. I was not reading about Caesar building a bridge across the Rhine. I was reading about a diver being attacked in a submarine cave by a gigantic octopus: *la Pieuvre!*

But how about the plays of Shakespeare? Surely they are different. I enjoyed the plays of Shakespeare, even at school, even under compulsion. So did most of us. We talked about them. We went downtown to see an amateur performance of *The Merchant of Venice,* and talked about that. And then there were a few other books which, even although obligatory, did not appear boring. We did penetrate to their value.

It is the same in other countries. We do not hear that French schoolboys object bitterly to reading Molière and Racine; that German boys despise Goethe when they are directed to study *Faust;* that the Italian youngsters think it is a waste of time when they begin Dante. They may kick at other compulsory books; but at those, no. On the whole, the young will read good books even if they are made compulsory, while they will object bitterly to reading inferior or obsolete books under the slightest degree of obligation.

Now, why is this? Is all compulsion hopeless in leading boys and girls to read? Or are there some books which ought to be compulsory, and can be made compulsory without creating permanent disgust? If so, what are they? Are there any methods of urging boys and girls to read which will gradually dispense with compulsion — in fact, change external pressure into self-perpetuating interest? Surely there must be some way of getting the young to read, without using Chinese tortures on them. Bribery, perhaps? No. A friend of mine recently told me that he paid his daughter ten dollars to read Walter Scott's *Ivanhoe.* Half way through she came and offered to return him five dollars if he would not make her finish the book. You see, bribery is expensive, and it does not work. There must be some other methods.

The first essential, it seems to me, is to choose books

which are not only good, but appealing: books which are authoritative, books which are already partly known, partly 'sold' to the young. Boys and girls have very narrow horizons. They know few books; they know few authors. Therefore it is no good giving them something remote and obsolete. They have never heard of George Eliot. Most of them have never even heard of T. S. Eliot (if you can imagine such a thing). The bright ones may care about T. S. None of them will care about George, and there is no real reason why they should. If they are to be interested in literature, they must be given *either* something by an absolutely first-rate writer, *or else* something by an author who is close to them in time and in interest. They will not reject Shakespeare. They will not reject Ernest Hemingway. With the one, they will know they are reading something of almost universal appeal. With the other, they will know that they are reading a lively and energetic contemporary. Most of them are not going to be professional students of literature. They will never write Ph.D. theses on 'The development of social consciousness in the nineteenth-century English novel as illustrated by George Eliot.' But Shakespeare will always be playing somewhere — on the stage, in motion pictures, or in other media; and every lively youngster will enjoy meeting the Nobel Prize winners of his own generation and his own country.

Then the second essential in this kind of reading is to encourage criticism. Many young people, at school and at college, are given books called The Classics, and are merely told to read them, as though they were expected to admire every single word in them. This is a mistake. No books are perfect. I remember still what a revelation it was to me at school when the master who taught us English literature poured scorn on Shakespeare's vulgar and corny jokes: those terrible puns, those cheap witticisms about sex —

true marks (he told us) of the brilliant but half-educated man catering to the groundlings. We were relieved to know that we did not *have* to laugh. But then (he went on), then the play of fancy when Shakespeare really gets off the ground, as in the Queen Mab speech in *Romeo and Juliet,* ah, *there.* . . . Thus we were taught to distinguish, even in the work of a great writer, between bad and good. A valuable lesson.

In the same way, I suffered a good deal from Walter Scott, and a certain amount from Charles Dickens. I ought to have been told the obvious facts, which I know now — that Scott was writing in a tearing hurry in order to make money, and often obeying conventions for which he did not particularly care; but that when he wrote what he liked best, battle scenes and moments of tense drama and bold speeches by peasants and simple folk, he was a great imaginative writer. Dickens's more complicated plots worried me to death, although *Oliver Twist* gripped me then as it grips me to this day. I should have been told that Dickens wrote them not as books, but as serials for magazines, and therefore committed faults of construction which I would have to overlook. A few hints like that would have made me ignore the bad parts of such books, and appreciate the good parts much more sincerely.

The third essential in encouraging the young to read is to explain, to analyze, to dissect without killing. Young men and women, boys and girls, are short-sighted. They cannot without guidance carry a whole book in their head, so as to see its structure and its entire meaning. Listen to them describing a motion picture — you will hear that they do it all in sequence: 'And then she comes in, and she has a gun, and he takes it out of her pocket while he's kissing her, but she doesn't know that, and then the light suddenly goes out and the door opens. . . .' They seem to have very little idea that anyone wrote the entire picture as a single work with a plan — what Hollywood calls 'continuity.' Therefore, one of the things best worth teaching them is to see a piece of history, or a motion picture, or a book, or the plan of their own lives, as a large continuous whole, with a structure which can be taken in by the mind and analyzed.

But it is useless simply to tell youngsters to read A Book. It is like telling them to go away and live for A Year. They should be told what to expect — week by week, section by section; they should be shown how to break down a big work into smaller parts, how to appreciate each part, and how to admire the skill with which the parts grow together into a single work of art. I am still grateful to the man who made me read Shakespeare's *Julius Caesar* when I was sixteen or so. I had scarcely even realized that all the men in the play were different, until he made me analyze the characters of Brutus and Cassius and Mark Antony, and how to find out — from their speeches alone — what made them tick. I had scarcely even realized that the play (and every play) had a measured movement, until he showed me how each act said something different in quality from all the others. At the end of that class, I not only understood the play of *Julius Caesar* better; I knew more about Shakespeare, I knew a little about the theater, and I was beginning to take an interest in psychology.

These are lessons which I have never forgotten. I have been trying to improve on them ever since.

Perhaps the lessons began with a little of the stick; but they ended with a delicious and nourishing carrot. And that is one of the main secrets of education — to hint at the stick, but to make sure the carrot is juicy. In the Book of Proverbs there is a fine poem in which Wisdom speaks to mankind. She does not say she is compulsory. She says she is attractive and valuable:

> Receive my instruction, and not silver; and knowledge rather than choice gold. For wisdom is better than rubies; and all the things that may be desired are not to be compared to it.

Criticoses

E VERY occupation moulds those who engage in it. You may recall that one of the first books written by Sherlock Holmes was 'a curious little work upon the influence of a trade upon the form of the hand, with lithotypes of the hands of slaters, sailors, cork-cutters, compositors, weavers, and diamond-polishers.' And so also every occupation has its characteristic diseases. Divers get the bends. Waiters suffer from flat feet — and deafness too, very often. Boxers are apt to become punch-drunk; sopranos suffer from delusions of grandeur; and so forth.

I have been a literary critic for quite a number of years now, and I am beginning to realize that people who read books in order to review them have their own set of occupational diseases. If there were only one of them, I might name it after myself, and join the proud ranks of Mr. Graves (the eponym of exophthalmic goiter), Mr. Parkinson, and Mr. Hansen. But there are quite a number of different ailments to which literary critics are subject, not all infecting the same person at the same time: so let us be simple and call them *criticoses*. (*Occasional* literary critics suffer from others: they have minor obsessions, repetition, and even glossolalia; but *permanent,* professional critics have criticoses.)

The first and commonest of these diseases, so widespread that it might be called endemic in every literate country, is *abulia*. Abulia means the inability to decide. It is induced by the fact that so many books are published every week. The average reader never sees or hears of most of them. The professional critic both hears of them and has to go over them and think about them. If you want to know something of what he suffers, open *The New York Times* on any average day, turn to the book review page, and there run through the 'List of Books Published Today.' You will see that there are ten, or twenty, or thirty, or sometimes fifty. All are no doubt worthy books, all the product of intensive effort on the part of authors, printers, and publishers, all demanding notice. What is the critic to do with them? When I was the literary critic for *Harper's Magazine,* I remember I used to go down to the office every Monday morning. A special table was kept for the books which came in for review. It was cleared every Monday; and by the next Monday it was full again, with anything from forty to a hundred books, sometimes more. I think I could have written a reasonable piece of literary criticism about any three of them, picked almost at random; but how about the other thirty-seven, or ninety-seven? Occasionally I felt the numbness of abulia coming over me, and I thought I detected it in other critics. It is the absolute inability to choose any one book out of a huge undifferentiated pile. The medieval philosopher Jean Buridan held that the will was entirely subject to the intellect (I wish that were true, don't you?); therefore his opponents reduced his doctrine to absurdity by making up the puzzle of Buridan's Donkey. They said that, according to his theory, a hungry donkey placed at absolutely equal distances from two bundles of hay of absolutely equal size would be bound to starve to death, since there was nothing to determine its will, nothing which its intellect could perceive as impelling it to the right rather than the left, the left rather than the right. It is convincing, isn't it? and yet Buridan was not wholly wrong. That is why the book publishers produce seductive book jackets to attract slightly bemused readers; and the cheaper the book, the livelier the jacket.

A second criticosis which really does affect me is *paronomasia*. This is confusion of names. For a long time I was not sure whether Antoine de Saint-Exupéry was a medieval painter, a modern balloonist, or a new way of preparing wild duck. The names of picaresque novels worried me terribly: I used to wake up saying, 'What Makes Sammy Run? What Makes Augie March? What Makes Saul Bellow?' It takes me a little leisure, and a little thought, and a little card-index, to distinguish between Vincent Sheean, Fulton Sheen, O'Casey Sheen, and Françoise (*Bonjour Jeunesse*) Shayan. Is it C.S. Hornblower who writes about Commodore Forester, or vice versa? It is not really possible for any critic to cure paronomasia: it is up to the authors and the publishers. Any author who wants to be remembered should choose a good name, preferably ending in k, like Kodak: Ruark, Burdick, Wouk: these imprint themselves on the memory.

Then there is a third critical disease. This seems to affect the reviewers of plays, motion pictures, and radio and TV, even worse than book reviewers. It is *acedia,* or not giving a hoot — not believing a single thing you see on the screen, on the stage, or within the pages of a book. It is the ailment of thinking that it is all cheap contrivance, worked out not by imaginative writers who are eager to offer a new vision of human life, but by hacks who merely write the Cinderella story over and over again, or at best repeat their own first work in slightly different periods and settings. I remember the first time this disease affected me. I was reading a long and elaborately constructed novel by a distinguished Southern lady. Its hero was introduced walking down the levee, on his way to a plantation he had just bought. He was tall. He was distinguished. He was rich. He was terribly handsome. He was beautifully dressed (his costume was described in detail, and authenticated in notes at the end of the book). His manner — ah, his manner was that of a man who had lived through grave ordeals and had (to coin a phrase) been hardened in the fiery crucible of life; and yet he was exquisitely, almost superhumanly well bred. And, do you know? he turned out to be a *gambler,* a *Mississippi River gambler* who had retired from his profession. Suddenly, just at that moment, I found myself unable to read a single page further. I put the book down and fell into a fine sound sleep. When I woke up fourteen hours later, I was healthy, cheerful, free from malaise or migraine — only, I couldn't read any more of that novel, or indeed of any book of fiction. It took me more than a week of dieting and exercise, devoted to the solid and substantial

products of the Bollingen Series, before I was fully recovered; and even then I ventured back into fiction only
with the greatest precautions, testing every step and every
handhold, and firmly roped to the latest volume of Will
Durant.

I have not yet been afflicted by the fourth of these criticoses, but other reviewers have told me that they do suffer
from it. It is *amnesia*. They cannot remember the books
they read. At the end of the year, when editors ask them
for the names of the three books they have enjoyed most
during the preceding twelve months, they have to look up
their own files and read their own clippings, in order to
find out. I knew one unfortunate critic who, after reading
eighteen historical novels about the rise of Christianity in
the Roman Empire, all equally false to fact and equally
corny in style, had to give up his occupation: he was convinced that the publishers were simply publishing *the same
book* over and over again, merely changing the name of
the author and the title on the jacket. He is quite happy
now. He is literary supervisor in the Campbell's Soup
factory: he supervises putting the labels on the different
cans of soup. Other critics, who are more successful because
they take more exercise and have more regular elimination,
have converted their occupational amnesia into an asset.
However stale a book may be, however obviously it may
be modeled on *Gone with the Wind* or *I Remember Mama*,
it still seems new to them, because they have forgotten
everything older than last week, and are able and willing
to treat it as new, fresh, original, a possible masterpiece.
Happy, happy, they! For ever panting, and for ever young!

Occasionally, however, I do suffer from *parachronism*.
All critics do, except those who live for ever in the past,

and are still trying to work out a definitive judgment of Henry James. Parachronism is confusion of times, and it affects all book reviewers because they have deadlines several weeks, or several months, ahead. Thus, you are sent a book in January, so that you can write your review of it in February and have it published in March or April. You do so. But by the first of March, you are apt to say 'That will be a splendid little book of adventure among the Indonesian guerrillas, wasn't it?' You are living in three or four months at once. This is made still worse if you write and publish books yourself: for then your book is finished in June, printed and proof-corrected and indexed in November, and manufactured complete in every detail in January, so that it can be published in March. You can see why people sometimes compare the process of authorship to the process (not more pleasant, but more natural) of having a baby; and why an author, when praised on his new book, sometimes looks as thoughtful as a young mother, when she gazes at her new baby and thinks, 'Well, here you are at last. You took a precious long time to get here!' To other people, it looks about a week old. To her it has existed for nearly a year.

Then again all critics have the uncanny sensation, for which as far as I know there is no regular pathological name, but which is called *déjà vu,* or 'This is where I came in.' You know the feeling. You go to a perfectly strange city on business. You register at a hotel. You go down to the dining room for dinner and are welcomed by a hostess with one hundred and twenty-eight teeth, several heads of hair, and a sleek black dress like a basking seal. You sit down and look at the menu; then you gaze round at the walls, the Early American decorations, spinning wheels, flintlock muskets, cobblers' benches, and so forth. Your eye catches the melancholy stare of an Italian-American waiter, peering forth from a background of handmade glass bottles and candle moulds; and suddenly you say, 'Where am I? I have been here before!' In the same way, I open a novel and find myself reading a chapter which begins, 'Henry looked around him. This was Harbor Place, but smaller, somehow meaner than he had remembered it. The people had not been so close to the ground when he was a little boy, and they had perhaps been cleaner or better dressed.' With the double-focus sensation of *déjà vu,* I look at the front cover. But no, the book was written (it says) by Oliver Mortimer Popp, and not by the author of whom it at once reminded me. Then I realize that once again I have been enjoying *The View from Marquand's Head.*

It is also possible to suffer from *aphasia.* Advertising men say it is endemic among them. The essence of this is that you read a book carefully and thoroughly, and then find the tongue paralyzed, the writing hand frozen stiff, the typewriter empty of words except 'The quick brown fox jumps over the lazy dog' and 'Now is the time for all good men to come to the aid of the party.' The English language, with its total vocabulary of one million words, shrinks away to nothing. All the adjectives dry up and blow away. Abstract nouns disappear like candles in a furnace. Sentences are impossible to form. Nothing can be said or written: nothing. One sufferer from this disease told me of a drastic remedy which, however, I have never ventured to employ. He said he wrote his review *before* reading the book, simply on the strength of the title and the name of the author. After the review was finished, then he read the book; the disparity between its contents and the review he had written stimulated his numbed brain. He took out his blue pencil; he changed *exciting* to *thoughtful,* and *power-*

ful to *delicate,* and *sexy* to *austere,* and *Chicago* to *Venezuela* (the book proved to be laid in Venezuela); he fixed up the proper names; and quite soon he had a rich pure fluent review, full of the charm of discovery.

Allied to this is the serious affliction called *polyphagia;* this amounts to reading everything indiscriminately, whether one can review it or not: it may go into *bulimia,* which is reading all the time, day and night. The only remedy for this is the cold turkey cure: to give the patient something so repulsive that it is unreadable. When I had a slight attack at one time I took up a best-selling story by that eminent author Mickey Spillane. In about two hours I had thrown the thing out of the window, and for at least two weeks I couldn't read anything except newspaper headlines and street numbers. (According to Alice Payne Hackett's *Sixty Years of Best Sellers,* seven of the ten American novels which have sold most copies during the last sixty years are by Mickey Spillane. If anyone represents modern taste, apparently he does, for not one of these books has sold less than 3,600,000 copies.)

This is not by any means a complete pathology of the criticoses, but it will perhaps be enough to make you sympathize with the members of an arduous and dangerous profession.

The look-it-up shelf

SOME years ago I was crossing the ocean in the off season. The ship was not very full, nor very gay; the sea was rough and disagreeable, as the North Atlantic nearly always is. I was alone. Fortunately I had brought plenty to read — for the ship's library was worse than mediocre, as it must be when the librarian never opens a book.

One long, dreary evening, I was sitting in the smoking-room, wishing that Somerset Maugham would appear in person and tell me one of his unpublished stories, when my ear was caught by an argument near by.

Three men were arguing about the Civil War. They had been going over the various battles, and now they were trying to remember when the surrender took place, the final surrender, at Appomattox. One of them said it was in

September 1865, one said in October, and a third in April. I thought it was in May, myself; but I did not enter, I merely listened. The argument went on and on and grew hotter and hotter. Drinks were consumed, and bets were laid and doubled. Finally the three men went off, steaming with competiveness and promising to settle the matter as soon as they touched land.

After the uproar had ceased, I read a few more chapters of my book and then drifted off. On the way out I spoke to the steward. I said, 'When do you think Lee surrendered? September or October?' He said, 'We'll soon see, sir,' and he reached into a drawer below the cigarette cupboard and produced a book of reference, a one-volume job. He looked up the index, found the Civil War, and told me: April 9th, 1865. I thanked him, and then said, 'But when you heard all that argument going on, why on earth didn't you bring out this book? You could have settled the whole thing in a matter of minutes.' 'Why,' he said, 'bless your 'eart, sir, the gentlemen was 'avin' a good time. Why should I spoil their little discussion?'

Now, how many arguments do you have, with your family, your friends, or yourself, which could be settled in a few minutes, if you only knew where to find the answer? Dozens, I imagine. In fact, I know — because several times every week somebody writes or telephones me at Columbia to ask some perfectly simple question which he himself could have solved straight away, if he had known where to look for the answer.

In all our personal libraries, there are many gaps. But the worst gap is usually in the shelf which ought to contain the answers to questions: the Look-it-up Shelf. Many people don't even have a dictionary in the house, which is ridiculous. Most people lack anything like a really well-equipped Look-it-up Shelf — not because they cannot afford to buy the necessary books, but partly because they do not fully realize how necessary the books are, and partly because they do not know which books to buy. This essay is meant to give an outline of the way to fill such a shelf.

Before you start to equip yourself, you should realize that there are many good reference books of nearly every type. You need not search. You need only choose. Go to a good bookstore and compare the possibilities; or go to your local library and ask your librarian to show you where they live; after handling them, decide which would be the most useful and comfortable for you to possess, and then compare prices.

The first two books you must have are a dictionary, to tell you the meanings and pronunciations of doubtful words, and an encyclopedia, to give you facts, explain complex subjects, and suggest where to get further information.

There are a number of excellent dictionaries available. There are also some dictionaries which go beyond the pronunciation and meaning of words, and add technical information; these are combined dictionaries and encyclopedias. To judge which is best for you, compare them all. Pick one word and look it up in several different volumes; then decide which tells you most clearly the kind of thing you want to know.

Suppose you choose *dynamo*. Look it up in *The American College Dictionary* (Random House, 1949). You will find a seven-line description of a dynamo, with pronunciation; the essential facts; no picture. Then try *Webster's New World Dictionary of the American Language* (World, 1951): it gives the pronunciation, derivation, and description in about six lines, but adds a picture, with details.

Next try *The Shorter Oxford English Dictionary:* you will find six lines of definition, plus derivation, plus the date when the word was first used; no picture. Then turn to *Funk and Wagnalls' New Standard Dictionary* (Martin & Murray, 1954): here you find an article of some fifty lines, with a complete explanation, a picture and many details, most of them highly technical. Last of all, you might look at *The Columbia Encyclopedia* (Columbia University Press, 2nd edition, 1950), where you will be referred to *generator,* and there find a very technical article half a column long, without a picture.

There are other dictionaries besides these. No one can tell which is the 'best.' One dictionary would be good for a man with scientific interests, another for a woman who enjoyed literature and music; a third for a boy in high school. You will have to look at the standard works yourself, and choose. If you pick a dictionary put out by a big reliable publishing house with an established reputation, you will seldom go far wrong.

You may have bought an encyclopedia when you were getting your dictionary. If not, you will have to have one, or else forever have your mind full of unanswered questions. Do you want a one-volume encyclopedia? Or would you rather have a big one, covering a dozen volumes or more, and of course much more expensive? You must decide. But there are two things which I myself always look for in estimating any encyclopedia: illustrations and bibliographies. It is not enough for a book to describe things; it should show you pictures and diagrams. Suppose you look up the *eye*: how can its structure and functions possibly be made clear to you without photographs and cross-sections? And it is not enough for such a book simply to state the central facts; it should also tell you where to find the evidence, and where to go for additional information.

Thus, if you look up *dynamo* in the *Encyclopaedia Britannica*, you will be told to go to *electric generator* (where you will learn that the word 'dynamo' is rather out of date); and there you will find an article on the electric generator running to seven and a half pages, with seven diagrams, one graph, five fine photographs, and a list of more than a dozen specialist books and articles on the subject. If you then look up the index volume of the same encyclopedia, you will find a long list of references to electric generators throughout the book — enough, if you read them all, to give you a sound theoretical knowledge of the entire subject.

There are dozens of encyclopedias. In one volume, you can scarcely do much better than *The Columbia Encyclopedia*. In many volumes, there are the *Encyclopaedia Britannica* — which is not wholly British, but is largely American, published in Chicago and continuously under revision; the *Encyclopedia Americana* (Americana Corporation, 1953), which is especially strong in science and technology; and *Chambers's Encyclopaedia* (Newnes, London). All are sound, and really it is possible to spend a pleasant hour merely browsing in any one of them. I defy anyone to look at the article on *Pottery and Porcelain* in the *Britannica* without being captivated by the charm of the subject and the grace of the pictures.

These are the essentials of your Look-it-up Shelf: a dictionary and an encyclopedia. These are the books which should be used every week, or even every day.

After them, where do your special interests lie? In people, places, or books?

People are described in *Who's Who in America* (kept up to date and published every second year by Marquis), together with many regional American and foreign *Who's*

Whos. Webster's Biographical Dictionary (Merriam, 1943) has some 40,000 names in it, about one-third being of living persons, the rest historical. Newspaper offices and big libraries have much larger works, such as *Current Biography* (Wilson), but the average man will not need those.

Places will be found and mapped in any of the big encyclopedias. They usually have a whole volume of maps toward the end, and an index of places, or gazetteer. But there are also special works on geography alone, the handiest being the Rand McNally *World Guide* (1953) — a collection of descriptive articles about countries, regions, and cities — and *Webster's Geographical Dictionary* (Merriam, 1949), a list of some 40,000 place names, with pronunciation, location, and essential facts, including history as far back as Biblical times. (Isn't it odd, though, that there is no geographical dictionary covering the entire United States?)

For books, the best thing I know is *Cassell's Encyclopedia of World Literature* (1953), which has over 500 pages of articles on general world literature, and about 2000 pages of biographies of authors in every literature of the whole world. Another indispensable shelf-book is a dictionary of quotations. In 1955 a new edition of *The Oxford Dictionary of Quotations* appeared, and also a new edition of *Bartlett's Familiar Quotations;* both are excellent. If you yourself are a writer, you probably ought to have *The Literary Market Place* (published annually by Bowker) to tell you where to sell your work; and you certainly ought to have the famous manual of style, Fowler's *Modern English Usage* (Oxford), and/or Margaret Nicholson's adaptation of it, *A Dictionary of American-English Usage* (also Oxford). (If you have gone so far in your career as to get a manuscript ready for the press, then you should have one or two of the essential advisory books written by experts on that subject; Oxford has a good little pocket-sized *Authors' and Printers' Dictionary,* and Appleton-Century-Crofts has a big manual called *Words into Type*.)

And music? and science? and art? business and industry? social problems? history? medicine? In all these fields there are valuable reference books. It depends on your own interests which you buy for your own Look-it-up Shelf. But there are two central books which you ought to consult whenever you are in any difficulty about books; they are books about books. One is *The Bookman's Manual* (published by Bowker, 7th edition, 1954). The other is *The Guide to Reference Books,* edited by Constance Winchell (American Library Association, 7th edition, 1951). These are not merely lists. They describe books in almost every conceivable subject; they evaluate them and compare them; they give publishers, prices, dates, and summaries. You can see them in any library, and if you want to build a good library of your own, you should start by taking one of them home. I mean, buying it in a bookstore, and paying for it, and taking it home.

But any shelf of this kind will be merely a decoration, like an antique cobbler's bench, unless you get into the habit of using it regularly. The Look-it-up Shelf is part of the equipment of every intelligent family. It discourages sloppy thinking. Not even the stubbornest adolescent can go on insisting that Einstein did his first work in Germany if there is a book handy which will show, with dates and other facts, that he did it in Switzerland. Not even the most reactionary father can continue to maintain that the distortions of modern art are simply a contemporary disease if his son can show him a reference book containing similar distortions in painting and sculpture dating back as far as the Stone Age. One of the dreariest aspects of family life is the long, purposeless arguments in which no one really exchanges any ideas, no one gives anyone any valuable information, but everyone asserts himself, with the old exclamatory preface, 'Well, *I* think. . . .' 'Well, *I* think. . . .' A single shelf of books, if properly chosen and used, will stop most of these arguments, futile as they always are, and perhaps direct our attention less to self-assertion and more toward learning the plain, clear, unemotional truth. It is all there, in the books, if we take the trouble to look for it.

Summer reading

SUMMER. Long days, not too busy (unless one is a professional baseball player or a mother with three young children — and even then the days are rewarding). Plenty of light, heavenly light. Peaceful evenings. Lazy week-ends. And, sometimes, quite long periods of emptiness. Vacant days. Week-ends which begin to be monotonous and even tedious. Evenings when husbands at home miss their wives in the country, or when wives looking after children in the country miss their husbands at home. Long weeks, too, when families are kept in town because the roads are crowded or the budget is cramped.

Summer is a time of leisure. But it is painful when summer becomes a time of tedium: emptiness, loss, and temporary death . . . the death of the spirit, far worse than the hibernation of the body in the remote arctic. It would be far better and more natural if summer became a time of adventure and expansion, a time for doing those long leisurely things which are impossible in winter because the days are too short and the evenings too crowded. The summer is the time for exploring: for visiting our own country or one of its regions; for seeing a foreign land; for learning more of nature; or, if we are tied to our home, then for entering a new world of skill, or art, or knowledge. Even if we are traveling, we sometimes need a quiet resting place for the spirit: not an intellectual motel, but a sanctuary — somewhere to rest, and live for ourselves, and think. Physically, it is not always possible to procure this. Mentally, it can be assured, if we have something to read.

I first found this out almost by accident. We had taken a house on the Cape for the summer. In a side pocket of my bag I had brought with me a single volume which contained the entire work of an interesting Roman poet whom I had never really read — something to be dipped into in off moments. However, it was a poor summer. It rained a lot. I got some books out of the local lending library, but they were not very rewarding. Then, in a shelf on a back porch, I found a twenty years' file of the *Reader's Digest*. I looked into it. The recent articles were quite familiar; the more distant pieces were rather strange; the twenty-year-old stuff was unbelievable — it might have come from a different world. During a week-end of solid rain, I set out to read them all straight through, the whole two hundred and forty issues. It took me quite a long time, but it was extraordinarily interesting, and gave me an entirely new view of the history of my own times.

Partly through the infectious force of example, I was compelled to take out the single-volume edition of my Roman poet, and I began to read it too. Before the summer ended I had read him straight through, without explanatory notes, from beginning to end. Now, classical scholars seldom do that. They specialize. They itemize. They analyze. They use a microscope. That is valuable; but it is also valuable to push directly through the works of a good author, trying to see them as a single creation, appreciating their wholeness and their uniqueness and leaving the details for later study.

That summer I got a great deal of experience from reading the back files of a national magazine, which were something like the material of current history, and from reading the entire work of a single genius. Going back home for the winter, it struck me that this was an extension of what I had been doing in music. For many years I had been trying to understand two difficult composers (Bach and Scriabin) and one elusive composer (Debussy); and it seemed to me that I had been making progress, by the resolute plan of playing my way through their works from opus 1 to the end. As I thought over this, it seemed to me that it was a good plan to follow every summer. Ever since then, I have read all through one important author from beginning to end during every summer vacation; and that, or something like that, is what I should like to recommend for summer reading.

You will ask what good this will do: whether it will be really enjoyable, or merely improving. Suppose you read all through Tolstoy's *War and Peace*, or even the whole of Tolstoy; all the novels of Hemingway or Thomas Mann — what real benefit will you receive?

In the first place, it is good for human beings to escape from themselves. The world is too much with us: the day's news, the family's problems, the excitements of Saturday evening and the worries of Monday morning loom too large if we can never look away from them toward a different time and place, toward a different mode of being. It is a rest for the spirit to plunge into some other period, into the mind of another human being — provided it is big enough and healthy enough. I should not recommend spending the summer in the mind of Nelson Algren or Calder Willingham.

Then, second, it is good for us to have sustained exercise for the mind, just as it is good for us to have regular exercise for the body. You know those fat people one sees sitting around on the beach: people who overeat and never walk a mile and oversmoke and never swim a hundred yards and are apparently content to listen to the functioning of their own viscera. You know how repulsive they look, and how unhealthy they are. Imagine (as Socrates says in Plato's *Republic*) that we could see their souls as clearly as we can see their bodies: surely we should see gross fat objects covered with heavy layers of spiritual adipose tissue, dulled and dimmed by many years of laziness, while other minds would look to us keen and deft like athletes, or lithe and graceful like dancers. The mind needs exercise if it is not to atrophy, and at last to putrefy.

Third, it is necessary for us to feed our subconscious mind: our imagination. It needs appropriate food, just as the body needs vitamins and fresh water. Everyone knows this vaguely. Everyone keeps something for his or her imagination to feed upon: fantasies of the future, memories of the past, visions of an ideal, fragments of a motion picture or a play or a novel, things as tiny and apparently unimportant as the rhythm of a dance tune or the words of a song; yet we feel them to be haunting and necessary. Very few of us realize that the subconscious has to be fed regularly, has to be supplied with material to nourish it.

For some of us, religion provides that food. In countries where there is much beautiful architecture, or in cities where there are museums full of fine pictures and sculpture, it is easy enough to feed the creative mind. But outside these regions we are often driven to take meager substitutes: routine movies, or movie magazines; games of chance; disconnected dreams; books of cheap excitement. Still, the best solution is to keep the subconscious mind constantly occupied in assimilating and manipulating imaginative material provided for it by a good artist. This will not make us good artists; but it will assuredly make us richer and happier people.

So then, the suggestions for summer reading are quite simple. The first is to read all the work of one single writer. But make sure that he is a big writer, and, as far as possible, a positive writer. (There are many voluble authors who write very forcibly, but who wish to die themselves and to inflict death on their readers: Céline and Malaparte, for instance. They should be read, but not taken as companions for a long period.) Another suggestion is to read largely about one single important and interesting subject: for instance, the paintings of the cave men; or the agony of modern music; or the rebirth of calligraphy; or recent theories of the creation and duration of the universe. Of course we should not, or not necessarily, take notes and read as a painstaking student, but rather read with our imaginations wide open, expecting many new stimuli to enter our minds, stimuli which the authors of the books themselves may not have known they were creating. Or, third, we might read a large selection of poems and prose passages selected in order to illustrate one single aspect of the world. One such volume would go into a pocket or a handbag and yet last all summer. Many soldiers have gone through an entire war with no other spiritual food than just such a volume. The most famous is *The Oxford Book of English Verse,* but there is also a sad and noble collection by Robert Bridges called *The Spirit of Man.* In the field of the classics the best thing is *The Oxford Book of Greek Verse in Translation,* which contains well over six hundred pages of good poetry well translated in readable English. And one of my own favorites is a beautiful anthology called simply *Love;* it was compiled by Walter de la Mare and published by Morrow in 1946. If you think love is glandular, or if you consider it — in more recent phrasing — a matter of 'outlets,' this is not for you; but if you believe in the fusion of body and spirit in the rapture we call love, then this book will put what you feel into eloquent words.

Then, fourth, one might decide to spend the summer with a single great or at least a single interesting man. For example, every doctor should know *The Life of Sir William Osler* by Harvey Cushing, and after reading that fine book he would enjoy himself if he went on to read Osler's own writings. Osler never tired of complaining that most doctors had minds too limited and too confined to the physical symptoms which they observed in the routine of their practice. He kept trying to enlarge his own mind and spirit, and his books will therefore enlarge the mind and spirit of his readers, whether they are of the medical profession or not.

In the same way, one might try to understand the character of Abraham Lincoln. It cannot be understood through reading any single biography: he was too complex for that. Why did he tell filthy stories to the members of his Cabinet at important meetings? And, at the same time, why was he so noble and so dignified in many of his public utterances? He invoked God often: what was his real attitude toward religion? Was he a single permanent character, or rather someone who went on changing continually until the day of his death? What was his true relation to his wife? Among his advisers, did any one man influence him at any time, or did he listen to them all and then ignore their advice? All these questions are important for those who seek to understand the history of our country and the character of great men — one book alone will not answer them.

There are many more books which might well occupy a happy summer, so many that I hardly have space to describe them, only to praise them. I myself spent one exciting vacation reading Spengler's *Decline of the West,* and now we have the final volumes of Toynbee's *A Study of History.* Only this year I found a wonderful anthology of fine literature called *The Limits of Art,* by Huntington Cairns, published in the Bollingen Series — I look forward to reading through it with slow appreciation. For thoughtful readers who like the Middle Ages, there is a fine historical novel by a Nobel Prize winner, Sigrid Undset's *Kristin Lavransdatter,* published by Knopf; and for fast readers who enjoy the sensual modern world, there is Jules Romains' *Men of Good Will* (from the same publisher, in at least a dozen volumes of romance and excitement).

People outside the United States sometimes accuse us of having too much and making too little of it: they say we have so much food that we throw a great deal of it away in the garbage. It is easier here than in most other countries for the ordinary man to get hold of good books full of invaluable nourishment. Sometimes he nibbles at them, sometimes he throws them away untouched, but more and more often in recent years he has realized that books are food for the mind — not only the intellect, but for all parts of that mysterious organ which raises us above the animals and makes us specifically human.

Permanent books

M Y profession is to read and teach the Greek and
Latin languages. I have other interests, but that is my
chief vocation. I have been studying the two languages
for just under forty years and teaching them for just under
thirty; I expect to go on teaching them for twenty years
more, and reading them for the rest of my life.

New acquaintances sometimes express surprise when
they hear what my job is. Occasionally they ask me why
I chose it, and now and then they even say something like
'What good does that do? What results do you expect to
produce?' Not so bluntly as that, of course, but in that
general direction. Such a question cannot be answered in
a single sentence, and not even in a single paragraph; but
it must be answered, and the answer will tell us something

important about the human mind. Here is what I would say in reply to such a question.

For civilized people, reading is an essential activity. Those who do not read, in the middle of a literate society, are in danger of making themselves into half-savages. Now, reading is of two different kinds. Some reading is temporary; some reading is what might be called permanent. The most obvious example of temporary reading is the daily newspaper, which is intended to last for only twenty-four hours (perhaps even less than that) and which is forgotten almost as soon as it is laid down. Weekly and monthly magazines belong to the same type, and so do most of the stories in them. They die soon. Many books that we read are temporary: detective stories, light romances, books of travel, most historical novels, and so forth. These are like modern motorcars and modern buildings, constructed to look bright and shiny and smart, to be worn out quickly, and to be replaced by something brighter and shinier in a few months or years.

But some books do not become obsolete. Some books are permanent. Usually they were built to last, by a writer who put everything he had into them, aiming at an audience not of one year or of one lifetime, but of centuries. Such are Dante's *Comedy* and Goethe's *Faust*. Sometimes, even if the author scarcely thought of the future, he happened to be so brilliant and to write with such grace and versatility and humanity that his work survived through generations which he could never have foreseen. Such are the plays of Shakespeare (which their author did not even bother to publish), the satire of Rabelais, and the greatest work in the Spanish language, *Don Quixote*. These books and others like them can be read by an intelligent man, not once, but many, many times at different periods throughout his life; they will never seem boring;

they will always give him some new intellectual and emotional experience; they are versatile companions and tireless teachers.

Now, most of the books preserved in Greek and Latin are permanent books of this kind. It does not matter that they are in languages which are not now spoken in those forms. Language is not meant only for speech; it is also meant for reading; and the thoughts contained in many of these books are inextinguishably valuable. That is why they are read; and that is why the languages in which they were written are still taught, and will continue to be taught and studied.

There are parallels for this in other arts. Take music. There is a great deal of temporary music, and there always has been. The scores of most musical comedies; the incidental music to most motion pictures and TV shows; popular dance tunes, comic songs, sentimental melodies; thousands of albums full of drawing-room music and *café* music, *Waltz of the Blue Butterflies, Memories at Sunset, Scènes Pittoresques, Hallowe'en Revels, Heimatsstimmen, Señorita Rita* — all these were written to divert for a time and then be forgotten. Nearly all the great composers produced such things in off moments; and many composers have written nothing else: think of Cécile Chaminade. But the music we really love is permanent music, and never becomes obsolete. No matter how many symphonies are written in the future, we shall always enjoy Mozart's *Jupiter* and Beethoven's Seventh and Brahms's Third. And everyone who wishes to study music (either in order to understand it better or in order to compose new music himself) is bound inevitably to examine these and similar works, movement by movement, page by page, bar by bar. Even the greatest conductor never tires of directing their performance, and always finds that playing and hearing them uplift and nourish his spirit.

So it is with drama. It appalls me sometimes to think of the enormous number of plays which have been written since the re-establishment of the popular theater in the fifteenth century, which have been put on film since the invention of the motion picture, and which are now pouring out of innumerable radio and television stations. Mostly trash; mostly junk. *Hoofbeats and Heartbeats. The Orphan's Revenge. Count Lamorak of Morden and his Specter Bride. Toujours l'Amour. The Mystery of the Old Mine. A Bungalow for Two. Only a Bootblack. The Clutching Hand.* No, that is not quite fair; not junk; merely temporary, run up to amuse audiences for a season, a week, or a night, and then to be forgotten. It would be worse than boredom, it would be actual torment, to be obliged to endure ninety-nine out of a hundred of the motion pictures, dramas, and television and radio plays which have been produced in the last four centuries. But, out of that enormous output, a few plays have actually lived, and lasted; and they still last. The Comédie Française never tires of playing Molière, and audiences never tire of seeing his delightful dramas. Shakespeare has been acted almost every single theatrical season since his reputation was established, and now, with the help of film and television, he is reaching a larger audience than ever before. No one who wants to appreciate, act, or write drama can pass by the plays of Molière and Shakespeare; he cannot imitate them, but he can learn from them much which he could not possibly learn elsewhere.

Then there is one kind of reading which almost everyone admits to be permanent: this is the reading of Scripture. No intelligent person would think of picking up the

Bible and reading twenty or thirty pages at the same speed as that with which he would read a magazine, and with the same divided and superficial attention. Those who read Scripture read it slowly and meditatively, verse by verse; and even if they have known a particular psalm or a particular chapter since childhood, they always sink deeply into it, as though reading it for the first time. The Bible, all of it — or nearly all of it (with the possible exception of the minor epistles) — was intended to be durable literature, and must therefore be read in a special way.

Of course, I should not dream of claiming that all the surviving books in Greek and Latin are worthy of such long and detailed attention. Some of them are little better than trash; some are frankly dull. But there is a surprising number of masterpieces: poems that can be compared with Dante's *Comedy*, plays equal to the best of Shakespeare, speeches such as no human being could now conceive or deliver, superb volumes of history and biography, philosophical works of unequaled subtlety and penetration. And nearly every one of these rewards any reader who goes over it the tenth time more than it did the first time. There are some poems by Horace, there are certain plays by Aristophanes, which I read again this year with astonishment and delight, although I first read them in 1925 and have often reread them since then. Now I believe that at the first reading I must have missed at least three quarters of their beauty and their wit; and yet even then I got enough to make me admire them enormously.

Now, this concept — that Greek and Latin books are meant not to be read through rapidly and then put aside, but to be studied with slow deliberation — usually comes as a surprise to many American and British students. It is much easier for French, Italian, and German students to assimilate, and it never even has to be explained to Jewish students, wherever they come from. This is because Jews are brought up with the idea that certain books are worth a lifetime of careful study: the Scriptures because they are sacred, the Talmud because it contains vast wisdom. Italians cannot go to high school without spending long and careful attention on the understanding of Dante's *Comedy,* and every educated Italian uses quotations from it in conversation with no feeling of affectation or strain. At the head of German literature stands Goethe's *Faust,* which took sixty years to write, and takes nearly as long to understand. And the French too are accustomed to revere a number of their own favorite works, which they justly call classics and spend much time on explaining in detail. But works of comparable difficulty are not studied in most American and British schools, so that many students are never exposed to the discipline of slow and careful study of a complicated book until they enter college — unless they take Greek or Latin in school, and even then they may not understand why slow and careful study is desirable, and may chafe when they cannot read fluently and superficially.

When it is explained to them (at least in college; I cannot speak for schools) they generally grasp the idea very rapidly. And in a Greek or Latin class it is easily explained. Any skilful teacher can spend an hour on a single page of Vergil: first of all, establishing the basic meaning; then bringing out the complex symbolism which Vergil loves to put in; then comparing the passage with the models the poet was using; next analyzing the style, which has something arrestingly unusual and original in every dozen lines; going over the melody and rhythm of the poetry, showing how sound is adapted to sense; working out the rhetorical elements which may be present, or tracing the philosophical assumptions behind the piece; and finally showing what part the passage plays in the entire structure of Vergil's work. Properly done, that would take more than a single hour; and the same teacher could spend another hour merely discussing the later poems and works of art, from the Middle Ages onward, which that single passage inspired. When the students have taken part in all this, and when in addition they are told that Vergil, although he was a fluent writer, edited and revised his work so carefully that one of his poems took him seven years to write, at the rate of less than two lines a day, they soon see why the only way to read such poetry is slowly and lovingly, with every faculty attentive.

But permanent literature such as that is not meant only for study in school or college. It is meant for all of us, always. Every one of us ought, as well as reading temporary books, to have a shelf or two of permanent companions, and keep one of them always going. To read part of one such book for a short time every day is a surprisingly tranquilizing and encouraging thing; it is admirable exercise; it raises one above routine; it leaves a pleasant residue of thought or imagination running in the mind like music. One single poem by Keats; one essay by Emerson; any of Browning's short monologues; a chapter of *Don Quixote* — these and many others will feed the mind for an entire day. The only time in my adult life I have ever passed without regular slow and thoughtful reading every day was when I was overseas on military service; and I swear I could feel my brain drying up and turning into excelsior; but my wife, bless her, sent me some permanent reading matter, choosing the books as carefully as food parcels; and the circulation soon resumed.

One more piece of advice is to have some such books to reread regularly every year or so. Never a summer passes that I do not work through some plays of Shakespeare which I have partially forgotten and seldom seen acted. Last summer it was *Cymbeline, Coriolanus,* and *Measure for Measure.* Next summer it will be *King John, The Winter's Tale,* and *Timon of Athens.*

And my final advice is to try, every week or so, to learn something by heart. A surprising amount will remain in the memory, and more and more as you train it; and then, as you walk or work or sit in the subway, you will have something more than daily trivialities to occupy your mind.

That is part of the answer to the question 'Why does one study and teach Greek and Latin?' It is because the best books are lasting books; many Greek and Latin books are lasting; and only such books are truly worth teaching for a lifetime, and studying for a lifetime.

The mystery of Zen

THE mind need never stop growing. Indeed, one of the few experiences which never pall is the experience of watching one's own mind, and observing how it produces new interests, responds to new stimuli, and develops new thoughts, apparently without effort and almost independently of one's own conscious control. I have seen this happen to myself a hundred times; and every time it happens again, I am equally fascinated and astonished.

Some years ago a publisher sent me a little book for review. I read it, and decided it was too remote from my main interests and too highly specialized. It was a brief account of how a young German philosopher living in Japan had learned how to shoot with a bow and arrow, and how this training had made it possible for him to understand the esoteric doctrines of the Zen sect of Buddhism. Really, what could be more alien to my own life, and to that of everyone I knew, than Zen Buddhism and Japanese archery? So I thought, and put the book away.

Yet I did not forget it. It was well written, and translated into good English. It was delightfully short, and implied much more than it said. Although its theme was extremely odd, it was at least highly individual; I had never read anything like it before or since. It remained in my mind. Its name was *Zen in the Art of Archery*, its author Eugen Herrigel, its publisher Pantheon of New York. One day I took it off the shelf and read it again; this time it seemed even stranger than before and even more unforgettable. Now it began to cohere with other interests of mine. Something I had read of the Japanese art of flower arrangement seemed to connect with it; and then, when I wrote an essay on the peculiar Japanese poems called *haiku*,* other links began to grow. Finally I had to read the book once more with care, and to go through some other works which illuminated the same subject. I am still grappling with the theme; I have not got anywhere near understanding it fully; but I have learned a good deal, and I am grateful to the little book which refused to be forgotten.

The author, a German philosopher, got a job teaching philosophy at the University of Tokyo (apparently between the wars), and he did what Germans in foreign countries do not usually do: he determined to adapt himself and to learn from his hosts. In particular, he had always been interested in mysticism — which, for every earnest philosopher, poses a problem that is all the more inescapable because it is virtually insoluble. Zen Buddhism is not the only

---

* This essay is 'Seventeen Syllables,' printed in *A Clerk of Oxenford* (Oxford University Press, 1954).

mystical doctrine to be found in the East, but it is one of the most highly developed and certainly one of the most difficult to approach. Herrigel knew that there were scarcely any books which did more than skirt the edge of the subject, and that the best of all books on Zen (those by the philosopher D. T. Suzuki) constantly emphasize that Zen can never be learned from books, can never be studied as we can study other disciplines such as logic or mathematics. Therefore he began to look for a Japanese thinker who could teach him directly.

At once he met with embarrassed refusals. His Japanese friends explained that he would gain nothing from trying to discuss Zen as a philosopher, that its theories could not be spread out for analysis by a detached mind, and in fact that the normal relationship of teacher and pupil simply did not exist within the sect, because the Zen masters felt it useless to explain things stage by stage and to argue about the various possible interpretations of their doctrine. Herrigel had read enough to be prepared for this. He replied that he did not want to dissect the teachings of the school, because he knew that would be useless. He wanted to become a Zen mystic himself. (This was highly intelligent of him. No one could really penetrate into Christian mysticism without being a devout Christian; no one could appreciate Hindu mystical doctrine without accepting the Hindu view of the universe.) At this, Herrigel's Japanese friends were more forthcoming. They told him that the best way, indeed the only way, for a European to approach Zen mysticism was to learn one of the arts which exemplified it. He was a fairly good rifle shot, so he determined to learn archery; and his wife co-operated with him by taking lessons in painting and flower arrangement. How any philosopher could investigate a mystical doctrine by learning to shoot with a bow and arrow and watching his wife arrange flowers, Herrigel did not ask. He had good sense.

A Zen master who was a teacher of archery agreed to take him as a pupil. The lessons lasted six years, during which he practiced every single day. There are many difficult courses of instruction in the world: the Jesuits, violin virtuosi, Talmudic scholars, all have long and hard training, which in one sense never comes to an end; but Herrigel's training in archery equaled them all in intensity. If I were trying to learn archery, I should expect to begin by looking at a target and shooting arrows at it. He was not even allowed to aim at a target for the first four years. He had to begin by learning how to hold the bow and arrow, and then how to release the arrow; this took ages. The Japanese bow is not like our sporting bow, and the stance of the archer in Japan is different from ours. We hold the bow at shoulder level, stretch our left arm out ahead, pull the string and the nocked arrow to a point either below the chin or sometimes past the right ear, and then shoot. The Japanese hold the bow above the head, and then pull the hands apart to left and right until the left hand comes down to eye level and the right hand comes to rest above the right shoulder; then there is a pause, during which the bow is held at full stretch, with the tip of the three-foot arrow projecting only a few inches beyond the bow; after that, the arrow is loosed. When Herrigel tried this, even without aiming, he found it was almost impossible. His hands trembled. His legs stiffened and grew cramped. His breathing became labored. And of course he could not possibly aim. Week after week he practiced this, with the Master watching him carefully and correcting his strained attitude; week after week he made no progress whatever. Finally he gave up and told his teacher that he could not learn: it was absolutely impossible for him to draw the bow and loose the arrow.

To his astonishment, the Master agreed. He said, 'Certainly you cannot. It is because you are not breathing correctly. You must learn to breathe in a steady rhythm, keeping your lungs full most of the time, and drawing in one rapid inspiration with each stage of the process, as you grasp the bow, fit the arrow, raise the bow, draw, pause, and loose the shot. If you do, you will both grow stronger and be able to relax.' To prove this, he himself drew his massive bow and told his pupil to feel the muscles of his arms: they were perfectly relaxed, as though he were doing no work whatever.

Herrigel now started breathing exercises; after some time he combined the new rhythm of breathing with the actions of drawing and shooting; and, much to his astonishment, he found that the whole thing, after this complicated process, had become much easier. Or rather, not easier, but different. At times it became quite unconscious. He says himself that he felt he was not breathing, but being breathed; and in time he felt that the occasional shot was not being dispatched by him, but shooting itself. The bow and arrow were in charge; he had become merely a part of them.

All this time, of course, Herrigel did not even attempt to discuss Zen doctrine with his Master. No doubt he knew that he was approaching it, but he concentrated solely on learning how to shoot. Every stage which he surmounted appeared to lead to another stage even more difficult. It took him months to learn how to loosen the bowstring. The problem was this. If he gripped the string and arrowhead tightly, either he froze, so that his hands were slowly pulled together and the shot was wasted, or else he jerked, so that the arrow flew up into the air or down into the ground; and if he was relaxed, then the bowstring and arrow simply *leaked* out of his grasp before he could reach full stretch, and the arrow went nowhere. He explained this problem to the Master. The Master understood perfectly well. He replied, 'You must hold the drawn bowstring like a child holding a grownup's finger. You know how firmly a child grips; and yet when it lets go, there is not the slightest jerk — because the child does not think of itself, it is not self-conscious, it does not say, 'I will now let go and do something else,' it merely acts instinctively. That is what you must learn to do. Practice, practice, and practice, and then the string will loose itself at the right moment. The shot will come as effortlessly as snow slipping from a leaf.' Day after day, week after week, month after month, Herrigel practiced this; and then, after one shot, the Master suddenly bowed and broke off the lesson. He said 'Just then *it* shot. Not you, but *it*.' And gradually thereafter more and more right shots achieved themselves; the young philosopher forgot himself, forgot that he was learning archery for some other purpose, forgot even that he was practicing archery, and became part of that unconsciously active complex, the bow, the string, the arrow, and the man.

Next came the target. After four years, Herrigel was allowed to shoot at the target. But he was strictly forbidden to aim at it. The Master explained that even he himself did not aim; and indeed, when he shot, he was so absorbed in the act, so selfless and unanxious, that his eyes were almost closed. It was difficult, almost impossible, for Herrigel to believe that such shooting could ever be effective; and he risked insulting the Master by suggesting that he ought to be able to hit the target blindfolded. But the Master accepted the challenge. That night, after a cup of tea and long meditation, he went into the archery hall, put on the lights at one end and left the target perfectly dark, with only a thin taper burning in front of it. Then, with habitual grace and precision, and with that strange, almost sleepwalking, selfless confidence that is the heart of Zen, he shot two arrows into the darkness. Herrigel went out to collect them. He found that the first had gone to the heart of the bull's eye, and that the second had actually hit the first arrow and splintered it. The Master showed no pride. He said, 'Perhaps, with unconscious memory of the position of the target, *I* shot the first arrow; but the second arrow? *It* shot the second arrow, and *it* brought it to the center of the target.'

At last Herrigel began to understand. His progress became faster and faster; easier, too. Perfect shots (perfect because perfectly unconscious) occurred at almost every lesson; and finally, after six years of incessant training, in a public display he was awarded the diploma. He needed no further instruction: he had himself become a Master. His wife meanwhile had become expert both in painting and in the arrangement of flowers — two of the finest of Japanese arts. (I wish she could be persuaded to write a companion volume, called *Zen in the Art of Flower Arrangement;* it would have a wider general appeal than her husband's work.) I gather also from a hint or two in his book that she had taken part in the archery lessons. During one of the most difficult periods in Herrigel's training, when his Master had practically refused to continue teaching him — because Herrigel had tried to cheat by *consciously* opening his hand at the moment of loosing the arrow — his wife had advised him against that solution, and sympathized with him when it was rejected. She in her own way had learned more quickly than he, and reached the final point together with him. All their effort had not been in vain: Herrigel and his wife had really acquired a new and valuable kind of wisdom. Only at this point, when he was about to abandon his lessons forever, did his Master treat him almost as an equal and hint at the innermost doctrines of Zen Buddhism. Only hints he gave; and yet, for the young philosopher who had now become a mystic, they were enough. Herrigel understood the doctrine, not with his logical mind, but with his entire being. He at any rate had solved the mystery of Zen.

Without going through a course of training as absorbing and as complete as Herrigel's, we can probably never penetrate the mystery. The doctrine of Zen cannot be analyzed from without: it must be lived.

But although it cannot be analyzed, it can be hinted at. All the hints that the adherents of this creed give us are interesting. Many are fantastic; some are practically incomprehensible, and yet unforgettable. Put together, they take us toward a way of life which is utterly impossible for westerners living in a western world, and nevertheless has a deep fascination and contains some values which we must respect.

The word Zen means 'meditation.' (It is the Japanese word, corresponding to the Chinese Ch'an and the Hindu Dhyana.) It is the central idea of a special sect of Buddhism which flourished in China during the Sung period (between 1000 and 1300 A.D.) and entered Japan in the twelfth century. Without knowing much about it, we might be certain that the Zen sect was a worthy and noble one, because it produced a quantity of highly distinguished art, specifically painting. And if we knew anything about Buddhism itself, we might say that Zen goes closer than other sects to the heart of Buddha's teaching: because Buddha was trying to found, not a religion with temples and rituals, but a way of life based on meditation. However, there is something eccentric about the Zen life which is hard to trace in Buddha's teaching; there is an active energy which he did not admire, there is a rough grasp on reality which he himself eschewed, there is something like a sense of humor, which he rarely displayed. The gravity and serenity of the Indian preacher are transformed, in Zen, to the earthy liveliness of Chinese and Japanese sages. The lotus brooding calmly on the water has turned into a knotted tree covered with spring blossoms.

In this sense, 'meditation' does not mean what we usually think of when we say a philosopher meditates: analysis of reality, a long-sustained effort to solve problems of religion and ethics, the logical dissection of the universe. It means something not divisive, but whole; not schematic, but organic; not long-drawn-out, but immediate. It means something more like our words 'intuition' and 'realization.' It means a way of life in which there is no division between thought and action; none of the painful gulf, so well known to all of us, between the unconscious and the conscious mind; and no absolute distinction between the self and the external world, even between the various parts of the external world and the whole.

When the German philosopher took six years of lessons in archery in order to approach the mystical significance of Zen, he was not given direct philosophical instruction. He was merely shown how to breathe, how to hold and loose the bowstring, and finally how to shoot in such a way that the bow and arrow used him as an instrument. There are many such stories about Zen teachers. The strangest I know is one about a fencing master who undertook to train a young man in the art of the sword. The relationship of teacher and pupil is very important, almost sacred, in the Far East; and the pupil hardly ever thinks of leaving a master or objecting to his methods, however extraordinary they may seem. Therefore this young fellow did not at first object when he was made to act as a servant, drawing water, sweeping floors, gathering wood for the fire, and cooking. But after some time he asked for more direct instruction. The master agreed to give it, but produced no swords. The routine went on just as before, except that every now and then the master would strike the young man with a stick. No matter what he was doing, sweeping the floor or weeding in the garden, a blow would descend on him apparently out of nowhere; he had always to be on the alert, and yet he was constantly receiving unexpected cracks on the head or shoulders. After some months of this, he saw his master stooping over a boiling pot full of vegetables; and he thought he would have his revenge. Silently he lifted a stick and brought it down; but without any effort, without even a glance in his direction, his master parried the blow with the lid of the cooking pot. At last, the pupil began to understand the instinctive alertness, the effortless perception and avoidance of danger, in which his master had been training him. As soon as he had achieved it, it was child's play for him to learn the management of the sword: he could parry every cut and turn every slash without anxiety, until his opponent, exhausted, left an opening for his counterattack. (The same principle was used by the elderly samurai for selecting his comrades, in the Japanese motion picture *The Magnificent Seven*.)

These stories show that Zen meditation does not mean sitting and thinking. On the contrary, it means acting with as little thought as possible. The fencing master trained his pupil to guard against every attack with the same immediate, instinctive rapidity with which our eyelid closes over our eye when something threatens it. His work was aimed at breaking down the wall between thought and act, at completely fusing body and senses and mind so that they might all work together rapidly and effortlessly. When a

Zen artist draws a picture, he does it in a rhythm almost the exact reverse of that which is followed by a Western artist. We begin by blocking out the design and then filling in the details, usually working more and more slowly as we approach the completion of the picture. The Zen artist sits down very calmly; examines his brush carefully; prepares his own ink; smooths out the paper on which he will work; falls into a profound silent ecstasy of contemplation — during which he does not think anxiously of various details, composition, brushwork, shades of tone, but rather attempts to become the vehicle through which the subject can express itself in painting; and then, very quickly and almost unconsciously, with sure effortless strokes, draws a picture containing the fewest and most effective lines. Most of the paper is left blank; only the essential is depicted, and that not completely. One long curving line will be enough to show a mountainside; seven streaks will become a group of bamboos bending in the wind; and yet, though technically incomplete, such pictures are unforgettably clear. They show the heart of reality.

All this we can sympathize with, because we can see the results. The young swordsman learns how to fence. The intuitional painter produces a fine picture. But the hardest thing for us to appreciate is that the Zen masters refuse to teach philosophy or religion directly, and deny logic. In fact, they despise logic as an artificial distortion of reality. Many philosophical teachers are difficult to understand because they analyze profound problems with subtle intricacy: such is Aristotle in his *Metaphysics*. Many mystical writers are difficult to understand because, as they themselves admit, they are attempting to use words to describe experiences which are too abstruse for words, so that they have to fall back on imagery and analogy, which they themselves recognize to be poor media, far coarser than the realities with which they have been in contact. But the Zen teachers seem to deny the power of language and thought altogether. For example, if you ask a Zen master what is the ultimate reality, he will answer, without the slightest hesitation, 'The bamboo grove at the foot of the hill' or 'A branch of plum blossom.' Apparently he means that these things, which we can see instantly without effort, or imagine in the flash of a second, are real with the ultimate reality; that nothing is more real than these; and that we ought to grasp ultimates as we grasp simple immediates. A Chinese master was once asked the central question, 'What is the Buddha?' He said nothing whatever, but held out his index finger. What did he mean? It is hard to explain; but apparently he meant 'Here. Now. Look and realize with the effortlessness of seeing. Do not try to use words. Do not think. Make no efforts toward withdrawal from the world. Expect no sublime ecstasies. Live. All *that* is the ultimate reality, and it can be understood from the motion of a finger as well as from the execution of any complex ritual, from any subtle argument, or from the circling of the starry universe.'

In making that gesture, the master was copying the Buddha himself, who once delivered a sermon which is famous, but was hardly understood by his pupils at the time. Without saying a word, he held up a flower and showed it to the gathering. One man, one alone, knew what he meant. The gesture became renowned as the Flower Sermon.

In the annals of Zen there are many cryptic answers to the final question, 'What is the Buddha?' — which in our terms means 'What is the meaning of life? What is truly real?' For example, one master, when asked 'What is the Buddha?' replied, 'Your name is Yecho.' Another said, 'Even the finest artist cannot paint him.' Another said, 'No nonsense here.' And another answered, 'The mouth is the gate of woe.' My favorite story is about the monk who said to a Master, 'Has a dog Buddha-nature too?' The Master replied, 'Wu' — which is what the dog himself would have said.

Now, some critics might attack Zen by saying that this is the creed of a savage or an animal. The adherents of Zen would deny that — or more probably they would ignore the criticism, or make some cryptic remark which meant that it was pointless. Their position — if they could ever be persuaded to put it into words — would be this. An animal is instinctively in touch with reality, and so far is living rightly, but it has never had a mind and so cannot perceive the Whole, only that part with which it is in touch. The philosopher sees both the Whole and the parts, and enjoys them all. As for the savage, he exists only through the group; he feels himself as part of a war party or a ceremonial dance team or a ploughing-and-sowing group or the Snake clan; he is not truly an individual at all, and therefore is less than fully human. Zen has at its heart an inner solitude; its aim is to teach us to live, as in the last resort we do all have to live, alone.

A more dangerous criticism of Zen would be that it is nihilism, that its purpose is to abolish thought altogether. (This criticism is handled, but not fully met, by the great Zen authority Suzuki in his *Introduction to Zen Buddhism*.) It can hardly be completely confuted, for after all the central doctrine of Buddhism is — Nothingness. And many of the sayings of Zen masters are truly nihilistic. The first patriarch of the sect in China was asked by the emperor what was the ultimate and holiest principle of Buddhism. He replied, 'Vast emptiness, and nothing holy in it.' Another who was asked the searching question 'Where is the abiding-place for the mind?' answered, 'Not in this dualism of good and evil, being and nonbeing, thought and matter.' In fact, thought is an activity which divides. It analyzes, it makes distinctions, it criticizes, it judges, it breaks reality into groups and classes and individuals. The aim of Zen is to abolish that kind of thinking, and to substitute — not unconsciousness, which would be death, but a consciousness that does not analyze but experiences life directly. Although it has no prescribed prayers, no sacred scriptures, no ceremonial rites, no personal god, and no interest in the soul's future destination, Zen is a religion rather than a philosophy. Jung points out that its aim is to produce a religious conversion, a 'transformation': and he adds, 'The transformation process is incommensurable with intellect.' Thought is always interesting, but often painful; Zen is calm and painless. Thought is incomplete; Zen enlightenment brings a sense of completeness. Thought is a process; Zen illumination is a state. But it is a state which cannot be defined. In the Buddhist scriptures there is a dialogue between a master and a pupil in which the pupil tries to discover the exact meaning of such a state. The master says to him, 'If a fire were blazing in front of you, would you know that it was blazing?'

'Yes, master.'

'And would you know the reason for its blazing?'

'Yes, because it had a supply of grass and sticks.'

'And would you know if it were to go out?'

'Yes, master.'

'And on its going out, would you know where the fire had gone? To the east, to the west, to the north, or to the south?'

'The question does not apply, master. For the fire blazed because it had a supply of grass and sticks. When it had consumed this and had no other fuel, then it went out.'

'In the same way,' replies the master, 'no question will

apply to the meaning of Nirvana, and no statement will explain it.'

Such, then, neither happy nor unhappy but beyond all divisive description, is the condition which students of Zen strive to attain. Small wonder that they can scarcely explain it to us, the unilluminated.

The world my prison

———————————

By the rivers of Babylon, there we sat down, yea, we wept, when we remembered Zion. We hanged our harps upon the willows in the midst thereof. For there they that carried us away captive required of us a song; and they that wasted us required of us mirth, saying, Sing us one of the songs of Zion. How shall we sing the Lord's song in a strange land?

S O says the writer of the 137th Psalm, in a short but agonizingly painful poem written after the Hebrews had been deported from Palestine to Babylonia — a poem which begins with a cry of anguish and ends with a curse. It is one of the earliest of a long and constantly growing group of poems and stories and meditations written in exile.

Exile is a hard punishment. It is hard on those who are young and look forward to making their career in a society familiar to their fathers and forefathers. It is still harder on those who have earned a good position and find it annulled by their expulsion. It is hardest of all when it is inflicted on an entire nation. That is why many of the saddest cries of the exile's anguish have come from the Jews — once bondsmen in Egypt, then wanderers in the desert, then settled in a land their ancestors had never seen, then bondsmen in Babylonia, then settled in their home again, and then wanderers for nearly two thousand years: a people typified in that horrible legend of the Middle Ages, the myth of the Wandering Jew.

Banishment sometimes makes a writer's work better, and sometimes it kills him. It seldom weakens him. (We must distinguish compulsory, punitive exile from voluntary exile. James Joyce, for instance, called himself an exile, but he was not: he could have returned to Ireland at any time. Like Bernard Shaw and Sean O'Casey, he chose to leave the country where he was born — but he was not expelled. Real exile, inflicted by a superior power, is a penalty, or a tyranny. It is not far different from imprisonment. The exiles in the Roman empire were really confined in a prison without bars; the very sky above them was like an unbreakable window.)

Many fine books have been written in exile. Since we live in a world which is increasingly full of DPs, it is likely that many more such books will be produced. Exile has evoked one of the best histories, one of the finest religious poems, one of the keenest political treatises, and some of the sharpest poetic satires in western literature.

There are many possible reactions to banishment, and it evokes many different kinds of books. The most unusual attitude is detachment. There was a Greek mine owner who, when the war broke out between Athens and Sparta, became a naval officer. His name was Thucydides. He commanded a squadron in northern waters; but — either through a misfortune such as unpredictable bad weather, or through a mistake such as Admiral Halsey almost committed at Leyte — he lost control of an important Athenian base. He was indicted and forced into exile. During the rest of the war he was a 'stateless person.' Those long years he passed in writing a magnificent history of the war itself. When we read it, we can scarcely tell where his sympathies lie. He scarcely mentions his own disaster. He utters no direct reproaches, although he describes the mistakes of both sides. He can sympathize both with the weaknesses and fears of the Spartans, and the intoxicating sense of victory that swept the Athenians off their feet. Still, there is a deep sympathy in the famous speech through which he immortalizes the unspoiled ideals of Athenian democracy; and when those ideals are debased, he does record the result with what sounds like rigidly controlled melancholy.

Another such book is *The Prince,* which the Florentine diplomat Machiavelli wrote after his career had been broken. He served his state in difficult and dangerous crises for many years. Suddenly he was dismissed, imprisoned, tortured, and ejected from Florence. He retired to his little farm in the country, with nothing to do but think — and, in the evenings, to play cards with the peasants in the village inn. He thought, realistically and coldly; and the result was the first modern treatise on the grim science of politics.

Most exiles do not take things so calmly. Many of them relapse into agonizing despair. Out of the depths they cry, and sometimes their cry, even in its pain, is beautiful. Such are the short poems miscalled 'The Lamentations of Jeremiah' in the Bible; such also are some chapters near the end of Isaiah. This kind of suffering is very near to the agonies of death. It afflicted a gay and charming Roman poet, Ovid, the singer of love and magic. In the prime of his life, at the height of his career, he was involved in a dreadful scandal. The details of his offense are still unknown, for he never dared to reveal them; but it focused on the emperor's own granddaughter. She was sent for life to a lonely island. Ovid was banished to the extreme limits of the civilized world, to a remote harbor on the Black Sea. From there he kept writing poetry, but it was now a continuous wail of misery, and an endless series of pleas for mercy. He was never forgiven.

If you are sent into exile, you need not weep. You can curse. Many exiles curse the land that threw them out. The greatest of Italian poets, Dante, was condemned to be burned to death if he ever set foot on the territory of his native city, Florence. He never returned; but when he wrote his wonderful vision of the world of eternity, he put many citizens of Florence in hell, and he made some of the dead utter grim denunciations of the Florentine people as a whole. His own teacher, Brunetto Latini, told him:

> That ungrateful and malignant people
> because of your good deeds will be your foe:
> small wonder, since among the bitter berries
> it is not right for the sweet fig to flourish.
>
> (*Inf.* 15.61, 64–6)

Victor Hugo similarly left France as soon as that second-rate dictator Napoleon III took it over. From his rocky 'eyrie' in the Channel Islands he poured out bitter and scornful denunciations of 'Napoleon the Little' — denunciations which proved to be right, which were justified by history. Hugo's banishment turned him into a far greater poet. One of the classical writers whom he most admired suffered a similar fate: the Roman poet Juvenal. In his early thirties, Juvenal was sent into distant exile for life, and had only a fate like that of Ovid to contemplate, when he was, almost miraculously, released by the assassination of the emperor who banished him. When he returned, he began to write his great satires: long and bitter exposures of the corruption of Roman society, which are filled with savage hatred of the despotic emperor Domitian, a tyrant almost as suspicious and as vengeful as Joseph Stalin. It is largely from that hatred that they draw their tremendous power. Similarly, Voltaire was banished to England, just when his career was about to dissipate itself in cheap success. The result was his *Philosophical Letters* — a far wiser and deeper book than he would ever have produced if he had been permitted to live on in France as a best-seller. It is a description of the British constitution and of the comparatively liberal British political system, which plunges a number of painful *banderillas* into the hide of French absolutism, and prepares for the final sword-thrust.

One famous voluntary exile produced several marvelous works of denunciation. This was Thomas Mann. In his *Doctor Faustus* he described the spread of disease and madness through the mind and body and art of a gifted musician, in such a way as to symbolize the growing degeneration, decay, and insanity of his own Germany. There must also be some symbolic relation between Mann's most extensive work — his reconstruction of the career of the exile Joseph — and Mann's attitude to his own family, to Germany, and even to the entire contemporary world; and any thorough biography of Mann will have to analyze it in detail. *The Magic Mountain,* set in a Swiss sanatorium; *Death in Venice,* describing the last phase of the life of a German visitor to the city where we are all strangers: these and others of Mann's most interesting stories are clearly studies of the problem of banishment.

Sometimes, however, men who are exiled almost go mad. One of the hardest trials of every prisoner is to resist insanity. General Dean, when his Communist guards prevented him from even seeing another American for three years, had to make tremendous efforts to preserve the balance of his mind. So also, in exile, the abrupt disappearance of home and family and friends and prosperity and consistency and purpose often makes a man's reason totter. During his years in Siberia, something terrible happened to the mind of Fyodor Dostoevski. It was enlarged and deepened, but was it not distorted? Was it ever quite sane afterwards? Something similar happened to a Roman writer, the philosopher Seneca. He was a brilliant young courtier, rising rapidly, when he was involved (like Ovid) in some court intrigue. Like Dostoevski, he was nearly executed out of hand, and was only saved by the skin of his teeth. Like Dostoevski, he was banished to a grim and lonely province of the empire. In a few years there was a palace revolution. Then Seneca was brought home to take what proved to be an almost equally dangerous position: that of tutor to the young emperor Nero. Seneca wrote a number of books upon philosophical and psychological subjects. They are persuasive enough, but they are strangely unquiet and anxious, as though their writer were trying to convince himself more than us. And in addition, Seneca produced nine terrible, morally anarchistic tragedies, which seem to vibrate with the pressure of madness forcing its way up like boiling magma through the blow-holes in a volcanic field. It was in the agonies of his exile, apparently, that Seneca became a Stoic, to avoid becoming a lunatic.

From such madness there are several ways of escape. We can, for instance, create a private world, full of truths and ecstasies not known to the outsiders. Then they are exiles, and we are at home. During the Middle Ages, certain Jewish thinkers built up a marvelously complex system of mysticism which is not exactly religion, not exactly philosophy, and not exactly myth. It is really a secret universe, called the Kabbalah. One of its weirdest qualities is its obsession with numbers. Since in Hebrew the letters of the alphabet also serve as numbers, the interpreters of the wisdom of the Kabbalah find mystical significances in the numerical shapes of certain words and the verbal translation of certain numbers. Dependence on numbers is often the sign of great intellectual activity combined with something very close to madness. Thus, an obsessed man will count his paces, or find mysterious significance in the figures of a street address, or determine to take a momentous decision only after he has met exactly seven red-haired men. The Kabbalah might be called a fantasy of exile.

Another way of escaping from exile is to re-create one's home. Many great experiences are appreciated only after they have ended. So exile sometimes makes us recall our past, to glorify and cherish it. This is one of the supreme strengths of much Jewish literature. It is strange to learn that now, after a Jewish national home has come into existence, some of its writers are expressing a nostalgia for the old life of the ghetto, which (we might have thought) they would have loathed and tried to forget. The Poles also have so often been invaded and occupied by brutal foreigners, and so many of their finest poets and artists have been thrust into exile, that the re-creation of their homeland is one of their principal themes. The greatest poem in the Polish language was written in exile: the 'epic idyll' *Pan Tadeusz*, filled with Polish gallantry, Polish humor, and Polish *style*. While Mickiewicz was composing it, one of his friendly rivals, Krasinski, was rising above the sufferings of his own exile to describe Poland, not merely as a land with a population of peasants and towns-folk, but as a profound spiritual fact; and Frédéric Cho-pin was changing the folk-dances and folk-songs of Poland, with their passion and vigor and melancholy and almost unshakable courage, into lofty and enduring musical art.

Finally, it is possible to abandon the idea of exile: to stop thinking that we are shut out, and to enjoy the discovery of a new world. In a sense, we are all exiles. Through our first parents we might have been inhabitants of the earthly paradise; but through their fault we were cast out. When Adam and Eve were expelled, they looked back, and saw

> the gate
> With dreadful faces thronged and fiery arms.

Yet even then they took courage.

> Some natural tears they dropped, but wiped them
> soon;
> The world was all before them, where to choose
> Their place of rest, and Providence their guide.

But we seldom think of that, and it is good that we should not: our home is here. Yet see how many people have ex-iled themselves, and then, with a difficult but heroic act of the spirit, have found, or made, a new home. There are many inspiring things in our past, but few are more inspiring than the story of the dangerous journeys and the long-sustained efforts undertaken by the immigrants to the North American continent: men and women who remade both the continent and themselves.

Immigrants

———————————

FOR Americans, there is one superb subject for literature
which hardly any other nation possesses. It is very difficult,
indeed impossible, to cover it all in a single book. It is
ample enough and various enough to inspire dozens of
different books, some comic and some pathetic, some coldly
factual and some warmly fanciful; and it is a subject which
will not be exhausted for many years yet. The theme is the
life of immigrants and their families: the people who
pulled up their roots in the Old World and came overseas
to put them down in new ground, drawing up new energy
through them, and nearly always producing new offshoots
which surprised even themselves. It touches all of us, this
theme; for we are all immigrants or the descendants of immigrants. (Even the American Indians are immigrants —

for it seems perfectly clear that they entered this continent from Asia in not very distant prehistoric times. Once you have grasped this fact, it alters your whole view of the Indians. I first realized its truth when I was watching a rodeo in the Crow Indian territory of southern Montana. Our party of four was the only white group present; all the competitors and the judges and the spectators were Indians. In an abstract sort of way I already knew about the ethnological links between the American Indians and certain peoples of central Asia; but it was only when I sat there and looked all round at the broad flat faces, the opaque black eyes, the straight black hair, the strong bones with a firm layer of fat over them, the weathered brown-and-russet skins, the heavily skirted women and the swaddled children and the powerful old men, the tents pitched in the camping ground and the dried meat hanging in strips near them, that I understood *actively* that these were transplanted Asians, and that their closest living relatives were the nomads of the great plains in and beyond Mongolia.)

We are all immigrants or the descendants of immigrants. But the adventure of immigration has been so very varied that it cannot possibly be brought into the compass of a single book, or even of a single bookshelf. Consider the different fates that led us here. Most of us, or our ancestors, came willingly and gladly. They loved the new land of freedom and could not be kept away from it. But one tenth of our population at least is made up of the descendants of unwilling immigrants: the Negroes, who were brought here by force, in chains. And a fair number of early white settlers were brought here more or less involuntarily, transported for such trivial offenses as stealing a silk handkerchief, or sold into apprenticeship when they were too young to have much say in the matter. A friend of mine spent some time studying the passenger lists of the ships which came out to the British colonies, and tracing the backgrounds of the men and women on them: the most amusing and pathetic consignment was simply described as 'four sweet singers' — evidently a quartet which had failed to get enough good engagements, and either determined or was obliged to seek a different fortune in the New World.

It could not be written as a single story. But it is enthralling to read the various episodes in it, even if they cannot be unified. Some of the most poignant works of American literature deal with them, and also some of the lightest. The adventures of fairly recent immigrants and their children were the theme of *Abie's Irish Rose,* which ran for an unheard-of time on the New York stage, and of *I Remember Mama,* which may still be running, in one form or another. Huge sociological studies have been written about immigrants; they have been worked over by anthropologists, penologists, historians, and almost every other kind of specialist. One of the saddest but most enlightening books on the theme is a study of the German and Austrian scholars, writers, and artists who came over to the United States during the era of Hitler: *The Refugee Intellectual,* by D.P. Kent (Columbia University Press, 1953). Fiction, nonfiction, and autobiography (which is somewhere between the two) can all be made out of the adventures of the immigrant.

Although it is impossible to make one story out of it, still, we do see certain broad patterns which emerge in the lives of most immigrants, certain recurrent experiences and problems.

The most important is that the vast majority of them feel a sense of expansion and freedom. Not all. Some are terrified by the power and magnitude of America and shrink into themselves. Some are too old to transplant, and never grow any further. But many original immigrants and the children of nearly all immigrants grow larger in body, and expand in spirit. They feel as though barriers had been broken down, walls pushed back, the ceiling lifted almost as high as the sky. (Sometimes they are dissatisfied and want still more walls broken and the ceiling lifted still higher; but they will usually admit that they have experienced a wonderful liberation.) There is a touching episode illustrating this in Vilhelm Moberg's book *Unto A Good Land* (translated by G. Lannestock, Simon & Schuster, 1954). It tells of a small group of Swedes leaving their own poverty-stricken country and entering the United States. One of them is a girl who has been miserably abused and downtrodden, viciously perverted and hated, in the old country; but in America she works hard, she changes her life, and at last she marries an American pastor. To symbolize her triumph, her resurrection, she performs a very important act. She buys a hat. In Sweden no such peasant girl could ever wear a hat; at best, a shawl over her head. In those days, hats were for great ladies. But now Ulrika is a free woman in a free country, and for her marriage she puts on — long-envied and now at last achieved, 'with long plumes and blooms and wedding bands' — a Hat.

Yet, one reason that immigration is so difficult and sets up so many psychical tensions is that often, along with this sense of freedom, the immigrant finds himself confronted by new and unexpected difficulties — so that he is forced at the same time to exercise fresh powers and to submit to fresh difficulties. The chief problem is language. Some immigrants never solve it. Few immigrants (unless they come in very young) ever solve it completely. Moberg expresses this difficulty very well when he says that his Swedish immigrant group, the moment they landed at the Battery, felt that they had been struck deaf and dumb, and partly blind, too. They could talk to no one, they could understand nothing that anyone said to them, and they could not read the papers or the street signs. They had become like little children.

The San Francisco restaurant keeper George Mardikian, who has written a delightful autobiography called *Song of America* (McGraw-Hill), tells some amazing stories about this problem as it affected his own group, the Armenian immigrants to the United States. One of his kinsmen, who had been many years in America, could speak only seven words of English. And what were they? Well, this character owned a street-corner flower stand in San Francisco. To every woman who passed, 'whether she was a pretty girl of eighteen, a stout middle-aged tourist, or a tottering great-grandmother,' he held out a flower, and he uttered his seven words: 'Lady, this flower is just like you.' From that he made a good living. Mr. Mardikian himself did not make the mistake made by some of his fellow-Armenians. He studied English hard at every moment he could. After starting as a dishwasher, he got a job as a counterman in a restaurant, and then began to expand (intellectually). At night in his hotel room, he used to practice calling out orders: 'Vee-al Coot-let! Corn-ud Bee-uf Hush! Pasht Ekks!' — until the neighbors hammered on the radiator pipes to make him stop.

This language problem is aggravated in many families of immigrants by the gap between the parents, thinking in their original language and speaking American English less than perfectly, and the children, thinking in American and speaking it most of the day with their friends. The playwright S. N. Behrman, in his autobiographical sketch

The Worcester Account (Random House), records how he was perplexed by finding it was difficult for him to talk with his own mother, after living away from home at Harvard for two years and in New York for six years; for she knew only Yiddish, and he says he had almost entirely forgotten it. Mr. Kent records that among the refugee families he studied, there were several where the children simply refused to speak the language of their parents, even when they were addressed in it. They would listen, and then answer in American English. This created an additional complication: the parents saw it as the breakdown of family discipline, and objected strenuously.

That is indeed a serious problem. The children always become Americanized much more rapidly than the parents. Although the situation is not strictly parallel, because Puerto Ricans are American citizens, I saw something like it the other day in New York, watching a couple of Puerto Rican women in a bus with their children. The little boys were chattering away to each other in brisk American, interspersed with a few Spanish phrases. Every now and then they would stop and explain to their mothers in Puerto Rican Spanish, kindly, not impertinently; and then rattle away again to each other in American English, while the mothers gazed at them with large astonished eyes. In Mr. Kent's book on the German and Austrian immigrants there is a touching story that illustrates the same point. It happened back in the days when Joe Louis was a champion boxer. The son of one of these immigrants was very enthusiastic about an important fight which was approaching, with Joe Louis as one of the contestants. (The book does not say which, but I imagine it must have been one of the Schmeling matches.)

> On the night of the event the son wanted to listen
> to the broadcast. His father, announcing that he did

not approve of prize fighting, forbade him to listen, and forced him to go to bed. The son went to bed, but refused to go to sleep until he was sure that the fight was over, even although he could not hear it. From his bedroom he talked to himself in tones loud enough for his father to hear: 'Down with foreigners! Foreigners are un-American!'

Poor father. He won that round, but he lost the contest.

One of the strangest obstacles which some immigrants encounter would not, I am sure, occur to most native-born Americans; if it did, they would strive to remove it. Some Europeans think Americans are coarse and blunt in speech. But many immigrants find Americans exceedingly, and even perplexingly, polite. They understand why, eventually. They know that it springs from the friendly nature of the American society — although they probably misunderstood that too at the beginning, having been taught that it was brutally and ruthlessly competitive. So some of the refugee immigrants of the Hitler era were bitterly disappointed when they were interviewed, and met with smiles and kind words, instead of the blunt and (to our ears) rude language of Germans. One of them has recorded his feelings:

An employer never says 'No job! I don't want you. You are not able enough for this job.' Rather he says: 'I'm awfully sorry, but right at this time we just don't have a vacancy in your line. However, we'll keep you in mind, and something may develop shortly. And we do appreciate your applying and are aware of your fine qualifications.' As Europeans we left feeling elated. When no call came, we were somewhat disillusioned. Now we recognize that this was a refusal just as much as the blunt rejection of a German employer. However, we left feeling good: not angry or bitter. . . . This is the genius of America.

One further difficulty which weighs heavy on some immigrants is the feeling that they are here only on sufferance, and that they can never hope to become full citizens. Mardikian says he knew many of his own group who went through all their lives without venturing on the citizenship test. Some of them, he says, 'had won a reputation in their neighborhood as wise men, yet in their hearts lay the fear that they couldn't answer the questions of the naturalization examiner.' This worried Mardikian; when he was preparing for his citizenship examination, he had nightmares in which the examiner asked him questions in some weird language like Chinese, and, when he failed, turned thumbs down. It worries everyone who takes the examination seriously. I remember that my wife and I, when we became citizens, were interviewed by a grave and wise judge who put many searching questions to us, which we answered with beating hearts. At last he turned away from me, and fixed his gaze upon my wife. After a painful pause, he said, 'Can you read and write?' Suppressing a gasp, she said, 'Yes, I can.' Then he relaxed for the first time; with a cheerful and welcoming smile he said, 'Yes, I know: I've read your novels!' She passed.

But for most incomers, these difficulties are small compared with the achievement of making a new life for themselves, and seeing their children grow up with more advantages than they themselves ever had. George Mardikian did better than most: he started with less and ended with more to his credit; he began as a penniless dishwasher, twelve hours a day six days a week, and at the end of his book he tells proudly how he was given the Medal of Freedom by President Truman and entertained at dinner at the White House by President Eisenhower. Yet the most intense moment of his entire career came when he was quite young, just after taking the oath of allegiance as an

American citizen. He rode out on the Sutter Street trolley as far as the terminus; he sat on the beach all alone, and looked at the Pacific Ocean, and felt his new life flowing through him. He says:

> You who have been born in America, I wish I could make you understand what it is like not to have been an American all your life, and then suddenly, with the words of a man in flowing robes, to be one, for that moment and for ever after. One moment, you belong with your fathers to a million dead yesterdays. The next, you belong with America to a million unborn tomorrows.

Index

Important references are shown by bold figures: **123**. A subject not explicitly named, but referred to indirectly, is signalized by a bracketed figure: (123).

Bacon, Francis, 104–5
Balzac, Honoré de, 271
baroque, 43–4
Barruel, Paul, *Birds of the World,* 4–5
Bartlett's Familiar Quotations, 290
baseball, how to abolish, 270
Baudelaire, Charles, 86
Beerbohm, Max, 64
Beethoven, Ludwig van, 5, 45, 302
Behrman, S. N., 336–7
Bemelmans, Ludwig, 186
Bernini, Giovanni Lorenzo, 44
Bible, 32, 93, (99), (125), 210, 223, 275–6, 303–4, 305, 323–4, 326
Biographical Dictionary, Webster's, 290
BISCUITS, TOPFLITE, 71
Blake, William, 28
Blood in the Gutter, 187–8
Bloody Frontier, 187–8
Bookman's Manual, The, 291
Bosch, Hieronymus, (27), 29–33
Boswell, James, 130, 261
Brahms, Johannes, 302
Bridges, Robert, 298
Brinnin, John Malcolm, 84–90
Britain, Great, 69, 127, 128, 129, 177, 304–5, 327, 333–4
Bronzino, Il, 6
Browning, Robert, 306
Bruegel, Pieter, 29, 34–40
Buchan, John, 203–4
Buddha, 315–16, 319–20
Buddhism, 308–22
Bunyan, John, 261
Buridan and his donkey, 279
Burney, Christopher, 259
Burns, Robert, 152
Buxtehude, Dietrich, 45
Byron, George Gordon, Lord, 64, 87, 235

C

Caesar, Gaius Julius, 271
Cairns, Huntington, 299
Callot, Jacques, 44, 59–62
Capri, 152, 154–7
Carlyle, Thomas, 203, 256
Casanova, Giovanni, 68
Cassell's Encyclopedia of World Literature, 290
cave men, 4, 10–17, 101–2, 172–3, 291, 297
Céline, Louis-Ferdinand, 297
Cellini, Benvenuto, 261
Cervantes, Miguel de, (301), (306)
Chambers's Encyclopaedia, 289
Chaminade, Cécile, 302
China, 27, 57, 315, 316, 319, 320
Chopin, Frédéric, 47, 330
Christianity, 31, 94–9, 196, 281, 310
church, the Roman Catholic, 75, 114, 145–6, 147, 153–5, 156
Churchill, Sir Winston, 247–8, 256–7, 258
Cobbett, William, 256
Coleridge, Samuel Taylor, 90–91, 175
Colette, 75–83, 201
Columbia College and University, 140, 263–4
Columbia Encyclopedia, The, 288, 289
Corvo, Baron, 144–50
Cowell, Henry, 49
Crowley, Aleister, 161–4
Current Biography, 290
Cushing, Harvey, 298

D

Dadaism, 163
Dali, Salvador, 28
Dante Alighieri, 32, 272, 301, 304, 305, 326